Best Wishes —

Margie Snowden North

FICTION NORTH, MARGIE SNOWDEN
NORTH

TO CHASE A DREAM

To Chase A Dream

By

Margie Snowden North

Copyright ©1989
First published in 1989 by Evans Publications, Perkins, OK 74059
All rights reserved. No part of this book may be reproduced except
for short excerpts for book review purposes.
Printed in the United States of America
Library of Congress Catalog Card Number: 89-83900
ISBN: 0-934188-26-2

Dedication

In memory of Papa, Alvin Leroy Snowden, who always believed in his five children, and

To Mama, Margie Berry Snowden (now Mrs. Roy Fowler) who is my most dedicated fan, and

To my husband, Ben, who is a great source of strength, and

To our five children, their spouses and our grandchildren,

Richard and Rhonda (Gregory) North and Lindsay,

Justin and Mary (Barfield) North, Ty, Melanie and Julie

Rickey and Judy (North) Greer, Levi and Malia

Ron and Mary (West) North and Kodie, and

Timothy Craig North

"Chasin' dreams—is like chasin' the wind, only harder. At least sometimes the wind stops. Dreams never do. They're always two steps outa reach."

(David)

Foreword

I sat down late in the afternoon to merely scan *To Chase A Dream* and quickly became so immersed in the story of the Easons I finished reading it word for word at 2 a.m. the next morning.

Even though I knew the book was fiction, I recognized the qualities of the author and her family background that made the words on its pages pour from her heart and pen. It seemed natural that she would write about a family bound closely together by ties of love and respect—a family where religious values and worship were the foundation—where a cheerful outlook lightened all of life—where children's respect and admiration for their parents cast a glow over the home.

The Easons were very real to me, not because the circumstances of their lives were those of the author's, but because the love and warmth within the family are what I remember of her own background. Hers was a special family, as I learned when she was one of my pupils the first year I taught, as were her sisters and brother eventually.

How were they special? They were a united family. A serious father with strong moral principles and a mother whose natural good nature and happy disposition made a good team. Each child was different—in looks and personality—but each was smart, well-mannered, co-operative, attractive. After the author's youthful marriage to a Beckham county boy, they continued the strong family life pattern. She has concentrated on her husband, children, home and church. In addition, while being a devoted homemaker, she has been a "closet" writer. The words seem to roll off her fingertips, whether or not there is anyone looking over her shoulder to read them.

Though *To Chase A Dream* is not the story of the author's family, the essence of the imaginary family was that of the real life one: "the rapport, the camaraderie, the loyalty" and the family members who "lived and loved and worked and dreamed."

The flavor of the people and area are familiar, too. Western Oklahomans are acknowledged to be different. This part of the state is young. It is an area of difficult weather and farming conditions. Life has not been easy, but people are therefore strong and hardworking. They are independent and self-reliant and enterprising. Religion and character are important. I "knew" the people in the book—they are truly the Western Oklahomans I have known for fifty years.

The only way I felt reconciled to leave the unresolved problems of the Easons when the book ended was that *To Chase A Dream* so evidently calls for a sequel. I look forward to that. When I hear it's available, I'll get a good night's sleep. Because when I get my hands on it, I know I won't be able to put it down till I finish it!

—Julie Ann Holmberg

Preface

Long ago a man called Pascal said, "Certain authors, when they speak of their work, say: 'My book, my commentary, my history' . . . They would do better to say 'our book, our commentary, our history,' since their writings generally contain more of other people's good things than of their own."

How true. Though this book is categorized as fiction, some of the things in it actually happened at one time or another to my family or to someone we knew. Every event, good or bad, every person I met, every word I heard, every philosophy I saw in action, was absorbed as I was growing up, and much of it has found its way into this book.

Most of the poems referred to were read to the Snowden children often by the oldest sister, Ava Jean. Perhaps I owe my appreciation of poetry to her. She and my other sisters, Donna Mae and Rose Marie, as well as my brother, Ransom, supplied material for "character studies" as I grew up. Analyzing people and traits always came naturally to me and has been helpful to me in my writing.

The gentle side of the personalities of "David" and "Papa" in this book were inspired by my on Papa's personality. Their mischievousness and their whimsical sayings were inspired by Papa also, as well as by my husband. Some of the viewpoints and sayings of "Mama" originated from my mother.

Many teachers helped shape my character during my growing up years and in so doing, helped indirectly to shape this book. To name a few: Mrs. J. M. Gamble, Mrs. J. S. Holmberg, Mrs. Verlin Glidewell, Miss Nelda Martin, Miss Ayliffe Garrett, Mr. Marvin Easley, Mr. Bill Dill, and Mr. Ed Horn, as well as a lovely red-haired Sunday School teacher whose name I can't recall, but whose glowing face and compassionate words convinced me God loved even the most homely and insignificant among us.

In 1947, the year in which this book is set, I was six years old. Papa and Mama were day laborers so that made their children day laborers, too. We worked long, hard hours in the field (as well as spending a year or two in California pea camps) and we lived for years in a two-room shanty with a tiny, tacked-on trailer house Papa had made. This served as a bedroom for the four girls.

Like the Easons in this book, we often played "thinking games" in the field. We laughed a lot, and we sang gospel songs together when we traveled. We ate plain food and read by lamp light and took baths in a galvanized tub. Even during the 40's and 50's most of our classmates had electricity and running water but the Snowdens weren't privileged with such luxuries until 1957 when I was a sophomore in high school.

Though back then I wished to be some glamorous creature who looked in the mirror and was stunned by her own beauty; who had only to act in movies, sing or do ballets or conduct orchestras before vast audiences, or write enthralling books and poems, I can truthfully say my early lifestyle was satisfying in many ways and that the things it caused me to learn are invaluable. Could it be that God knew exactly what I needed all along?

It is my hope that as you read this book it will bring back memories or help you learn of a certain era of history and of a particular segment of society about which not a lot has been written. If you have never personally experienced the feelings and events common to day laborers or sharecroppers, may you experience them now through the reading of this book.

EXCELSIOR
Henry Wadsworth Longfellow

The shades of night were falling fast,
As through an Alpine village passed
A youth, who bore, 'mid snow and ice,
A banner with the strange device,
        Excelsior!

His brow was sad; his eye beneath,
Flashed like a falchion from its sheath,
And like a silver clarion rung
The accents of that unknown tongue,
        Excelsior!

In happy homes he saw the light
Of household fires gleam warm and bright;
Above, the spectral glaciers shone,
And from his lips escaped a groan,
        Excelsior!

"Try not the Pass!" the old man said;
"Dark lowers the tempest overhead,
The roaring torrent is deep and wide!"
And loud that clarion voice replied,
        Excelsior!

"Oh stay," the maiden said, "and rest
Thy weary head upon this breast!"
A tear stood in his bright blue eye,
But still he answered, with a sigh,
        Excelsior!

"Beware the pine-tree's withered branch!
Beware the awful avalanche!"
This was the peasant's last good-night,
A voice replied, far up the height,
     Excelsior!

At break of day, as heavenward
The pious monks of Saint Bernard
Uttered the oft-repeated prayer,
A voice cried through the startled air,
     Excelsior!

A traveller, by the faithful hound,
Half-buried in the snow was found,
Still grasping in his hand of ice
That banner with the strange device,
     Excelsior!

There in the twilight cold and gray,
Lifeless, but beautiful, he lay,
And from the sky, serene and far,
A voice fell, like a falling star,
     Excelsior!

Prologue

By 1947 the United States was making a slow but sure recovery from the trauma and expense of a war overseas. Optimism ran high. Those who came out of World War II were idealistic, sincerely believing they were coming home to build a new and better world. In many ways they succeeded.

However, in rural areas the poor were staying poor, or getting poorer. There were those trapped in the cycle of near-poverty—namely the sharecroppers and common farm laborers—simply because they were born there. For some this life was reasonably adequate; plain food to eat, but generally enough of it, worn clothes to wear, but routinely scrubbed clean, a roof over heads (leaky though it usually was). A major goal might involve a five-dollar bill and a free Saturday night, or some other occasionally attainable end.

But for most of those in the lower economic bracket, for those who had not quelled expectations and ambitions until they lay dormant and wounded or dead, there was a more distant dream. Not necessarily the same dream, for aspirations differ according to interests or needs or talents, but a dream nevertheless.

The dream might be purely materialistic, or it might be spiritual or it might be intellectual or it might encompass all three realms. It might be definable, or it might not. The significant factor is that it was there, causing men to attempt to press forward even while existing conditions either held them fast or greatly impeded advancement.

Dreams foster progress in every facet of life and living, causing men on every social or economic level to do and discover the unthinkable. They are the reason wars are fought and won for freedom, the reason new realms and methods are explored, the reason people seek the spiritual and aspire to heaven. The scriptures say, "Where there is no vision the people perish."

Following good and noble dreams by individuals as well as nations then, is neither uncommon nor impractical. On the contrary, following dreams, even for those whose future seems woefully pre-determined, is as natural as eating and breathing—and for the most part, just as necessary.

Chapter One

DAVID'S BLUE eyes glistened as he said angrily to Papa, "You taught us to be one thing, and now you're sayin' maybe it's okay to bend the law just a little."

Abby had just hooked the enamel dish pan on the nail near the cabinet and was spreading the dish rag over it to dry. Her brother's words seemed so unlike him. She looked around quickly to make sure it was really him. His face was rigid, his mouth a thin line.

Without looking up, Mama tautly sifted through the dried beans searching for tiny rocks and other foreign particles. Her bottom lip was compressed between her teeth. She reacted as though the words were expected— as if she had intuitively known this confrontation was inevitable.

Lucy Belle dangled her rubber doll by its one arm, staring curiously at her brother.

Papa winced under the indictment. Then his face became, like David's, a mask that was unreadably frightening. His voice was even more menacing than David's as he said, "I won't have no son of mine a-tellin' me I'm a crook!"

Now that angry words were being spoken, David was quick to continue. "You always said call a spade a spade. In my books you're breakin' the law, and a man that breaks the law is a crook."

"I said there won't be no name-callin' in this house." The emotion caused a tremor in Papa's voice, "I didn't raise up my young'uns to spout off to their elders."

"I'm speakin' the truth, Papa, and you know it." There was a hardness in David's voice and in his eyes, and his hands were clenched into big fists at his side as he instinctively prepared to defend himself.

Abby saw two faces, unmoved, dark and angry—faces that once laughed at one another, and held respect for one another—that could anticipate each other even when there weren't always words spoken. The two faces were looking more and more alike as David entered into manhood. Two pairs of clear blue eyes that had before exuded understanding and a deep, abiding father-son love. Now they were piercing each other with hostility and a thing almost akin to hate.

"I brung you up to respect me and your Mama," Papa said, and his voice rang out with authority. "Now you git that settled in your mind right here and now, once't and for all."

"Travis!" That one word came from Mama, almost inaudible, and no one turned to look at her because the horror of what was taking place before them had riveted each of their gazes to Papa and David.

With all his unfamiliarity with anger and wrath, David had seemed to become an expert overnight. Now he took deliberate aim, hitting his mark with the next statement, "You expect me to respect a bootlegger? A cheap, law-breakin' bootlegger?"

To steady herself, Abby touched her fingertips to the scarred counter of the wooden cabinet. She was suddenly giddy and sick. It was a nightmare. This could not be David who used to tease them silly and pull her one long braid and help her plant ox-eye daisies around the doorstep.

Mama gripped the bean pot with both hands, her small body tense, unmoving in its shapeless and faded feed-sack dress, the color leaving her face. Lucy's mouth twisted into a puzzled consternation, for not once during her young life had scenes of this nature taken place in the Eason house. In Abby's almost sixteen years it had not, and suddenly she felt as numb and lifeless as the scratchy-faced doll Lucy still clutched haphazardly in her hand.

There was the clatter of Papa's belt buckle coming loose, and all eyes turned toward him in disbelief at what was taking place. The belt slid from the loops like a snake. A thing that had not happened since David was twelve, and now he was a young man and had grown those clumsy, long arms and legs and even had sprouted a few hairs on his chest and chin.

"Travis. Not here. Not now," Mama half asked, half pleaded.

The belt, the one David had made for Papa a year ago Christmas, hung from Papa's hand while his chest heaved and constricted in little angry gasps. Then, as though he were moved by some invisible force, Papa strode jerkily over to David, who was staring at the floor now, resigned, unafraid, waiting. In an odd, uncoordinated motion, Papa grasped David's arm with work-hardened, vise-like fingers and raised the belt.

In alarm, Lucy had crept over to Abby and whispered convulsively, "What's Papa doin', Abby?"

Abby was unable to draw a breath for a moment. Her heart was trying to tear out of her chest, but being born a protector even in traumatic times, she managed to say through her paralyzed throat, "Lucy, we got to git them catalogs and things put up we was lookin' at before supper."

She heard the first blow without seeing it. Lucy was protesting, pulling away like a colt on a rope, even while her deep blue eyes widened at the scene she was witnessing behind Abby's back.

"Lucy—"

But Lucy was stubborn, immobilized by fear, and Abby, still clutching her younger sister's shoulder, turned to watch with her in terrified disbelief. The muscles in Papa's arms bulged and jerked with each blow—there were a half dozen more of them—and his face was convulsed with a rage that they had never seen before.

David stood stoically, hardened, steeled against the blows, his finely-chiseled features fixed into an emotionless mask, his chin high, his eyes looking ahead not seeing anything or anyone.

In all her life Abby had never wanted so desperately to help her brother, even while she simultaneously longed to console and reassure Papa. This was not their way, this angry retaliation. The spankings he had given David before were insignificant in comparison, and she herself had never received more than a swat with his hand on her backside when she was a very young child. He had always disciplined with words, stories and examples.

When Papa cracked the belt the last time over David's lower back, it slowly fell to his side. David looked at Papa through a hurt, half-smile of a smirk and swaggered out the door in a deadly silence. There were no other sounds in the room except Papa's shallow, labored breathing. He turned to Mama. Their eyes met, each searching the other for some understanding. He gasped, "It had to be did, Maudie."

Mama whispered through stiff, pale lips, "Maybe you should'a jist talked to him."

Papa acted like he did not hear. "It was the only way," he said.

Like a defeated man he moved toward the round kitchen table, slumping into one of the slat-backed chairs, the one that was cracked that usually only Lucy sat in. Abby saw the chair give just a little as his big frame settled into it. "He—over-stepped hisself, don't you see. He . . ."

He brushed a hand over his lined, sun-browned forehead, and his eyes were clouded and full of hurting, but it was the irregular breathing that bothered Abby the most. She wanted desperately to hold her ears and to never have to hear it again.

"Lucy," she said softly, and her breathing was almost like Papa's. She was going to explode if she didn't get away. But she had to think of Lucy, who was still huddled next to her in wide-eyed silence. "We got to git them catalogs put up. And we got to git ourself in bed . . ."

She lay stiffly in the double bed in the front room, with Lucy finally silent and settled next to her. The events of the last few moments played relentlessly in her mind. The whacks of the belt. The sounds of Papa's breathing.

It had been a little like the war she had read about in the papers. But that war—the one with Germany and Japan and Italy—had already been fought and won, and had not touched them personally. It had only been a vague worry in the backs of their minds, heightened at certain times when they must face the rationing of gasoline or shoes or sugar along with everyone else, or when Aunt Myrtle wrote that she hadn't heard from Uncle Lewis since he landed on a beach at Anzio. Papa's and David's war was taking place right in their home, and she knew it was not over. What would happen now?

Trembling, she pulled the worn covers over her head trying to close out the words and the sounds that still rang in her ears. This tragedy would have to be reckoned with tomorrow. It was too late tonight.

She would think of other times instead. She would remember how all of them used to laugh together, how they had all been so close and loyal to one another, especially Papa and David; how all of them had played thinking games and wishing games and had lived and loved and worked and dreamed. She would remember those times when heartbreak never touched the Easons.

- - - -

"Papa, what would you wish for if you could have anything in the world?" Lucy Belle had asked often during those better times. And always her deep blue eyes were wide with expectancy, her pink cheeks glowing, framed by light brown curls that had been coaxed into pigtails at the back.

On this particular occasion they were all finished eating, all of them lazy and satisfied and lingering at the big round table with the worn red and white checkered oil cloth. Mama's small but strong hands were always busy, and she was scraping the smattering of cornbread crumbs and bean drippings from each plain, white plate as it was passed to her.

Acting as though he had never considered such a far-fetched question before, Papa studied for a minute, his light blue squinting eyes looking off into space, his fine-textured, fawn-colored hair slightly mussed as usual, and trying his best to conceal the look of a mischievously inclined school-boy.

"Well, daughter," he began (these were always his first words because it was never David that asked, but always Lucy or Abby). "I b'lieve I'd have me a cotton-candy machine," he mused thoughtfully, rubbing his slightly whiskery square jaw, "and take it out to the fields and we'd all of us have a puff of it at the end of ever' row." He winked at Mama, his eyes laughing. "Now, that oughta put a squirt of want-to in Lucy Belle's workin' gear."

"I haven't never been convinced she's got a workin'

gear," David declared wryly, with the obvious intention of making them laugh, which they all did, even Lucy, who was so hopefully enchanted with Papa's idea she didn't notice David's remark was less than complimentary.

Lucy, who was almost nine, had made up the wishing game. That was fitting, Abby thought, because she was a pretender. Looking at the rows of perfumes, lipsticks, and nail polish at the ten-cent store, for instance, was enough to send her imagination spinning, and it was from these episodes that David had pointed out her lack of a "working gear."

But Papa's answers were always fascinating and exciting. He might say, "I'd have that-there cow that can jump over the moon—bless her hide, if she ain't too tuckered out by now. She ought to be good for maybe sixty bucks a month down to John Ringling North's circus."

Or, "I'd have me a rainbow, a *Regenbogen,* if you please, and give ever'body in the fam'ly a ribbon of color off of it. Lucy'd git the red to match her cheeks. Abby'd git the blue to go with her eyes. Mama'd git the violet cause that's her fav'rite flower. And David, well, I guess he'd jist have to settle for the green and let Mama cut him out a shirt. As for the pot of gold at the end, we'd divvy it out between us all and give the good Lord His share down to the church."

It was always Mama's turn to wish after Papa. Being practical and cautious, she never asked for anything that wasn't serviceable or sensible. While busily brushing cornbread crumbs from the table to a plate, or wrapping the milk jar in its "cooling" cloth, she might ask for "A life supply of coal oil for the lamps and cookstove," or "Some of them new kind of dishes that'll scarcely break even if you try." This time she simply wanted new linoleums like they had seen one Saturday afternoon down at Cooper's Furniture and Undertaking.

In the dim glow of the coal oil lamp, Abby looked at the floor, seeing it through Mama's eyes. It was strewn over as usual with fine sand that moved in the ceaseless winds outside and forced its way in around deteriorated window casings and under poorly fitted doors. Like the floor coverings laid in every house in which they had lived, this linoleum didn't even appear to be a linoleum anymore. The scuffle of too many feet for too many years had worn the original bright, outer pattern right down to the blackened burlap backing and conformed the covering to every hump and buckle of the floor itself. Only by looking in the corners and at the narrow strip along the walls where no one walked, could the original, now faded colors be detected. Abby agreed with Mama that new linoleums would seem lively, even a bit awesome, but she was not sure she would want to walk on them for fear of scarring them up.

Lucy's turn was next, since she was the youngest. "I want some of them 'namel dishes like's at the ten-cent store," she said. "With flowers on 'em, and spoons and forks and little loaves of bread to put on the plates, and a little bitty tea kittle that you can really set on the stove and boil water in."

Lucy had seen the enamel dishes Saturday at Mullin's Five and Dime and had rattled on about them ever since as though there was really a possibility she might someday have them. She was forever wanting things that could be bought down at the ten-cent store.

Abby was next. She thought deeply now, seriously, as Papa always did, frowning in order to emphasize her deliberation, knowing all the while she wasn't going to be able to say what she really, truly, achingly wanted.

So she came up with something else. "I'd have me a milk cow for ever'body," she said. "Then we'd always have all the milk and butter and cream we needed 'cause they surely wouldn't all go dry at one time. And we could sell the extry at Harp's Creamery over'n Shawnee."

David didn't usually approve of Abby's wishes and he mumbled, "A cow, my achin' back," because, as he often pointed out, everything Abby wanted called for more work for everybody. It was one thing to commit the unpardonable by enjoying physical work rather than merely tolerating it, but it was something else to dream up work for everyone.

Then in relishing his own wish he forgot his impatience and said grandly, squinting off across the dusky room as though he were seeing it, "I'll take one of them new, 1947 air-conditioned Lincoln Continental Cabriolets like they're fixin' to come out with, like Mr. Tolsey, the math teacher's thinkin' about gittin'. Custom coach with power-operated windows and foam rubber seat cushions and independent wheel suspension . . ."

The wishing game was a favorite for them all, but they didn't play it too often because Papa thought it would lose its fascination for them. The games they played most often were thinking games—those that would build minds, 'cause Papa said thinking was what made a brain strong, just the same as working made the back strong.

He had always held with Robert Browning in condemning the "unlit lamp and the ungirt loin," and thought a fellow ought to keep his shirt sleeves rolled up and a light in his mind. (The *Licht,* because Papa was one-quarter German and occasionally slipped in one of Grandma's words.) He said anybody could pick out a goal, but only the smart, diligent and single-minded could plan for it, work toward it, and finally attain it.

Abby realized that Papa, at thirty-nine, had never reached his goal—that of becoming self-sufficient—but they all thought he would one day. His own Pa had died a sharecropper, died early, and that had put him at a distinct disadvantage. He had dropped out of school at fourteen intending to go back when times got better, but Grandpa's death had made it necessary for Papa to go to work full time at seventeen to help support a family of six.

But despite that, Papa was smart. Abby never ceased to be amazed at his mental recall and reasoning. He was common smart. He could rattle off all thirty-three presidents and all forty-eight states and capitals and could quote dozens of poems and scriptures. He could debate Keats' famous line, "Beauty is truth, truth is beauty," with the best of them—an ability Mama frankly labeled "a bunch of hawgwarsh." "If Mr. Keats had wanted anyone to know what the saying meant he should have spelled it out plainer," she would say. She doubted the poet, himself, could explain it if he were actually confronted.

But Papa was intrigued by deep things that way, and Abby knew he wanted his kids to have plenty of opportunity to seek such things, too. To that end, he expertly kept little minds in motion, but in a way that none of them were aware of what he was up to until they were older. Mental delving came to her as naturally as a game of horseshoes or "clap in, clap out," and it took the mind off aching muscles and boredom when they worked all day, row after row, in the field.

For as long as she could remember they had played thinking games. The wishing game came later, the same year they moved to Tecumseh. That was April 1945, about the time the newspapers were saying U. S. troops had landed in Okinawa, and during the season that farmers began in earnest preparing the ground for planting.

The Easons had spent a year in California picking peas and cherries, and had had their fill of being called fruit tramps and Okies. ("Okie" was the derisive label Californians placed upon all outsiders, even those from Arkansas or Kansas or Texas.) Back in Oklahoma, they wanted nothing more than to get settled into the familiar sharecropper routine, a family working the ground, planting the seed, battling the weeds and harvesting the crop. This was a cycle that was strenuous, but not as dreary or frustrating as non-farmers might have thought —at least it wasn't to Abby. Cropping was so deeply entrenched into her life-pattern that it was accepted without thought or reservation.

If there were vague frustrations connected to farming, it was because she understood all too well that the land they worked so diligently belonged to their various landlords. When it came time for the harvest of their labor to be sold and divvied, their returns were piteously small. Abby knew all the wishing games in the world wouldn't change that.

But the optimistic spirit with which Abby had been born led her to believe that somehow, some way, the Easons would one day be landowners and not just croppers. It would not be a matter of just wishing, and probably not even of intelligence, but one of trusting the good Lord, of perseverance and time to let it happen.

Chapter Two

P APA'S APPROACH to thinking games proved to be a sound one, Abby reflected. All three of the Eason children made above-average grades, even though David's grades came almost spontaneously.

David was constantly amazing his teachers as long as Abby could remember. In his grade school days his papers came home with gold stars. There were glowing notes jotted on his report cards. He had the lead parts in school programs, and was leader of this and captain of that. Teachers visited Mama and Papa in order to commend them.

In Tecumseh the pattern continued. The principal asked David to coach other students during his study halls, and even brought him out of regular classes for tutoring when there was a special need. Mr. Tolsey, the math teacher, had taken a special interest in him and had invited him to accompany his wife and him on several outings, some educational and some purely for enjoyment.

So on that fall day when the Tolseys drove up to the Easons' three room shack in their expensively restored 1915 Ford Couplet, it was not too unusual. Abby supposed they were going to invite David to another antique car show, or maybe to pay another visit to the Historical Building in Oklahoma City.

She and Lucy had just gathered a washtub of green tomatoes which Mama would use to make chow-chow, and David had carried it to the house for them. Papa had brought in two buckets of fresh well water and they were all getting cool drinks and wiping sweat and laughing over something when the Tolseys stopped out front. Mama started worrying, as usual, about the kitchen.

"Lucy, git your play-purties put up. Abby, take that jar of sour milk to the back room. David, quick, scoot that tub of tomatoes over outa the way . . ."

Abby set the jar on the dresser amidst the combs, liniment jar, hair oil bottle and the dust, and glanced quickly into the mirror. Because of the heat, her face was pink through the tan and sprinkle of freckles, and just a bit grimy. She wiped at it with her dress tail, then studied her hair. It was in its usual disarray, with prairie-straw colored strands of it flying free from the one long braid hanging down her back. She smoothed and patted it, and straightened her dress collar. The Tolseys were rich, everyone said anyway. They probably wouldn't notice her, but she didn't want them thinking she didn't take any thought of her appearance.

In the kitchen, Papa was standing by the washstand looking out the window. Abby looked too, and saw the Tolseys meticulously picking their way through the drying weeds and over the baked red dirt that constituted the Easons' front yard.

"Should of got those thistles hoed out this summer," Papa said thoughtfully.

When he answered the door, Abby tried not to seem overly curious. While Mama and Mrs. Tolsey exchanged hellos and the men shook hands, she sat at the table and began quartering the largest of the tomatoes so they could be run through the grinder.

"Will you take a chair?" Papa asked, but Mr. Tolsey declined politely.

He was a tanned, muscular man, lean and fit-looking, and he seemed to dwarf them all, even Papa. Gripping his narrow-brimmed derby with strong, brown fingers, and standing with his feet slightly apart, he seemed somewhat ill-at-ease. Occasionally he shuffled positions on the blackened linoleum, or darted a glance toward his wife. But when he spoke, his voice sounded calm and sure.

"I'll get right to the point of the visit, Mr. and Mrs. Eason, but first let me mention how we appreciated those times that you allowed David to take part in our various excursions. We enjoyed him immensely."

When Papa nodded, smiling, Mr. Tolsey returned the smile benevolently and said somewhat tentatively, "We've watched David closely in the months we've known him, and I must say we're very impressed."

Papa and Mama exchanged brief, pleased smiles. "Well, we're proud of our young'uns," Papa responded.

Almost as if he were merely making conversation while calculating things of more importance on his mind, Mr. Tolsey continued, "You people are in the tenant farming business, I understand. Pretty widely traveled, I assume?"

"It's what they call an occupational hazard," Papa acknowledged, grinning in his usual friendly way.

Mr. Tolsey smiled with him, a bit absently, and mused, "Cropping in Oklahoma is educational in one sense of the word, but rather rigorous—perhaps even detrimental—in terms of formal training. But, then— that isn't what we're here for . . ."

Mrs. Tolsey touched her husband's well-developed forearm gently and he relinquished the floor to her without hesitation, almost as though he were grateful. "Winburn and I are not impulsive people," she began softly. She was a dainty thing, dressed in a deep blue gabardine with an inset of delicate tatting about the throat. Her face was small and heart-shaped, the chin softly rounded, but it was the eyes that attracted. They were very large and baby-blue, and filled with quiet confidence. "And though we've never had children of our own, I feel we've been kindly endowed from heaven with the hearts of parents. And, in a sense, Winburn has had many, many sons and daughters." She laughed, a soft, melodious sound, and everyone laughed with her, though Abby wasn't sure exactly what they were laughing about, and she was getting a tiny, uneasy feeling. For a moment her knife remained motionless in one hand and a huge, green tomato in the other while she tried to analyze the feeling, at the same time furtively admiring Mrs. Tolsey's fashionable black and white wing-tip high heeled shoes.

"He's been teaching for almost 20 years," Mrs. Tolsey went on. "Not that that is of great importance, but it should qualify him for something, don't you think?" Another gay laugh. "But I simply must emphasize once again—before Winburn continues—that we never do things rashly, without much careful consideration."

A tiny, adoring smile towards her husband signaled him the floor was his once again. "Kathleen and I have been doing some very serious thinking," he said. He cleared his throat, re-rolled the brim of his hat, and changed positions. "We—ah, have been watching David, as I said earlier . . ."

A strange tenseness was growing in the room. It was being propagated, Abby sensed, by some feeling other than the usual discomfort caused by the presence of regality. She and David looked at each other then, and all at once she had the distinct feeling that he knew already the reason for the Tolseys' visit.

"Your son shows exceeding promise," Mr. Tolsey said gravely, his gaze fixed somewhere behind Papa. "I can say without reservation that I've never seen a finer mind for computation. I believe I can safely say he is a mathematical wizard. I have no doubt in my mind that, given the proper guidance, he will go far. Perhaps even more than we can comprehend at this point."

Papa nodded, as he had done occasionally, but there was a slight, wary look settling upon his face. Mama's expression registered a similar look, and she fussed with her hair for a moment, nervously pushing the brunette strands back into the bobby pins that were holding the rest of it back out of her face. David stood motionless, his hands thrust into his pants pockets, his tanned, strong-jawed face strangely intent, his eyes full of wonderment and curiosity.

"We'd like to make an offer," Mr. Tolsey continued. "Perhaps you may think it an unusual offer—and I hasten to add that it is done with all due respect toward you folks."

Again the petite Mrs. Tolsey placed a gentle hand on his arm. "And please know that we have thought this over so very carefully . . ."

Mr. Tolsey continued, "We feel strongly that David should be totally immersed in an environment of—learning, of dedication to the acquiring and the assimilation of knowledge. We feel he should be developed mentally and intellectually to his fullest potential. We believe we can offer such an environment."

Mrs. Tolsey smiled upon them prettily, a vague pleading in her wide, baby-blue eyes. "In our home David would be given total freedom to explore, to expand, to discover. There would be no distractions, monetary or otherwise. Winburn and I feel it would almost be criminal to allow such brilliance to—in a sense—fall by the wayside. And we don't say this with any intention whatsoever of casting a reflection upon you good people, but there are unusual mental capabilities at stake here. Taking everything into consideration it is even an aesthetic thing. Yet there is much, much more to our concern than that. And—even now—we look upon David as we would a son . . ."

Absolute quiet prevailed for the longest time. The only one stirring was Lucy, who was playing dolls beneath the table, and occasionally gazed at Mrs. Tolsey in deepest admiration and wonderment. Papa's shoulders drooped and he was looking past Mr. Tolsey, concentrating hard to find the right words. "So, what you're saying is . . ." he began slowly.

When he hesitated, Mrs. Tolsey said softly, "We would be honored to take the responsibility of David's education into our hands. He simply must go to college, Mr. and Mrs. Eason. Educationally, he must have all the advantages that money can provide. In today's society—well, higher education is hardly a matter of choice, especially for one with such a brilliant mind."

"We don't expect you good folks to make the decision today," Mr. Tolsey concluded magnanimously. Now that his message had been stated in full detail, he seemed completely at ease. "But we believe when every angle is considered, every possibility examined—"

Papa almost had to force his way back into the conversation, but he did so with the gentleness that was part of his nature. "We know you folks mean well, and we can see your side, but we don't need no time to make no decision. Our decision's done already been made before you-all walked in the door. Before we ever even knowed you. Back to the time when David was first borned. There ain't no way a man can part with his flesh and blood jist at the drop of a hat. I'd sooner cut off one of my arms and offer it to you folks as I would one of my young'uns. I don't mean to be ungrateful, but it's jist the way things is."

Mrs. Tolsey's hand rose slowly to her throat, and she lightly clasped her husband's arm as she worked to regain her composure. Mr. Tolsey patted the tiny hand with his big one and said with calm self-confidence, "Can we leave the matter open, please? It is only five miles between our homes, so it isn't as though you wouldn't see him often. But perhaps it was a more staggering proposal than we had first thought. Nevertheless, the invitation, you understand, will be valid indefinitely . . ."

When they were gone, Mama sat rather abruptly in one of the slat-backed chairs and murmured dazedly, "Well, I do vow."

Lucy was at the window, staring, and Papa and Abby looked, too, as the Ford Couplet with its blue-black mirror paint job and real leather top, drove away in a little cloud of red dust. David had talked about the Couplet before, as well as the Lincoln Continental Cabriolet the Tolseys were considering buying. He knew a lot about them, and their plans for the future. Abby found herself wondering worriedly if he and the Tolseys were on even closer terms than any of them had known. Papa must have been thinking the same thing. He turned to David, who was gently scuffing the blackened linoleum with the toe of one worn shoe.

"They shouldn't of said it out in front of you, Davey," he said quietly. "Unless they'd already said it to you in private."

David moved restlessly over to get another drink from the water bucket and he kept his back turned. "They asked me if I would like to, is all," he said reluctantly.

Papa thought about that for a moment. "And they shouldn't of talked to you before they talked to me and Mama in private first."

"They didn't mean no harm, Papa," David said. As though the whole matter was hardly worthy of consideration, he shrugged his wide bony shoulders, saying, "It was jist talk, anyhows."

Papa started to say something more, then changed his mind. "We got chores," he reminded.

"It jist—ain't natural," Mama was saying, more to herself than to anyone else.

And that was the drift of their conversation, hers and Papa's, later on that night, even after all of them were in bed. It was as though the idea weighed upon them so heavily that they couldn't quite put it out of their minds. Talking about it seemed to serve as a release. In the double bed with Lucy, Abby listened through the thin one-by-twelve walls and felt their anxiety keenly.

She wondered how David felt. All his life he had been enough like Papa that he kept most of his big thoughts and feelings to himself. During supper he had tried with dogged determination to set them at ease with his banter. It was almost as though he was apologizing for the episode.

Then after supper, while Abby and Mama and Lucy cleaned up the kitchen and Papa soldered the handle back on a stewer, David had gone outside. As Abby washed dishes (and cautioned Lucy not to drop them as she dried) she watched him through the window. He was down at the cow lot in the gathering dusk, leaning on the sagging board fence, just staring.

There were several stars twinkling in the sky and a breeze was softly sweeping away the heat of the day when Abby hesitantly made her way down to the cow lot. David didn't seem to notice she was there. He was absently pricking the board fence with his pocketknife. The cows were stirring, lowing softly to calves or merely to each other, and that warm cow-smell was all about them. Abby slipped through the fence and put her arms around one named Elsie. She leaned there comfortably and scratched Elsie's neck and watched David's shadowy form out of the corner of her eye.

"Did you want to go?"

He didn't look up, just plucked the knife blade into the fence. "I dunno."

That could mean a dozen things. It could have meant yes, no or varying degrees between. Abby kept scruffling Elsie's neck gently and tried again. "It'd be like they was your parents. How would you like that?"

"Aw, it ain't nothing like that," David scoffed. "They jist want me to have a chance to learn. That's all."

"You'd like that, not workin' in the field," Abby said, testing. She found herself waiting to breathe until David answered, half hoping he would say he would a thousand times over rather be with his own family, even if the work was hard. But he didn't. Still looking into the darkness, he merely said, "Yeah, it'd be okay, I guess."

"It wouldn't be the same around here, though," Abby said, still giving him a chance to mention that he wouldn't leave his family for anything.

Instead, he suddenly grinned a little, his squinted blue eyes glimmering. "Lucy'd be glad, I bet."

Thinking of the way David always warted Lucy to death, Abby grinned back at him. "I bet she'd help you pack."

Then they both laughed some. Abby was more or less convinced that David would have gone with the Tolseys if the choice had been his.

For several days the Tolseys' visit cast a slight pall over their lives. But it was fall, and the first bolls of cotton were opening. Papa and David were busy repairing the old cotton trailers for the landlord, Dutch Turner, and getting the last of the wheat sowed. Mama and Abby and Lucy finished making chow-chow from the last of the green tomatoes in the garden, and pickled okra and canned the final batch of peas. In between times, they made new straps for the cotton sacks and reinforced the underside of some of them with new duckin' so they would be ready for the first picking of cotton.

Gradually the preposterous proposal of the Tolseys paled, as most unpleasant situations do. As fall passed into winter, and hands and minds were preoccupied with harvest, the conversation about David's future was all but forgotten.

Chapter Three

ABBY WAS getting chill bumps in spite of several layers of David's old shirts. The stinging wind sweeping down through native elm and post oak along Squirrel Creek whipped her long braid around into her face and pulled at her clothes, forceful enough to bend the resisting stalks of cotton over against her occasionally.

She made herself keep moving, ignoring the frequent blasts of red dust peppering her face, methodically snapping bolls with experienced, canvas-gloved hands. When she had several, she would push them with one hand down into the duckin' sack she was dragging with a wide shoulder strap, while reaching for more bolls with the other hand.

It was an automatic process—snapping, transferring, and emptying—that might seem fascinating, or at least slightly complicated to a novice. To Abby, it was more like breathing or swallowing. She did it without considering it while her mind relived last night's checker game or the Amos 'n Andy program they occasionally heard on the car radio, or Heath Martin's smile.

Pulling bolls was second nature to cropper's children because as babies they rode along on their Mama's cotton sack (baby-settin', Papa called it, mimicking the term the very rich used when they went off cavorting at town and left their children behind with a paid "sitter"). From age three or four they pulled in their Mama's sacks, scurrying along the row ahead with a syrup pail or lard bucket to fill. Around age four or five they were presented with a sack all their own, complete with shoulder strap made from the backs of worn-out Levi's or overalls. Even the very young or the weak-minded could snap cotton if his back was strong and his will controlled. The children of sharecroppers were usually noted for their snappin' abilities, if not much else.

It was early January and the cotton stalks were long dead, the leaves curled and brown, but every boll on the stalk, even the tiny, dried-up ones, had to be gathered. Abby had learned at an early age that when the stalks were small they could be stripped with both hands in one motion. It was no problem for the cotton gin over in Shawnee to separate the dried leaves and pieces of stalk from the cotton, as well as the seeds and hulls, thanks to Eli Whitney's genius.

When a norther was on, as it was today, Abby tried to gather the first few pounds in a hurry. Otherwise, the wind would lift the cotton sack right off the ground in a swirl of red dirt and bits of dry leaves, sometimes with enough velocity that it almost took her with it. Of course, she wasn't very large for her age. "No bigger'n a minute," Mama often said of her. "Hafta stand up twice't to make a shadow," Papa would agree. Only he called it *"Schatten"* in that thick accent to make them laugh.

Because it was unusually cold and windy for boll-pullin', Papa had bargained with them at the scales a few minutes earlier. "One more good weighin'," he had said above the gusts of wind. "David, you git at least sixty pounds, Abby forty-five, Lucy twenty."

"What about Mama?" Lucy asked pertly, holding a gloved hand over her reddened nose in order to warm it.

Papa had winked at Mama and said to Lucy, "I got a lotta confidence in Mama. She don't never play ducks and drakes with her time the way some of us around here does. Now, let's git our rows and light a shuck. I bet Mama'll make us some good hot 'tater soup when we git home. And I'd bet my day's wages she's got some peanuts we can stick in the oven for later on around the fire."

David was dawdling, as he had been doing more and more of late. Maybe it was his age? Abby had heard Papa tell Mama one night that sixteen was a *rauh* age, for boys especially, and they would just have to be patient until it passed. Or maybe David still secretly thought about the Tolseys' visit back in the fall. Since that time Abby had half-expected them to come again and reaffirm their mind-boggling proposal. On the other hand, she was confident Papa's refusal had been potent enough that they would think twice before continuing to pursue such an obviously futile venture.

Crouched down on his knees, apparently oblivious to the unusual onslaught of wind, David studied a strand of cotton, stretching it out slowly from the boll. He could have been trying to figure out how Eli Whitney had devised the mechanism for getting out the seeds. On the other hand, Abby would have bet his mind was miles away, over at Norman at the University, or at nearby Shawnee where the Baptists had a college. Random remarks he had made lately, casual though they were, indicated he was doing some deep thinking about higher education.

And Lucy, a pathetic little figure in her faded and outgrown red wool coat, was hunkered up against the cold, just standing. Her sack, made especially for her by Mama out of a burlap bag that had first held a hundred pounds of potatoes, was whippng and billowing out behind her because she hadn't put much into it yet.

"Lucy," Abby said with quiet cunning. "Think about somethin' good when you're cold and don't wanta work."

"Ain't nothin' good right now," Lucy said, looking around dejectedly at the row upon row of dead cotton stalks loaded with bolls that awaited their hands.

"Remember when Gran'ma Eason was here Christmas a year past?"

Lucy twisted her mouth, thinking. "I wonder if our little Dresden dolls she gave us are still put up in the closet," she asked.

"Sure," Abby said. "Where else would they be?"

"We oughta see if Mama'd let us git 'em out," Lucy said, becoming interested.

"Maybe we could ask her sometime," Abby agreed. She thought about the tiny Dresden dolls that Mama had smothered in muslin and tucked away under some quilts. Dolls that Grandma had cherished (but never handled) as a young girl and that her German mama had owned before that. The little, perfect Dresdens were not for playing with or for holding, Mama explained, but just to think about and pass on from generation to generation. Only twice since that Christmas had Mama gotten the dolls out and allowed the girls to look and exclaim for a few minutes and cautiously caress the tiny features with gentle fingertips. Abby sometimes wondered if beautiful things were worth having when you were so seldom allowed to see or touch them.

"Remember how the Christmas tree looked?" Lucy said, getting into the spirit of remembering.

"The *Tannenbaum*," Abby murmured, nodding. That's what Grandma called it, being half-German, and making it sound like a little catchy phrase of music.

"*Der Tannenbaum*—it vud be *besser* dis high," she had said once when they had chopped a tree too small for her liking. "Dey are to fill *der Heim* viss dere *frohlocken*, not *der* corner only!" *Heim,* they all knew, meant home and Papa explained with his usual patience that *frohlocken* meant joy and gladness.

Grandma had been a Holmsdorfer and had spent her first twenty-three years in Germany, which explained why she had never been able to pick up much more of the English language than she needed to become a citizen. She spoke a strange mixture of her own that they could usually understand if they listened closely. If not, Papa would interpret, though he never used the language except for occasional teasing, or when he was disturbed or upset, which was not often. Mama said deep things always brought out the Holmsdorfer in him.

But the *Tannenbaum*. Papa and David had cut it, a scratchy, fragrant cedar from down by Squirrel Creek. They had found an extra large one in case Grandma got to come, though the weatherman on the radio said the snows would keep right on coming and leave half of Oklahoma snowbound. Making it a family affair, they had strung popcorn and red-orange possum berries, and made bright chains by cutting the colored pages of the catalog into strips and pasting them with flour and water into loops. Mama had mixed more flour and water and brushed the tops of some of the branches, giving the enchanting appearance of clinging snow.

"And the candles, Abby," Lucy said eagerly. "D'you think we could make candles like Gran'ma's for next Christmas? We shoulda thought of it this year."

"If we could git some wax we might," Abby said. Grandma called her candles *Kerzen,* and kept them for Christmas only, for "Vhat is *der Tannenbaum* viss-out *Kerzen*?" They were handmade by Grandma, herself, when she was still in her teens and each year if circumstances allowed her to visit at Christmastime, always the candles came, too. They had holders, all twenty-four of them, that could be attached to the tree branches. Mama had lighted them for a few, brief moments that Christmas before last, and the beauty of it had almost taken Abby's breath away.

While the tiny flames were flickering and bobbing, causing pleasant shadows to dance across the walls and all their faces, Papa had read the Christmas story from the gospel of Luke. Then holding hands, they had all sung, "Silent Night, Holy Night," with Grandma's high, quavery voice joining in. Only she was saying, *"Stille Nacht, Heilige Nacht"*. . .

"Why didn't Gran'ma come this Christmas?" Lucy asked, not because she didn't know already, but because she realized Abby had been idle longer than usual and would be shortly prodding her to get busy. A bit of ingenuity was clearly in order.

"It's a long drive from Tulsa and there was that blizzard," Abby answered, coming away from the glow of the Christmas memory reluctantly. "Maybe next Christmas she can. Now, Lucy," and she tried to ease into it gently, "We've got to git busy or we're never gonna git through."

Lucy sighed deeply. "We ain't never gonna git through, anyways." But she set to work resolutely—at least for the time being.

Because his back bothered him too much to bend over for long periods, Abby noticed Papa was doing his work walking along on his knees in the powdery red dust. He stopped now to adjust a strap on one of his knee pads and glanced back at David. He studied the situation for a minute, then said distinctly, in a low but rollicking voice, " 'I sprang to the stirrup, and Joris, and he; I galloped, Dirck galloped, we galloped all three.' "

David had glanced up quickly at the first word, and was grinning with interest. "Robert Browning," he said.

" 'How They Brought The Good News From Ghent to Aix.' "

Papa nodded, his eyes looking at his cotton row, a little smile playing about his lips. "Let's do some gallopin,' " he suggested mildly.

Then, toward Lucy, who was standing idle again, " 'Whatsoever thy hand findeth to do, do it with thy might.' "

Lucy, shivering inside her red coat, looked at Abby. "I don't remember," she whispered anxiously.

"Ecclesiastes," Abby prodded, pushing a handful of bolls into her sack.

"Ecclesiastes . . ." Lucy relayed to Papa, who was looking stern only because his blue eyes were trained so steadily upon his work.

"9:10," Abby finished softly.

"9:10," Lucy echoed loudly, so everyone could hear.

"Put your hands to work a-grabbin' them bolls, Lucy Belle," Papa admonished blandly. "Twenty pounds ain't too much for a big gal like you."

Abby thought at first Papa wasn't going to give her one, then in a somber rumble he began, " 'Theirs not to make reply, Theirs not to reason why—' "

" 'Theirs but to do and die,' " Abby finished for him smartly. "Tennyson, 'The Charge of the Light Brigade.' "

Papa nodded, pleased. "We'll be tradin' daylight for dark if we keep dawdlin'. Let's all light a corn shuck, now."

David began working like a house afire, which was the way he did things. With him it was either all or none, Papa often said, and would usually shake his head wondering, though at times he freely admitted to the same tendencies as a boy.

Lucy reached out and picked two bolls tentatively, apparently not quite enough inspired. "Give Mama one," she cajoled.

Mama threw Papa a glance, tugging her tightly fastened wool head-rag into place, a hesitant smile on her wind-reddened face. She was never very comfortable when they were doing mind-building exercises. She had had schooling to the eighth grade, the same as Papa, but she had never been much on reading. Like Papa said, a book in the hand was worth two dozen in the shelf.

"Give her an easy 'un," Lucy added charitably. Then she grabbed for her sack as it flew straight up with a sharp gust of wind.

Papa thought for a minute, all the while thrusting big handfuls of bolls into his sack, the points of the dried bolls shrieking softly as they passed over the coarse material.

" 'In happy homes he saw the light of household fires gleam warm and bright.' "

Mama considered for only an instant, then shook her head. "You know me, Travis," she said apologetically. "Mind about as quick as a hog-tied turtle. I can remember hearin' you read it, but that's as far as it goes." She nervously tucked a stray wisp of brown hair under the wool head-rag and went back to work.

"Give her a hint," Abby said, confident that Mama could get this one with a little pushing.

Papa studied for another second. " 'His brow was sad, his eye beneath, flashed like a falchion from its sheath.' "

Still smiling gamely, Mama shrugged her narrow shoulders hopelessly.

" 'Excelsior!' " Lucy cried then, triumphantly. "Anybody should know that 'un!"

"Jist because it's your favorite," Abby chided her

quietly. "Mama caint help it if she's not especially good at memorizing," she said in Mama's defense.

"Henry Longworth Wadsfellow!" Lucy continued, gloating.

David looked back and guffawed at the mix-up in Longfellow's name, and Abby giggled behind her glove. With laughter sparkling out of her deep blue eyes, Mama said consolingly, "That's still better'n I did, pun'kin," and Papa corrected the crestfallen Lucy, managing to keep most of his smile contained.

Then, because not one of them was doing his or her job by then, he said pointedly, "Excelsior, now!"

Of course they knew the word meant 'ever upward' in Latin, which meant Papa was still hinting broadly at them to get to work and even that struck them as humorous. Luckily, working came as naturally to them as funning, and they all set their minds with renewed vigor to cotton snapping.

They were still in high spirits when they arrived back at the house several pounds of cotton later. It was almost like a holiday quitting the fields in the middle of the afternoon and getting out of the weather that Papa said wasn't fit for man nor beast. Mama and Abby immediately started paring vegetables for the soup, and Lucy set the table.

David went to get several arms of dry shinnery roots from behind the house so Papa could build a fire in the Franklin. They were roots picked up out of the fields in the spring, both for use later and because they got in the way of the plows. When Lucy had given her usual dim view of the back-breaking task, Papa had asked her with twinkling blue eyes, "Did anybody ever tell you why the good Lord made shinnery trees, Lucy Belle?"

"It wouldn't make no difference to me," Lucy said frankly.

So that Papa's feelings would be spared, and because she was always curious, Abby had asked, "How come, Papa?"

"So's pore folks would have heat in their house come winter!" he said. "Rich folks, they've gotta go down to the railroad yard and pay out good money for a load of coal and the rest of us jist goes out and picks our fuel right off the land. Ain't nobody gonna tell me Oklahoma ain't rich in natural resources!"

"He sure outdid Hisself on this field," David had commented, looking out across the sandy ridges at the impressive scattering of roots, both loose ones and those still attached that were sticking up at various angles. "Ever' time the wind blows fifteen minutes, it uncovers another wagon-load."

And now the dried roots of the shinnery were proving their worth again, as they had—and would—every day of winter, providing a roaring hot fire. Papa always said nothing, not even the city dude's coal, could burn as hot as shinnery roots. Of course, they weren't very long-lived so that a good deal of time was spent feeding the fire and running out back for another armload.

Very soon the chill was off the kitchen and the Easons could stop shivering and peel off two or three layers of clothes, hanging them on the row of nails near the front door. Each had his own nail, and each was responsible for keeping his own 'outside' clothes hung their neatly, ready for use the next day.

Stirring butter into the soup and breathing in the tantalizing aroma of boiling potatoes and onions, Abby thought contentedly, 'In happy homes he saw the light of household fires gleam warm and bright.' She pictured the youth in "Excelsior," wondering if he hadn't been sorely tempted to stop in those snug homes by the household fires instead of pressing ever upward. Of course, it wouldn't have made much of a poem if he had.

David was like that. He had that same drive, that burning zeal that had sent that youth on through snow and ice despite warnings about the Pass and the avalanche, even despite the gentle persuading of the maiden and the prayers of the monks. The youth had pressed on and on and in the end his fervor for struggling ever upward had cost him his life. That was the part of the poem that left a little hollow sadness in Abby's throat and she promptly put it all out of her mind now by sinking back into the warm and cozy atmosphere of the Eason kitchen, with the crackling and popping of the fire, the fragrance of cooking food, the security of family.

If it weren't for the uncertainties and occasional futileness of sharecropping, she wouldn't change places with anybody in the world. And when they were all together like this, content and happy, even sharecropping was entirely bearable.

Chapter Four

"WELL, I'LL swan," David said blandly. "Would you look at what was in Lucy Belle's ear."

They had just boarded the school bus to go home. Everyone within David's hearing distance looked as he held up a penny.

Lucy gave him a disdainful glance. "I ain't that dumb."

"I've a good mind to see if there's more in there," David mused, his blue eyes glinting with suppressed mirth. Then his long arm snaked out and hovered near Lucy's ear again and another penny appeared.

There were hoots of approving laughter. The day before they had seen The Great Marvoni perform magic at a school assembly. Now, somehow here was that David Eason doing one of the same tricks with every bit as much skill.

"I don't no more b'lieve that than a man in the moon," Lucy declared, reaching up and feeling experimentally of her right ear.

"I bet you've got enough in there to buy you a Baby Ruth candy bar," David said thoughtfully. And sure enough, he plucked out another penny.

"Quit it," Lucy said, glaring. "Ever'body knows it's not real."

"Why, it looks real to me," David said, examining the penny. "Don't it look real to you, Rick?"

Rick thought it did. Everyone was grinning at David's little game and some urged him on. Even in a world that thought sharecroppers were a little less than most, David had a flair for being the center of attention and he always played it to the fullest.

A newcomer named Linette was sitting by Abby and she asked softly, her gaze resting on David, "Does he have a girlfriend?"

Abby smiled and felt a touch of pride, as though she had something to do with his looks and personality. "I don't know. He never talks about girls."

"I bet he thinks about them."

"Maybe." But Abby really doubted it. As far as she knew, David had always steered clear of girls, preferring to mull over the intricacies of those newly invented power-operated car windows or the principles of Newton's laws of motion or some other boring theory.

"Would you find out if he thinks I'm pretty or not?" Linette continued, apparently quite smitten.

Even knowing it was useless, Abby agreed benevolently. No matter where they had lived, girls always reacted that way to David. Pied Piper, Papa called him, seeming to get a bigger kick out of all the stricken girls than David did. Even high-brow girls—daughters of bankers and such—cast longing glances his way, though they were careful not to admit it.

The bus slowed and Abby absently surveyed the unkempt yard and tumble-down shack as the Barkley girl got off. Vickie Barkley was frail and skinny and had the look of a loser. Bo Barkley, it was said, slapped and booted his kids around. Abby had seen it when they were working in adjoining fields. Bo Barkley cursed and ranted if he imagined any of his children slacked up.

Kate Barkley was no better, smoking, drinking and cursing like a sailor. Complexion like bull-hide leather from the effects of tobacco smoke, but mostly from being out in the weather without bothering to cream her face at night the way Mama tried to do. Mama had heard Mrs. Barkley was caught up in reading movie magazines and dime novels when she wasn't in the fields. She changed bedcovers and swept out the house once or twice a year whether it needed it or not, Mama had said quite sarcastically once, adding that it was people like them Barkleys that gave sharecroppers a bad name. A little dirt was expected, Mama allowed, what with Oklahoma dust storms and precious little time for cleaning, but a pig-pen existence was another story. Even though the Easons sometimes shared extra milk or garden produce with neighbors such as these, Mama said it was pretty nigh impossible to help somebody that wouldn't help themselves.

"Well, I'll be," David was saying smoothly as another penny appeared miraculously. "No wonder Lucy's head's been rattlin' so much."

"My head ain't been rattlin' near as much as yours has," Lucy said indignantly. Then she escaped to the front of the bus, even though they were in motion and the bus driver frowned as he looked through the mirror.

David's laugh triggered a hearty response by his admirers. Then utilizing that dash of charisma that always attracted a following, David demonstrated the trick several times until the others had mastered it. That was David—in spite of his lowly status as a sharecropper's son, he was always surrounded by admirers—made up of all classes of people, often even placed on a pedestal, yet more often than not, willing and eager to share a bit of himself with others.

Mama had said not long ago that it wasn't good for David to have things so easy, to be used as an example by teachers and other grown-ups that should know better. Could go to his head, she said, and give him highfalutin' notions and make him go against his raisin'. A body needed to know how to work for things, sweating out the hard ones, instead of having them fall into his hands like so many perfect apples.

Papa had laughed heartily and said that for a little half-pint heifer she could do some tall worrying. David could take care of hisself, he said. His head had always been on straight, hadn't it? Why fret before any milk was even spilt? Mama had agreed, but not wholly convinced.

A letter came from Aunt Myrtle that week. It was filled, as usual, with exclamation points and parentheses and underlined words—just as the way Aunt Myrtle talked. Papa read it aloud to them, his deep, resonant voice lending substance to the lighthearted prattle.

> "On our way to Dallas. Nasty business trip. You know Lewis and his holdings. He can't seem to get all his eggs into one basket (you see! I *am* on to the sayings of you farmers! ha!) Mother Eason *insists* on seeing you. Lewis wanted her to wait till spring, but she has her mind set. (She's an *Eason*, after all!) It's been over a year, she keeps reminding us. We'll drop her on the way unless we hear from you otherwise. If you were fixing to take off for Europe or somewhere, we understand! (ha!) Looking forward to seeing you Saturday afternoon, twenty-third of January. Don't cook for us—we'll grab a bite in the city."

Uncle Lewis' holdings, Papa had explained long ago, were the oil interests that Aunt Myrtle's father had passed on to them back when she and Uncle Lewis first married. Because of this 'tidy living,' as Aunt Myrtle called it, Uncle Lewis had not farmed a day in his life since he left home at twenty.

Grandma still mentioned it occasionally, bewildered by the departure of her son from that which he rightfully should be. It had upset and confused her back then because her family over in Germany had all been farmers, toilers of the land, for generations.

"*Besser* it iss to be *der Pachter*," she said often. Better to be a farmer. Because *Pachters* made the world go. They filled hungry stomachs and put clothes on bare backs.

And for their closeness to the Land, *Pachters* were better people than the average. "It jist iss so," Grandma said, not with pride or arrogance, but with quiet certainty and staunch loyalty.

When Uncle Lewis would laughingly try to tell her of oil prices and market reports and gushers and the like, Grandma became even more stubborn.

"Takin' *der* insides out from *der* Land," she said, clicking her tongue and shaking her head. "Someday *der* Land vill come in, like *der*—like *der*—" and her searching eyes found the balloons she had presented to her grandchildren, which Lucy and Abby were busily blowing up, "—like *der* play-purty viss-out *der* air."

At that precise moment one of the balloons had popped, giving Grandma a terrible start and causing her to throw her hands into the air, after which she laughed at herself, but with much relief, "Already I'm tinkin' *der* Land hass come in!"

And Uncle Lewis, as well as the rest of them, laughed heartily at Grandma's assumption that the earth was filled with oil and would eventually collapse if it were all drawn out.

"Mama," he said fondly, "if it was left up to you there wouldn't be an oil well in the state. Then where would we be? Look at it this-a-way. I'm a farmer, too, only I go deeper for my crop." He thought for a moment and seemed pleased with this spur-of-the-moment analogy, and enlarged a bit. "Oil's the fruit and we're diggin' for it like Travis, here, digs for potatoes. I'm a farmer, Mama. An oil *Pachter!*"

Grandma only shook her head and later she confided to Abby, as though only the two of them could understand, "Iss *besser* to *Holten* to *der* Land, Abby-*Madchen*." *Holten* meant to 'hold,' of course, and Abby pictured someone lying on the ground and digging his hands determinedly into the soil, holding on for dear life.

That was almost the way Papa felt toward the land, the way Abby, herself, felt. Still, sharecropping held little hope for the simple reason that croppers never owned the farms they toiled over year after year. Somehow, there was a vast difference in owning and tending.

From across the way Abby could see the Barkleys at the cotton trailer for a weighing. Vickie Barkley had pulled her sack of cotton in under the scale and was now sitting languidly against the wheel while her father weighed and her brothers did the emptying.

The north breeze brought Bo Barkley's loudness near as he barked out the weights with an occasional epithet thrown in for good measure. Abby could see in her mind his beady eyes, mean even in his jesting, a whiskery cheek bulging with a chew of tobacco. Today his mood was apparently jovial and uncouth instead of angry and uncouth—a slight improvement.

On the Easons' side of the fence, Mama and Papa were a little way ahead, as well as Lucy, who often worked on any row she preferred instead of having one of her own. Abby had dropped back to help David, since he was dawdling again. In fact, he was now standing there in the middle of his row with one arm and hand hanging loosely in the opening of his cotton-sack, obviously a thousand miles away.

Without breaking her cotton-snapping rhythm, Abby said, "Linette Hopper said you was cute."

David didn't move a muscle. Didn't even bat an eye.

"She said she'd give her eye tooth for a picture of you."

Nothing from David.

"D'you think she's purty?"

David, having apparently not heard a word, began

to move slowly and reached thoughtfully for a boll. "Ab, you ever heard of Vannevar Bush?"

"No. What grade's he in?"

David rolled his eyes upward in agony at such stupidity. "He's not in a grade. He's a full-grown man, president of the Carnegie Institution since '39."

"Well, how'm I supposed to know?" Abby huffed. "Does he live around here, or what?"

"What would he be doin' around here, if he's president of the Carnegie Institution? Besides, have you ever heard of any famous college president bein' from Tecumseh, Oklahoma?"

"I never heard of him, so he must not be very famous," Abby came back. "And Papa's lookin' to see how come you're not workin'."

David started pulling bolls right and left and his almost-full cotton-sack followed him in little zig-zags. "It told about him in the *Oklahoma Times* newspaper Mr. Tolsey brought to school one day."

"Who—Papa?"

Abby giggled at her joke, but David didn't seem to notice. "He makes machines called differential analysers."

"If they'll pick cotton, I'll take two," Abby intoned, the way Bob Hope would have.

But David was somehow humorously disinclined today. He went on, "They can calculate figures as good as a person."

"Oh, sure. I guess they have brains, maybe," Abby said, thinking David was probably gradually working up to a punch-line. But his eyes weren't giving him away as they usually did. They were cold sober and deeply thoughtful.

"It's somethin' like a brain, I guess. But I figure I can make a better one. You know, like people always say they're gonna build a better mousetrap. Only I'm really gonna do it."

"Build a better trap?" Abby asked innocently.

David scorched her with one of his famous looks and Abby wished she would be more sensible, since David apparently was for once. Rarely did he ever share anything that amounted to a hill of peas. Usually he was either going on like a comedian, or lately, treating Abby as though she—and everyone else—were slightly deranged beneath his dignity. Like Mama and Papa, she was ready for David's *rauh* age to pass.

But she was feeling good today. Cotton was almost over. Grandma was coming. And perhaps best of all, Heath Martin had smiled at her from across the room in a special way several times at school. She had a lot to be happy about, a lot to think about. But those things could wait, and she turned her attention to David, asking quite sanely, "What does one of them things look like?"

"Oh, I dunno for sure. The newspaper didn't show a picture, but I think they're big, maybe as big as an icebox. The one I'm gonna try to make'll be little enough to carry around in your hand."

"What for?"

"It'll be a lot handier."

'Hand' and 'handier?' Abby looked at David closely to see if that could be a joke, but it apparently wasn't, so she merely asked, "Where'd you git such a notion?"

'From readin' about it and studyin' it out. Only you have to have college to work at that kinda stuff."

Abby nodded thoughtfully while pausing to shake down her sack. "Well, there's Winburn Tolsey."

"Yeah," David slowed again, stared some more, thinking deep.

"I bet he'd give you college, even if Papa didn't let

him board you," Abby encouraged. Though she had to admit it to herself it seemed as though Mr. Tolsey was as interested in a son substitute as he was a student. And she remembered how Mrs. Tolsey, immaculately dressed and standing no taller than Mama even in her fashionable wing-tip high heels, had mentioned something about the son they never had.

"That's what I've been a-thinkin'," David said. He's my only chance, the way things is. What I aim to do is see if he'd jist help me git started that first year or two. I could work part-time, but there's no way I could make enough for it all. It costs four dollars a credit hour at Oklahoma University. And the books and eats and things is extry. They say you need four hundred dollars for one semester, countin' ever'thing."

"I don't know anybody that's got that much money," Abby said. Grabbing bolls with her usual industriousness, she added, "Except Winburn Tolsey."

"Yeah," David agreed as he picked another boll or two. "When I git out and git a good-payin' job I could pay him back."

Abby waited a moment then tried half-heartedly again, "Linette Hopper wants to know if you think she's purty."

But David was somewhere else again, deeply solemn. Somehow he looked older and more mature and unfathomly wise. Abby wondered suddenly if he had 'crossed over.' They always talked about it. "When I git grown up," they would say. And the thoughts they added to this vaguely unsettling time always implied a certain magical stepping over into a new, mystical world.

Maybe a world of movie stars, or singing songs over the radio, or going to the Olympics as a participant, or even dancing the ballet. Out in the pasture where no one could see, Abby often twirled and glided, hearing beautiful melodies and performing for a vast, appreciative, invisible audience. David had pompously planned to be president of the United States, or set a world record, or write science and math manuals, or become a big-wig who told union bosses where to get off so there wouldn't be anymore strikes. And in particular, he would tell John L. Lewis, the coal boss, just how the cow eats the cabbage.

All those dreams had been far-fetched, perhaps even laughable. But this college thing—that might be within reach, even for a sharecropper's son. Especially one looked on so favorably by so many, who had Winburn Tolsey on his side.

Abby stole another glance at David, his blue eyes squinting into a slight frown, looking intently at nothing. Thoughts and dreams and plans were no doubt turning in his head. She was going to miss the old David, now that he had crossed over.

But a few minutes later, down at the scale while Papa was weighing the sacks of cotton, she gave a sigh of relief when David started warting them—pulling all sorts of things out of Lucy's ear—a key, even the tiny pocket knife he had gotten for Christmas, until Lucy was thoroughly frustrated and sullen up under the edge of the cotton trailer.

From the far side, David peered under, looking at her and chanting softly and craftily,

> Mirror, Mirror, on the wall,
> Who's the baby of 'em all?
> Lucy Belle, without a doubt!
> Likes to whimper, likes to pout!

"Shut it up!"

> Likes to goo and likes to prattle,
> Likes to shake her baby rattle!

"You make me sick, David Eason! You got a cowlick stickin' up right in the back! Ugly as a mud fence!"

> Tie her bib and change her diaper,
> Wish to Pete someone would swipe her!

"Mama, shut him up! I'm afixin' to hit him good!"

"There won't be no hittin'," Mama said, studying the little paper where she was jotting down the weights. "David, settle down. Wish you had half the energy for pullin' bolls as you do for pullin' legs."

David marched around the trailer obediently, clicked his heels and saluted smartly. "Yes, ma'am, right away, ma'am."

"And no sass," Mama reminded, laboriously trying to total her columns.

Lucy stuck her tongue out at David, who responded, his eyes dancing, "I wish your face'd freeze that-a-way. It'd sure make Frankenstein feel better about hisself."

"Git your sack emptied, David," Papa ordered from the top of the wagonload of cotton.

David caught hold of the makeshift ladder on the side of the trailer and gave Lucy a parting shot.

> Hubba, hubba, hey, hey
> Lucy Belle went that-a-way!

Over in the next field, Bo Barkley was getting worked up about something and his booming voice could be heard, foul language and all. The family didn't seem to be paying him much mind until Kate Barkley began getting heated up and the two of them exchanged unbelievable insults.

"He's crazy, smooth crazy," David muttered, pitching down his empty sack and picking up Lucy's limp, half-filled one and emptying it with one or two jerks of a hand.

"It's not so much that, as it is he knows so much that ain't so," Papa said mildly.

"Somebody oughta put the hindrance to him," David suggested, climbing down the ladder.

Papa followed. "You cain't reason with a bunch of baloney."

"Yeah, I forgot," David said, grinning over at Lucy. "I guess that's why I ain't havin' much success with Lucy Belle today. She's jist full of it, ain't she?"

At that, Lucy lunged and pinched David's hip with energy, declaring loudly, "David's the ridiculousest boy I ever knowed."

Mama said patiently, "Davey-boy, I think that's enough funnin' for now. Lucy Belle, you smooth down your hackles and git on your toleratin' face. Let's try to git another good weighin' before sundown."

David wriggled his head and one arm through the duckin' strap of his cotton sack and said softly, "Lucy's a jim-dandy pinch-hitter. If she can't hit you, she'll pinch you!" He added, smirking, "But she's got a problem. She don't know a gen-u-wine rooster tail from a cowlick!"

And as the Easons found their rows and resumed boll-pulling, their laughter and talk easily drowned out the harsh and meaningless arguing and mean talk from the field across the fence.

Chapter Five

ON FRIDAY, the twenty-second, the sun was out at last, distant and pale, and during the night the wind had laid. It would have been a perfect winter day for dragging cotton sacks. David would have said with fine-honed sarcasm that "perfect" and "cotton" should never be mentioned in the same breath. However, they had finished the last field the day before, so it wasn't necessary.

"We'll dress some hens for tomorrow," Mama said as soon as breakfast was over. She smiled as she added, "Myrtle always says not to cook, but she'd be thunderstruck if I didn't."

Then she stood, thinking, her lips pursed. "We'll warsh the windows—jist the insides, since it's still so cold. We'll hafta mop. I let it go too long as it is, what with the cotton and all. And I b'lieve we'll use some of them dried apples for a cobbler."

They put a boiler of water on the stove to heat for scalding the hens and started the breakfast dishes while Papa and David went out to catch two hen. In order to pick out only those that were not laying at present, they would test them by measuring across the lower back bones. If the bones were three fingers apart the hen was likely a good layer. If less than that, then she probably was falling down on her job. The lazier hens were usually fatter anyway, and would make the best dumplings.

When the water was almost to the boiling point, Papa carried it outside where he dunked each hen, now headless, just long enough to loosen the feathers, yet not long enough to damage the plump skin. Steam and the wet feather smell rose all about them as they hurriedly plucked off the feathers, putting the tough tail and wing feathers into one pile to be discarded and the soft ones in a gunny sack to be hung over the clothesline to fluff and dry. Someday, when enough of them were collected, they would either make more pillows or an entire feather mattress, a *Matratze*, like Grandma's.

"I'm hard-put to tell why they call this-here dressin' chickens," Papa said, his breath making little puffs of vapor in the cold. 'Looks to me like we're undressin' 'em!"

"It'd make a fine burlesque show," David drawled, as though he knew all about such things. "At least it would for a rooster!"

Mama was scandalized at that and told David to watch his tongue and he and Papa looked at each other and laughed silently. And though Abby only had a vague notion as to what a burlesque show was, she couldn't help thinking it was funny too, especially when David forced one of the stiffening hens to do an imitation of a chorus girl, kicking her leg high. He accompanied her by singing a snatch of the chicken song that was getting so popular nowadays:

> Chickery-chick cha-la cha-la
> Check-a-la-re in a ba-nan-i-ka . . .

"'Tonsil-tanglin' nonsense," Mama called the song, shaking her head sadly over the decline of modern children. "Why they don't write words that make sense these days is beyond me." And probably, if it hadn't been so disagreeably cold and if they hadn't been in such a hurry to finish, she would have added a few choice words about the descent of decency and 'right thinkin' ' in the United States, and how it always came out in the latest songs and movies you heard about and the outlandish books people were said to be writing.

Papa quickly rinsed the hens with a bucket of water out of the barrel in the well house while telling about a gal he knew from back east who married a rabbit farmer. "He asked his new wife if she could dress a rabbit," Papa claimed, "and she reckoned she could dress one as good as the next fellow, and she showed him. She put the purtiest little pair of pants and shirt on that rabbit you ever saw."

Everyone was about as stiff as the hens by now. Inside again, it was necessary to warm near the roaring Franklin before they could manipulate their hands enough to finish cleaning the pin feathers and entrails. At last the entire mess was tidied up and the hens boiling briskly on the cookstove.

"Lucy Belle," Mama directed, "git an old sock outa the rag-bag and clean off the dresser and things. Now mind, do a good job and don't leave streaks. Abby girl, you git out the clean scarfs for ever'thing, then you warsh the windows. Put some vinegar in your water to cut the grime. David, you fetch two more buckets of water and git some kerosene to fill up the lamps. Trim the wicks while you're at it, but wipe the black off the scissor blades after."

Sounding like Lucy, Papa joshed, "What I gotta do, Mama?"

Mama joshed back, "Jist try to be a good boy and stay outa Mama's way."

Papa got the broom then, whistling "Sally Was A Good Ole Girl," and started sweeping so vigorously that little swirls of dust rose all about him. Mama put a new rag in the mop-head, all the while bantering back and forth with Papa, who was pretending he had the bad end of the deal, having to stoop to housework.

"But such is life," he said philosophically, "when you live with a half-pint *Hausfrau* and a *Hausful* of kids."

"And whose fault would it all be?" Mama demanded gaily.

"Why, the good Lord's, of course," Papa drawled.

With her dust rag idle, Lucy asked curiously, "Papa, would you ruther to have Mama or that movie girl we seen a picture of once't?"

"You mean Jane Russell?" Abby asked, giggling a little and waiting with interest for Papa's answer.

"You want the honest truth, Lucy Belle?" Papa asked, scooping up the sand and trash onto a piece of cardboard. "Or d'ya want me to story a little bit?"

"The truth!" Lucy hollered in gleeful anticipation.

"Well..." Papa winked at Abby and took his time answering, dumping the trash into a galvanized bucket that set in the corner for that purpose, and tucked the cardboard behind the cabinet.

Pouring Lysol into the bucket of sudsy mop water, Mama didn't look very worried even though by her own testimony Papa used to be quite a lady's man with every eligible sharecropper's daughter within twenty-five miles giving him the eagle-eye—and even a few upper-crust ones, too. Once she said she always wondered why Papa picked her, and Papa, in order to make them all laugh, allowed as to how he'd been wondering the same thing.

"Papa," Lucy prodded impatiently.

Papa grinned at her, his blue eyes twinkling merrily. "The truth is always better, Lucy Belle. So I'd have to say I'd ruther have your Mama here, than *two* Jane Russells. Them silver-spangled, high-steppin', moon-eyed wimmen are a dime a dozen, don't you know. There's not a one of 'em as purty as your Mama."

Mama's cheeks were pink. "Travis Eason, who're you tryin' to fool? If one of them movie stars stepped in this door right now you'd fall all over yourself a-tryin' to show 'em your colors. It'd be, 'Ma'am, can I git you a chair?' or 'Let me take your mink coat, little lady, and lay it in the back room.' I know you 'cause I seen you workin' all them little tricks back before we was married!"

Lucy was looking at Mama closely, no doubt to see if she was really that pretty and Abby and David were laughing along with Papa. "Why, fancy wimmen don't move me," he said jauntily. "I like 'em that's got a good head on their shoulders."

David stopped pouring kerosene into the lamp and spoke up knowingly, "Well, I seen that picture and Jane Russell's got a good enough head on her shoulders for me. And the shoulders, theirself, ain't all that bad."

Mama looked at David as though he weren't supposed to notice such things, but the rest of them were laughing, and Mama, too, when Lucy declared frankly, "I would of picked the movie girl, anyways!"

With everything done except the mopping, Papa got a prose and poetry book to read aloud and they all sat on the bed there in the corner of the kitchen in their stocking feet while Mama deftly pushed and pulled the mop over the ridged and blackened linoleums.

"Do 'Excelsior,'" Lucy suggested, her dark blue eyes sparkling.

Papa began:

> The shades of night were fallin' fast,
> As through an Alpine village passed
> A youth, who bore, 'mid snow and ice,
> A banner with the strange device,
> Excelsior!
> His brow was sad; his eye beneath,
> Flashed like a falchion from its
>   sheath...

Half-listening, Abby's gazed intently over the room

inspecting everything. She always did that when they were going to have company, as though she were seeing things through different eyes and could experience what others thought about the plain, well-used appearance of everything.

Steam and a good aroma arose from the stewer of hens on the black and white kerosene cookstove. They'd had the stove a good many years and the oven racks and burners were covered with baked-on grease, but it had served them well. Once a year, in the springtime, Mama took it all apart and soaked it up with lye and got the crusts scraped off until it looked almost as good as new.

Next to that was the cabinet Papa had built years ago from one-by-twelve scraps which held the sugar and flour and cornmeal and such, as well as the dishes. Near the door was the washstand. Hanging on nails above it were a dipper and towel and washrag, and setting on top of it was the wash pan, the two buckets of water, a glass holding five toothbrushes, the box of soda for brushing, and a grimy bar of soap in a saucer. Mama often said, "Jist farmers and mechanics knows what it's like to have to warsh the bar of soap before he warshes his hands." Abby would try and remember to wash the soap before Aunt Myrtle and Uncle Lewis came.

Above the bed where they sat was a picture of Jesus sitting with chubby, adorable children on his lap and gathered around him. At the bottom it said in fancy hand-writing, "Suffer the little children to come unto me." Lucy always said she'd be scared to get that close to Jesus, but Abby knew she wouldn't be able to resist anymore than the children in the picture.

Near the bed was the old mahogany rocker, scarred with time, but well-polished by Mama's furniture wax that was saved for that one purpose only. In the seat of it, over the worn springs and upholstery, was a square feather pillow with a patchwork cover to make it nice and soft for Grandma when she came.

On the other side of the room was the table with the red checkered oilcloth, worn and abused until it was more white than red now, and the six slat-back chairs, three of them minus a rung. One of them had its back leg wired on so deftly that it was scarcely noticeable, but it was rather weak and Lucy was the only one who sat in it.

Sitting on the table near the saltcellar and lamp was a jar of water that contained several sprays of mistletoe, the translucent, bead-like berries and waxy leaves glistening in the pale sun streaming in at the window. Abby had gathered the mistletoe the day before down by Squirrel Creek, where it grew in abundance, green and alive, clinging with tenacity to winter-dead trees.

Mistletoe was a parasite, according to the books, living furtively off the lives of other growing things. But the plant itself was beautiful, and the true story Papa had told them about it enhanced it further. Back in the fall of 1891, the second run for homesteads of Oklahoma Territory took place, he said, part of the land being surplus of the Shawnee and Pottawatomie Indians. In the bleak, cold winter days afterward, a young wife died of pneumonia. Her grieving husband laid her to rest in the frozen ground lying in a handmade coffin. In the absence of flowers to soften the starkness of bareboards, sprays of mistletoe were gathered and tenderly placed on the lid of the coffin. The man's neighbor comforted him, saying, "George, if I ever see this territory become a state, I'll see that the mistletoe is its state flower." And this he did, Papa said, as a member of the Constitutional Convention later on. Abby never saw a spray of mistletoe without pondering for a moment on that anguished young husband, and how he was perhaps comforted a little by the beauty of a plant some considered useless.

Next to the table was the yellowish-white icebox, seldom in use for its original purpose because blocks of ice cost more than they could afford to pay. Papa once said how ironical it was that poor folks could have all the ice they needed—in the winter when they didn't need it! If they wanted to keep something cold, it was taken to the back room by a window.

This was their home, cozy, safe and comfortable even if it was plain and worn. Home, as declared boldly in the crossstitch Grandma had given Abby to make for Mama's and Papa's Christmas present when she was twelve. It hung over the head of their bed so that she could see it now. It stated at the top, over a red rose bouquet, *God Bless Our Home.* At the bottom it echoed in German, *Gott Segne Unser Heim.* And the good Lord had blessed their home, Mama said often. "We may not be rich, but we got vittles, clothes on our back and a roof over our head. We've got respect for law and order and we've got each other. What more could a body ever want?"

Abby's thoughts went back to Papa now as his voice slowed, sober and dramatic,

> There in the twilight cold and gray,
> Lifeless, but beautiful, he lay,
> And from the sky, serene and far,
> A voice fell, like a falling star,
> Excelsior!

Lucy sighed resolutely, deeply. Perched on top of the end bed rail, David stirred, his muscles reflecting the restless energy of a boy in the process of becoming a man. Mama was finished mopping and she said cheerfully, "Who-all wants some popcorn and hot tea? I bet if I walk easy, I can fix some and still not leave a single track."

"And can we have sugar in the tea?" Lucy asked anxiously.

"Look at Lucy's hair," David said thoughtfully. "It's like silk. Corn silk."

"Why, I bet we can find some sugar," Mama answered.

That settled, Lucy turned to Papa, ignoring David, "And can we hear 'The Highwayman' while we're a-waitin'?"

"And her eyes are like pools," David analysed softly. "Cess pools!"

"I don't see no reason not to," Papa said to Lucy, winking at David.

"Her teeth reminds me of stars," David went on, becoming deeply pensive. "They come out at night."

Abby giggled and Mama said smilingly, "Enough's enough, Davey-boy."

Lucy shrugged and said with much contempt, "I don't give a hoot in a hailstorm what he says, anyways."

So, with Mama shaking the popcorn in a skillet and the house warm and wonderful with the smells of it, Papa began in a measured, resonant voice,

> The wind was a torrent of darkness among the gusty trees,
> The moon was a ghostly galleon tossed upon cloudy seas,
> The road was a ribbon of moonlight over the purple moor,
> The highwayman came riding, up to the old inn-door . . .

Chapter Six

"Now, WE can't stay but a minute," Aunt Myrtle reminded them as they made their way into the house after the first flurry of greetings.

David carried Grandma's box while Papa helped her to the rocker where she always sat, her faded blue eyes alert and interested. She clutched her black purse. Everyone knew better than to ask Grandma if they could put away her purse. At night she even kept it under the edge of her mattress, the feather one, the *Matratze*. Papa said it wasn't because there was anything especially valuable in it, because she had only a monthly old-age pension check that covered necessities and nothing more. It was just that old people got that way about their belongings, especially if they had been through a lot of hard times like Grandma had. She didn't trust banks—she hadn't in Germany and she wouldn't in the United States—but she trusted the security of the underside of the feather *Matratze*.

With Aunt Myrtle around it was hard to get in a word. "—a committee meeting," she was saying now, tugging off her soft black kid gloves. "Then holder's meetings for the next two days. At least two banquets. I packed enough clothes for a month of Sundays! Just a mad dash around town the whole week long, like a chicken with its head cut off!"

She laughed merrily and everyone else did, too. Abby could see in her mind yesterday's headless chickens being dunked into the steaming water and wondered if Aunt Myrtle had ever seen a chicken without its head.

"I *do* hope you didn't cook for us, Maudie," she said as she glanced toward the stove where the aroma of dumplings was rising in the steam that reached all the way to the dingy, fly-specked ceiling and dampened it with droplets of moisture. Then, though it was too early for supper, she ate a bowlful of the dumplings, the *Huhner Kloss*, Grandma called them, as they had all known she would.

While she was eating, Uncle Lewis finally got an opportunity to talk without interruption. He was a quiet man, not so much by nature as by circumstances, but there was usually a little glint of mischievousness in his blue eyes, just like Papa's and David's. That was the only way he and Papa resembled. Uncle Lewis was short and wiry like Grandma, while Papa was tall and rather big-boned, but slender.

Uncle Lewis and Papa and David had been back in a corner discussing oil production (125,000,000 barrels in Oklahoma this year, and yes siree, one or two of 'em was Lewis Eason's!) and differential analyzers (think they're a passin' fad, or here for the duration?) and the effects of last year's United Auto Worker's strikes (they claimed the 18½ cent an hour raise they got made it possible to feed the kids and nothin' more, and who am I to say?).

It was just a matter of time before the subject of the military would be brought up (if not by Uncle Lewis's whim, then by Abby's design). He had explained before that his years in the 45th Infantry Division were almost sacred to him, but the explanation had been unnecessary; it was evident by the look on his face when he spoke of his experiences therein. The 45th, he said, was made up largely of Okies: city dudes, cotton farmers, (and oil *Pachters*) school teachers, clerks, even chili pickers and sheep herders. Just good ole boys, standard-issue citizens turned soldier. And 511 combat days during the second war alone! Even George Patton, hisself, had said of the 45th with unusual fervor, "Born at sea, baptized in blood, your fame shall never die."

When there was a slight lull in the conversation, Abby asked, "Uncle Lewis, what was the name of that ship you rode on after the war was over?"

Uncle Lewis's face lit up. "Ah, yes. Queen Mary, Abby girl. Quite a ship she was, too. Designed to accommodate two thousand. Would you believe there was fifteen thousand, two hundred and seventy-eight of us crammed in there? Truman said he wanted to git us all back home to the states on the double and he was a man of his word!"

Abby had heard it all before, but the slight awe in her voice was real. "How did you all fit in, Uncle Lewis?"

"Why, we slept in bunks three and four tiers high, that's how. Packed in there like sardines. Everywhere you turned, you rubbed backs and elbows. Only got two meals a day. Franks and sauerkraut for breakfast and sauerkraut and franks for the other meal!"

Everyone laughed.

"Tell them about our new business," Aunt Myrtle said, looking at the big pot of dumplings again.

"Biggest business venture of the 20th century," Uncle Lewis acknowledged. "The iron and steel business." He paused, the way he always did when he was about to deliver a punch line. "She's gonna take in ironin' and I'm gonna take up stealin'."

They all laughed, Grandma too, even though she had no idea what was funny. She didn't understand jokes too well because everything was serious to her, and if the conversation was bandied about at too fast a clip, she became lost in the conversation. Therefore, until she was ready to put in her two cents worth (often on another subject altogether), she merely nodded and smiled and laughed when the others did.

"Dafid," she said a bit slyly, "bring *der Kasten.*"

"Box," Papa motioned automatically to David, who brought the pasteboard box he had put in the back room, and set it on the floor beside Grandma. Lucy ran and dropped to her knees beside the chair but Abby made herself stay by her place near the Franklin and tried not to act overly interested.

If she had been Lucy's age she would have been right down there with her, but one of the unspoken but stifling rules for young ladies going on sixteen, was that they must keep eagerness about surprises suppressed, pretending to be more interested in pushing back a cuticle or checking with outstretched hand the amount of heat coming from the fire.

Grandma's old, wrinkled hands were unfirm, and she fidgeted at the tucked box flaps for several minutes. All of them wanted to help, but no one dared to offer lest she think them over-anxious.

At last she gave up, raised her face and said in her high voice, "Dafid?" and David knew then it was permissible for him to open the box for her.

Very slowly she withdrew a small round something, carefully wrapped in a catalogue page, and handed it to Lucy, then one just like it to Abby, who received it primly and properly and went back to her seat by the fire. The last one went to David. Abby unwrapped hers and could hardly believe her eyes. It was a pear—huge, plump, juicy-looking pear without a blemish on it, right here in the dead of winter.

"Mama's been keepin' those for you young'uns since October," Uncle Lewis explained, smiling broadly. "Wrapped 'em up and put 'em in the cellar where it's cool so they wouldn't git over-ripe, but not too cool so's they don't freeze."

"Thank you, Gran'ma," Abby said smiling,

caressing the smooth, yellow skin with the tiny brown flecks. She wanted to bite into it immediately, yet she hated to spoil the delicious beauty of it. Lucy and David said their thank-you's, too, and each already had a mouthful.

"Dank you, *auch*," Grandma echoed, looking pleased.

"I believe I'll have just a taste of that apple pie before we go," Aunt Myrtle was saying at the table, a taste to her usually being a very large piece.

"Myrtle's watchin' her figger," Uncle Lewis announced, winking at Abby. "It's finally got out there where she can watch it without any trouble a'tall!"

"Now looky here, Lewis," Aunt Myrtle warned good naturedly. "You know I'm on a sea-food diet. Everytime I see food, I eat it!"

Joining in the laughter, Abby thought how pleasant it would have been if Grandpa Eason could have been present with them. It was such a tragedy for Papa to have lived more of his life without a father than with one.

Grandma said of all her five boys it was Papa that took after Grandpa the most. She had a picture—one of the entire family standing sober-faced and proper in front of someone's Model T—to prove it. The tallness, the bigness, the clean-cut facial features with square jawline, the light blue squinting eyes and fawn-colored hair that was always a bit unruly—they were Grandpa all over again.

Only Grandpa wore overalls instead of Levi's, and his face seemed uncommonly stern. Papa said that was because back then everyone thought it was presumptuous to smile for a photograph. He said he'd wager that the minute the shutter was snapped, his Papa was either hoo-rahing someone or chuckling over someone else's wit.

Sanftmutig, Grandma called them, Grandpa and Papa. Gentle and mild was what it meant. And she would usually add mischievously, "But spice dey are not viss-out, *auch*." "*Gleich Vater, Gleich Sohn*," she said, too. Like father, like son. "If *du* vud know Gran'vater," she once added, "Vud be no difference." Papa said Grandma was saying if they had known Grandpa it would be just like knowing your own Papa.

That had fascinated Abby. She wondered if Mama would someday say that about Papa and David. They looked like twins born twenty-three years apart. They acted alike, too. Closemouthed about deep things that mattered, so that it often was not clear just how they felt except by looking carefully in their eyes, or by listening for undercurrents in what they were saying. Both of them were always going on and saying the frivolous or the foolish to make everyone laugh, as though they never had a serious thought in their heads.

Only, lately, and unlike Papa, David seemed to be saying haughty and impatient things almost as much as the pleasant, as though no one had any sense except him, and maybe Papa. Like the other night when she had misunderstood a thing in her studies and was floundering off in one direction when she should have been going the other, and he had said pompously, "That makes about as much sense as George the Third droppin' into Boston on the evenin' of the tea party. At least he was kinfolks."

It was not the saying exactly (for under ordinary circumstances it would have been funny) but the way it was said. It was never the laughing with, but the laughing at that she minded. Nevertheless, she had managed to laugh, and allowed him to get her back on track, all the while feeling dimwitted and childish due to the sarcastic way David was carrying on. Papa had finally shown mercy and called him down in that mild, yet firm way he had.

The fact that she and David were only a year apart in age perhaps made her occasional feeling of inferiority more acute. She tried to keep in mind that David was at the *rauh* age Papa had mentioned and to be charitable in her evaluations because of it. The roughness would someday pass and in the meantime she would try to be patient with him.

After supper, the *Huhner Kloss* and *Apfel Pastete*, Grandma sat in the rocker again looking around at them with her bright, inquisitive eyes.

"Vel, Dafid, *du* are growin'k tall. *Du* are ter'teen, maybe?"

David snickered, a bit embarrassed, and more than a little incredulous, probably thinking how he was almost up with Papa in height now and surely didn't look that much like a mere kid. "No, Granny, I was thirteen three years ago. I'm jist about seventeen."

"Seben-teen?" Grandma exlaimed. "How can *ist* be so? Und Abby *Madchen*, so *klein* she is, lit-tle. *Du* are ter-teen, den?"

Abby giggled over at David and corrected her, "Fifteen, Gran'ma."

Grandma shook her head in disbelief. "An, und little Lutchy. Almost *wie* Abby. *Du* are ter-teen, Lutchy-*Madchen*?"

It always took Lucy a while to get over her shyness of Grandma, and hardly ever could she understand what was being said. Now she only looked puzzled and hunched her shoulders in a hesitant shrug. Abby explained, "Gran'ma wants to know if you're thirteen."

Lucy tittered, abashed and uncertain. "Tell her I'm goin' on ten," she said, as though Grandma couldn't hear.

"Tell her yourself," Abby whispered.

Lucy hunched her shoulders again and said shyly, "Nine, Gran'ma."

"Nine, it iss?" Grandma said surprised. "Big, she iss, Lutchy."

"Abby's gonna be little and I'm gonna be big," Lucy remarked with obvious pride and speculation.

"It iss *besser* to grow big for *der* vork," Grandma nodded. Growing big for the work had always been a concern in Germany, Papa once said. Then Grandma seemed suddenly to remember Abby's smallness and added, "Lit-tle iss *besser, auch. Klein*—lit-tle—ole Granny iss, as Abby. Und funf..." and she raised five fingers, slightly gnarled and very workworn, "*funf Sohns* she brung up." She smiled, blinking and smiling hopefully, " Abby vill, maybe, bring up *funf Sohns, auch*?"

Abby glanced at Papa for help and he explained Grandma was asking if she was planning to raise five sons.

"No, ma'am," Abby said firmly to Grandma. "I wouldn't have five boys if you paid me. Jist one girl— if I git married at all." She held up one finger.

"Vhat iss? Only *ein*—one? How vill she den gid in her share *der* crop?" (For sharecroppers—especially in Old Country—expected both by providence and happenstance to rear many children in order to work the Land, Grandma had pointed out before. This had been when she was expressing her concern and curiosity over Papa's only rearing three children, healthy man that he was, with both the ability to produce and more importantly, the need for additional hands. For what would they do, pray tell, when David was gone someday?)

"I'm not gonna be a sharecropper, Gran'ma."

"Vhat?" Grandma asked, puzzled. "Tsk, tsk. Ve must *Holten* to *der* Land, Abby-*Madchen*."

"I'll hold to the land," Abby promised. "But not share it."

Grandma, after studying a minute, was satisfied. "And Dafid?"

"No farmin' for me," he said emphatically. "Goin' to the moon in a rowboat, maybe. Or settlin' John L. Lewis' hash. Or—college." He shrugged at this last, becoming careless and even indifferent, as though the thought had popped out of its own accord and his only recourse was to pretend it was hardly worthy of notice, as likely as manning the aforementioned rowboat.

And Abby knew he was still thinking of the Tolsey offer. She saw Mama give Papa a quick glance. He got up, abruptly it seemed to Abby, and went over to the stove to pour himself a cup of coffee. It seemed even the mention of college—or Winburn Tolsey's name—brought an uneasiness to Papa anymore. "He didn't have no right," Papa had told Mama that night. "No right to step in that-a-way and try to outshine David's own fam'ly and make him think he's a-missin' out on things."

"Vhat?" Grandma asked, frowning. "Kol, kol . . ."

"College," David repeated, smiling, still very casual. "You know, where the rich dudes go. See, me and ole Vannevar Bush is thinkin' about goin' in partners on differential analyzers."

"Vhat?" Grandma asked again, thoroughly confused by now.

"They're machines," David explained, deftly turning the entire matter into a joke. "They can calculate figures—whole lines of 'em—better'n a man can. Or a woman, for that matter." And he laughed, his blue eyes squinting toward Papa, who smiled with him as he stirred cream into his coffee.

Grandma merely blinked and remained silent, trying to digest this new bit of information.

"But you gotta have college first, and git your brain dislocated and shot fulla book-learnin' and uppity-bunk. You gotta git your head overhauled, in other words, before you can compete with the rich dudes and git your finger in their kinda pie."

Then David shrugged and laughed a little again, suddenly aware that maybe he had shared his hopes too freely—no matter that it was done in such a flippant way that a casual listener wouldn't have recognized it as reflecting a hope. And no matter that all of them were smiling with him and all of them—except Papa, perhaps—were enjoying his nonsensical views.

He added disparagingly, so that his rationale would not remain in question, "And I look for all this to happen about the same time that feller dips cut the last thimbleful of water from the ocean."

"Vhat is mat-chinks, Dafid," Grandma queried. "Are dey at Kol—are dey—vhere are dey?"

"Lissen, Granny," David said, suddenly acting very decisive and serious. "You need to learn to talk American-style so *du* could understand *besser*." He threw a little triumphant look at Papa because he had just used the German words for 'you' and 'better,' and with Grandma's heavy accent. Papa shared his achievement with another gentle, half-smile.

Abby knew David loved Grandma. He knelt his lanky frame down beside her chair and looked into her eyes, smiling. "David's goin' to college—like a pig's eye. Now, you say it, Gran'ma."

Grandma smiled back, uncertain, determined to

form her words meticulously. "Dafid's goin'—*zu* Kolleghc—like *der* pigs-zie?"

"That's right, Gran'ma!" David whooped over everyone's laughter. "Now say the chicken was good."

"*Der* chincken vas—gute, No?"

"Say 'good', Gran'ma."

"Gu-ute!"

"Try a little harder, Granny," David begged hilariously. "Say 'good' real plain."

"Goo-udt," she complied delightfully, joining in the fun.

Everyone was listening, laughing and encouraging Grandma on with her English lesson. After a few more lively attempts, which Grandma seemed to enjoy tremendously, rocking and laughing and occasionally slapping her knee with the rest of them, David said, grinning sneakily, "Now say, 'Gran'ma is a goose'."

And, with everyone hollering with mirth, Grandma said obediently, "Gran-ma iss—*der*—goosch!"

Chapter Seven

AFTER GRANDMA had been settled in Mama's and Papa's bed, dressed in her heavy flannel gown and nightcap, Papa revealed some unwelcome news. It was news he had been carrying quietly, except for telling Mama, since that morning when the landlord stopped in front of the house and the two of them had sat in the car for thirty minutes talking, Abby assumed, about the cotton yields and other farm matters.

Dutch Turner was selling out because of failing health, which meant the Easons would have to move on because the new owners weren't going to keep croppers on the place. They had six children, three of them almost grown, and would do all the work themselves.

Everyone looked at Papa, and Abby asked for them all, in a voice suddenly subdued, "When, Papa?"

"First of May, about the time school's out. Maybe a week or two sooner."

The news was unexpected and unsettling, like falling through a trap door. It was such a stark contrast to the delightful day they had just experienced. They had all made some friends in Tecumseh after spending that gloomy, near-friendless year in California. The last thing Abby wanted to do was to move away and start all over again, as she had six times already during her ten years of schooling. But, as bad as that was, the worst thing about moving was David, because of his hopes concerning Mr. Tolsey and college.

Just now he was staring a hole in the floor, a little muscle moving in his jaw each time his teeth clenched together. 'His brow was sad, his eye beneath, flashed like a falchion from its sheath,' Abby was reminded.

Only David's brow wasn't so much sad as it was disappointed, silently protesting.

"Where to?" Abby asked Papa soberly.

"We're moving to Erick. It's over by the state line, west on Highway 9. A feller by name of Wade Collins is needin' tenants and Turner put in a good word for us. They used to know each other, back durin' the first war. They'll need us come plantin'."

"But ain't we gonna finish school first?" Lucy frowned up at Papa anxiously from the pallet of quilts on the floor, her bed, and Abby's, as long as Grandma stayed.

"We hafta go when we're needed," Papa explained apologetically. "Cotton cain't wait when the ground's warm. You kids is all smart enough to pass without that last week or two."

"I thought we wasn't—" David began. Then he shrugged and looked down again. Abby caught the look of frustration in his eyes—eyes that had been laughing and twinkling only moments before. David was looking and sounding just the way she felt—as though he had been slapped unexpectedly, and without justification.

Papa glanced his way and gave voice to what David was thinking. "I thought when we come here we'd git to stay on for good. I planned on it. Otherwise, I wouldn't of told you that. But you jist cain't outguess fate. Dutch Turner didn't know he was gonna git sick, and neither did I."

David sighed heavily. "I don't see why we cain't just git a decent job and forgit about farmin'. Ain't no way to make a livin', if you ask me."

The remark was bound to hurt Papa, Abby knew, feeling as he did about the land, but he didn't say anything for a minute, and when he did speak he didn't acknowledge even hearing David. "Turner offered to sell me the farm here 'while back. But—the crops wasn't very strong this year so our part didn't amount to much. Still, if we jist had somethin' to put up for security, we could borry some money from the bank . . ." He was rubbing his jaw and looking unseeingly off across the room. "It takes money to borry money, to change up an old sayin'.'

"We got the car, Travis," Mama reminded him softly.

"It ain't enough," Papa said. "It's gittin' old. The tires is wore out. The crankcase is leakin' oil." He paused, thinking deeply, "But—someday. . ." And he didn't try to go on.

The unfinished thought hung in the room like a judgement, even after Mama got up and announced with a forced cheerfulness that it was bedtime for school children. Though Papa's discouragements were seldom revealed to any of them except possibly Mama, discouragement was clearly written on his face now. To Abby, the realization of it was a little upsetting and she wasn't sure why. Maybe because it reminded her too much of the time in California when, she remembered, Papa had not been able to remain calm and sure of himself.

It had been all those negative outside influences then, the lack of work, or the disagreeableness of it when it was available, the fighting in the camps, the open discriminations. Now, it was something else. Something very subtle. Something concerning David, possibly. Papa's boy needed him now, and Papa wasn't going to be able to provide.

Papa got up and put more wood on the fire, even though it was plenty warm already, popping and crackling merrily. It was as though he was restless and needed to be stirring around. For some reason the lines from 'Excelsior' flitted through Abby's mind once again. 'In happy homes he saw the light of household fires gleam warm and bright.' But now, suddenly, despite the roaring flames in the Franklin as the fresh wood caught and took off, it seemed as though their fire was somehow burning colder.

— — — —

David had stared silently out the bus window the entire route, his mind far from the chattering, laughing school children with their rattling papers and stacks of books. To the few riders who attempted to banter as usual with him, he only gave a token smile or a half-hearted come-back until they had taken the hint and left him alone.

When most of the children were off and no one else was around them, Abby asked quietly, "What'll you do about college now, David?"

"Without, I imagine," he said, tight-lipped.

"Mr. Tolsey'll know where you live. You could still—"

"Mr. Tolsey ain't gonna care no longer if I move plumb across the state."

"Is Erick that far away?"

"A hundred and fifty miles past Oklahoma City, is all."

"Mama and Papa is sorry about it," she consoled. They hadn't said that, of course, but she knew they were. David's disappointment and disapproval had affected them all the last two days. No one knew what to make of his unusual sobriety and lack of bantering. "It's not their fault, anyways."

"Sorry don't change nothin'," David answered curtly.

"Besides, you got over a year to think about goin' to college."

"More likely I got a whole lifetime to think about it. Unless I stay here."

"Stay?" she asked incredulously.

"I've a mind to."

"Papa won't let you stay," Abby said, feeling her insides sinking slowly, the same way they had when the Tolseys first came up with their preposterous plan. She had seen David and Mr. Tolsey talking in the commerce room that very morning. Usually when she saw them they would be laughing or casually chatting, whether they were poring over something in a book or newspaper, or merely walking down the hall. Now she wondered if Mr. Tolsey had had the gall to reissue his ridiculous offer since this newest development in David's life. And for a moment she felt a little of Papa's hostility toward the carefree couple who not only had money and opportunities and a Ford Couplet—but David's admiration and loyalty as well.

"I'm not a ten year old," David pointed out flatly. "I've got some ideas of my own."

"But they wouldn't let you before," Abby insisted anxiously. "And it would of jist been a few miles away to the Tolseys."

David shook his head slightly and said nothing.

Abby held to the seat back as they rounded a corner, listening to her heart beat sluggishly in her ears. David didn't care, for some reason. He would choose college and the Tolseys over his own family. That was almost impossible to comprehend. He didn't even care that they would be separated, not a real family anymore, like so many other sharecroppers they knew.

Like Dub Lamb down the road, who farmed his kids out because he couldn't find anybody that would let him farm on the shares anymore. Everybody knew he was lit up most of the time, and couldn't make a hand because of it. And Zeb Epstein, who Mama said just up and left his bunch. There were six kids and Marge Epstein was in the family way again. And Ransom and Ramiro Dickson were just sixteen and seventeen, but everyone talked about how they lit out for California not long ago and left the rest of the Dicksons in an awful bind because it had been during cotton snapping. Then there was Harold Ferguson. He hadn't right out and left his bunch, eight young'uns that included David's good friend, Terry, but he'd gone up by Tulsa and got in the oilfields and only came home twice a month, but he did bring money when he came. And there was Brian Hawley's bunch that didn't have a mother. They said Retta Hawley died from over-doing. Killed herself sharecropping, was what they said. And that was always a sobering thought in itself, but Abby passed over it lightly this time, because of the gravity of the situation her own family might have to face.

"We wouldn't never git to see you," she said in a small voice.

He shrugged. "Wouldn't be any different than goin' off to college or leavin' home to git married or go to war or somethin'."

"You're too young, though."

"Who said?"

Who said? Papa, that's who, Abby told herself, and leaned back against the bus seat only a little comforted with that thought.

"Now I ain't gonna be unreasonable," Papa said. You would have thought he was talking about the weather, or how good or poor the stand of cotton was that year, instead of something that could change the whole course of a life. "But I had my say to Mr. Tolsey the other time, and my say is still the same."

David kept looking at the floor, his face shadowy in the lamp glow. "How come?" he asked, not belligerent or disrespectful, but calmly, with only the little vibration in his voice to show what a strain he was under. His square jaw was set.

Papa's jaw was set, too. "We don't need to rehash all the reasons, son. We ain't gonna break up the fam'ly for no better cause than that. Mr. Tolsey jist— overstepped his bounds is all."

Lucy was asleep on the pallet. Abby was supposed to be, but she was instead, lying rigidly, listening and worrying herself sick. Why couldn't David just stop fretting and tormenting himself over college and be content with his lot? Of course, she knew the answer to that, because he was an Eason and had his mind set, and because he was like the young man in "Excelsior," always pushing to climb higher. 'Above, the spectral glaciers shone, and from his lips escaped a groan, Excelsior!'

"Davey-*Knabe*," Mama said gently, using Papa's little-boy name for him, "you got a lotta time. We could start tryin' to save some money to'ard it."

David pushed at the unruly, fawn-colored hair on his forehead. His voice was level, just a bit impatient, and still quivering ever so slightly. "Money for college— when we jist barely git by, year after year?"

"Your Papa—we're all of us a-doin' our best," Mama admonished.

David's voice rose, "Mama, I'm not sayin' nothin' against that."

"Watch the tone of your voice around your Mama," Papa said sternly.

Silence, heavy and troubled followed.

"I got to get to college," David said, and his voice was low and urgent now, fraught with deep feeling. David, who never could stand for anyone to know he felt much of anything that was weighty or serious, was pleading. "And I got to start planning now instead of waitin' till it's time."

"I know you do," Papa said. His voice was sounding just like David's, as though he was trembling inside too, and trying hard to keep it under control. "And we're gonna try and see you do, but not like you're wantin'. You're not stayin' here while we move that far away."

"Mr. Tolsey said I still could," David continued doggedly. "If I could git you all's say-so."

Papa was taken aback. "You mean you talked to him again? Lately?"

"This mornin'," David admitted, instantly unsure of his ground.

Papa drew an unsteady breath. "You talked to him again without askin' me or your Mama first?"

Barely above a whisper, David answered, "I guess so."

Papa got up restlessly and walked to the window and looked out at the dark and shadows of the night for a moment, then turned back around. "That ain't no way to go about it, behind our back."

"I knew what you'd say."

"Then you didn't have no business goin' ahead with it." Papa was angry now. It was the thought of what Winburn Tolsey had started, and the knowledge he could be losing control of the situation.

"Travis . . ." Mama said, troubled.

"I didn't see no harm—" David upheld stubbornly.

"Well, I'm a-tellin' you now, it's all settled," Papa cut him off brusquely.

David was staring at the floor again, the little knot

of muscle appearing and reappearing in his jaw. "I— I'm gonna stay, though," he said, and to Abby he sounded more like a scared little boy than a defiant one. It was the only time she could remember that he had ever set himself against Papa, and it made her close her eyes tight and squeeze her hands into fists and wish desperately that all the misunderstanding could vanish like magic, with everybody satisfied and happy again.

Papa must have been thunderstruck at what David had said so deliberately. He said nothing, but Abby could hear the rise and fall of his breathing in the silence.

David pushed on determinedly, "I'm old enough to decide things for myself. I know what I want. I ain't gonna be no sharecropper all my life, Papa, and use myself up workin' the crops for somebody else, and not never havin' nothin' to show for any of it."

Don't let Papa get mad again, Abby thought to herself, because she knew they might lose David for good if he did.

Papa must have sensed it, too. He breathed deeply again and his voice was calm suddenly, everything either under control or at least well-masked. "Sharecroppin' ain't the question, son," he said. "I ain't expectin' you to be no cropper. But I'm expectin' you to mind what I set out for you to do—till you're of age. Then, if Mr. Tolsey wants to give you college, well, then that's his tub of peas, not mine."

Silence again.

Very quietly, "You hearin' me now, David?"

"Yessir," David said, his voice thick with emotion— disappointment and hopelessness, and some anger. "I heard you."

"Okay," Papa said, and his voice matched David's again, only maybe it was relief or pain or something that caused the thickness. "Bed, then. And you be sure and tell Winburn Tolsey tomorrow. Tell him it's done settled and that I don't want nothin' else said about it, ever."

For a long time after the others had gone to bed, Abby lay on the hard pallet, tense and unable to sleep. David would be doing the same, seething inside probably, wanting his way. Maybe still angry, he might even run away. That unexpected thought caused her to raise up in a reflex of alarm and look around the room.

Papa and Mama were asleep. In the moonlight from the window Papa's chest moved slowly and rhythmically under the covers. The entire room seemed remote and strange, shadowy dark. There were no sounds except those of breathing and the loud ticking of the clock.

David's sleeping room was set against the outside of the kitchen, a tiny, tacked-on square not much bigger than the bed, made of scrap lumber Papa had gathered from here and there. He could walk away if he took a notion, and not one of them would know it until morning.

But David wouldn't run away. How could he? He had always done what Papa and Mama wanted, always especially seemed to want to please Papa. It had been that way ever since Abby could remember. She recalled a young David, trying new things, "See me jump, Papa? I can go highest of any!" "Papa, I can stand on my head till you count to a hundred!" "Watch me, I can throw a ball further than any kid in third grade!"

And he hadn't changed, still wanting to do new, exciting things, to see how far he could go, still expecting Papa's blessing. Only now, Papa wouldn't give his blessing for reasons they perhaps would not understand until they stood in a parent's shoes. And practicality must surely play a part; their means of livelihood, very simply, would be greatly hampered if they were forced to do without David's strength and abilities.

They had to have him, surely he understood that. On the other hand . . .

Abby lay back against her pillow wearily. She would think pleasant thoughts and maybe drop off to sleep. She would think of Grandma and how she made them all laugh. Yesterday, after school she had held to Abby's arm and shuffled all over the two rooms examining everything minutely as she did every visit. In the back room she had approved the faded pink chenile bedspread, then rubbed some liniment on the back of her neck from the jar on the dresser. Near the applecrate bookshelf she had examined the stiffly starched scarf with its yellowed tatting, had held the Bible reverently, then pondered a worn copy of "In His Steps," though Abby knew she could not read at all.

In the kitchen she had thumped the number three galvanized washtub used once a week for washing clothes, and twice a week for washing bodies. It hung by a nail on the wall. She cracked her knuckles smartly against the rubboard on which Abby had scrubbed about a thousand socks and almost that many underdrawers. At the table, still grasping Abby's arm firmly, Grandma had studied the sprays of mistletoe for so long that Abby's shoulder began to cramp.

In the back room again she stood before the 'God Bless Our Home' cross stitch for sometime. *"Du* finish it, Abby-*Madchen?"*

Abby had nodded, and said as she had several times over the years, because Grandma kept forgetting, "I finished it, Gran'ma. I gave it to Mama and Papa for Christmas one year. Remember?"

"It iss *Weihnachten* again?" Grandma asked in surprise.

Abby shook her head, smothering a giggle. "No, Gran'ma. Christmas is over for another year."

"Vel, *dank gutten*,' Grandma chuckled. "Ve vud haf no gifs!"

They had laughed heartily together, thinking of the strangeness of a Christmas with no gifts. How could life so quickly go from one extreme to the other, that on one day you would laugh easily, and the next you felt as though you might never laugh again? Then Grandma had softly repeated the words from the cross-stitch. *"Gott segne unser Heim,"* and nodded. *"Gott* iss *gute,* Abby-*Madchen. Erinnern sich."* God is good, Abby-girl. Remember.

Abby clenched her hands now, and made herself remember how good God was. So good that never would He allow their family to be split apart, some of them here and some of them there—or even worse, to be split apart and yet all living under the same roof.

"God bless our home," she whispered impassionately into her feather pillow. Then, like an echo in her mind, came Grandma's part of the benediction, *"Gott segne unser Heim."*

Chapter Eight

THE CREAKY, TWO-WHEELED trailer that had traveled over various parts of Oklahoma and made a trip to California and back, was piled high again. As they were loading, Abby thought it would be impossible to get everything in—the bed rails and springs, the cook stove, the Franklin, the one-by-twelve cabinet, the kitchen table. But everything fitted. Papa placed Grandma's rocker right on top, upside down and strapped it tight with a rope.

Good-byes had been said. At school Abby told only her best friend, Ava, because she knew that to most people a sharecropper's wanderings were to be expected and not much cause for interest. If it had been the regular kids, somebody would have given what was called a going-away party. In December, Donna Oren had received a beautiful lacy, nylon blouse because her daddy's company was transferring him and they were moving to Stillwater. When Donna wore the blouse on her last day at school, Abby had looked at it from afar and admired it, but she had harbored very little envy and no grudges at all even though she had moved six times without having received a single gift for it. Croppers didn't expect gifts or favors, or even much respect, though she sometimes thought it would be nice.

She and Ava had exchanged addresses, despite the fact that there would not often be stamp money for writing, nor tablets, nor envelopes. Abby had a whole list of names, written on a blank page carefully extracted from the front of an old prose and poetry book. They were addresses of friends from places all over Oklahoma, and even one from California, who was also a fruit tramp and a misplaced Okie. Each time she thought about writing she knew it was futile because those friends would be drifting from place to place, too, and probably not one of her addresses was current now.

Heath Martin found out that the Easons were moving. Abby was in the room cleaning out her desk after the last bell when he came in and started absently looking through some books on the library shelf. She could see in her mind right now his dark brown hair and those beautiful eyes that could be so thoughtful and serious one moment only to crinkle into a friendly smile the next. She knew he was watching her out of the corner of his eye. When she dropped her notebook paper and it scattered up and down the aisle, he hurried over and started helping pick it up. It was while they were both kneeling there, wanting to, but trying not to look at each other, that he asked with studied casualness, "Do you think you might move back to Tecumseh some day?"

"I doubt it."

"Do you have a picture?"

Abby's cheeks turned pink as she told him she didn't. Though the picture takers came to the schools year after year and though she usually had her picture taken right along with everyone else, and even though they were often at the same school long enough to receive the pictures back, never had they been able to afford to buy any of them. She didn't even ask Mama and Papa. The only pictures she had of herself were a few faded snapshots taken along with the rest of the family by Aunt Myrtle over the years, and just now they were packed away in the tattered black photo album under layers of furniture and bedding and clothes.

They still hadn't looked at each other but it was going to happen because they were gathering up the last of the papers. "You're prettier than Deborah Lynn Witt ever thought about being," Heath blurted out.

The words came in such a rush that Abby wasn't sure she had heard correctly, and if she had, she wondered briefly if Heath had a problem seeing clearly. She fussed with the papers, straightening them, and asked softly, "What?"

"I don't care if you *are* a cropper," he mumbled on.

"Most ever'body else does," Abby said as a fact.

"Well, croppers are people," he said defensively.

They looked at each other quickly, then away from each other, and Abby smiled.

"That sounded stupid I guess, didn't it?" he asked.

She answered, "No. It sounded nice."

"And you are nice, too," he announced with sudden boldness.

"If you say so, Heath."

They laughed again then, stiffly, establishing brief eye contact. They smiled, their faces just inches apart. Abby knew that was their goodbye. She knew, barring a miracle, she would never see Heath again, but she carefully filed away the memories of what he had said and how he had looked at her in case she ever wanted to draw them out and use them some day when the fields and the heat or cold, or the backaches were almost unbearable.

On the bus Abby told Vickie Barkley about the move, mostly to have something to say. She had pitied Vickie since first knowing her, but the girl's seclusive nature wasn't conducive to close friendships, especially since Abby was not exactly outgoing herself.

All Vickie said was, "I wisht I was goin' somewheres, too."

"You mean you like movin'?" Abby asked curiously.

"I jist wanta git away from home," Vickie said softly. "And I'm goin' to—someday. Even if I have to git married or run off."

"You're jist in the ninth," Abby reminded her.

"I don't care, Abby, I'm a goin' someday."

The bus was slowing for her stop and Abby felt compelled to offer some sort of encouragement, but nothing came to mind immediately. A few words weren't going to help that much in a hard situation like Vickie's anyway. But as Vickie stood to walk towards the bus door, Abby whispered hurriedly, "Maybe someday he'll change."

Vickie shook her head knowingly, and Abby watched her glide down the bus steps. She looked out to where Bo Barkley was chopping wood, chips of it flying all about him, without glancing up at his only daughter coming home from school, a daughter he had lost somewhere in the shuffle of his callousness and mean spirit, and probably didn't even know it, nor care.

Little Rose Marie Lamb, down the road, cried when Abby told her they were moving. Abby almost wanted to cry with her, but of course, she couldn't. She understood that Papa didn't really have a choice. He was only doing what he thought was best in an unexpected situation. It was David that worried her.

She found him that last evening after everything was loaded out behind the dilapidated, old chicken house, sitting on a rusty half-barrel and whittling a stick. She stood quietly, watching him working away at the stick until the last piece of it was gone and he was just sitting, feeling of the knife blade gingerly, without really thinking about it.

All at once a stream of tobacco juice shot from his direction and landed a yard or so from Abby's foot. Startled, she stared at him. His cheek was round with the quid of tobacco and his eyes were filled with a touch of silent defiance.

"David, where did you git that nasty stuff?" She demanded sternly.

His answer was another squirt in her direction, closer this time.

Her lips pressed together in disgust and distaste and a dozen emotions raged inside until, subdued by compassion for David and his folly, she quickly wilted. "Papa and Mama feels bad enough," she admonished softly. "Don't you think your pity party's lasted long enough?"

He surveyed her quietly, knowing she was right. He worked the tobacco into the other cheek. "Jist where do you git off tryin' to run my business?"

"You are ever'body's business when what you do affects us all," she reminded him sharply. Abby hadn't meant to tell him what to do exactly, but David was carrying his emotions just a little too far.

"I think I can handle it," he said.

"I don't think you're handlin' it very good," she told him, "Sullin' up and chewin' tobacco."

"That's easy enough for you to say," he scoffed and spat again in her direction. "You don't stand to lose nothin' by movin'."

Abby thought of Heath, and of her best friend, Ava, and tears came to her eyes at the finality of having to leave. Boys don't know anything about how girls feel, she thought. She answered softly, "We jist got to try and pull together, David."

"We been pulling together for all these years and we don't have nothing to show for it yet," he growled, rolling the quid around in his mouth again.

"How can you say that?" she asked softly, rubbing a tear from her eye. "We got each other." Funny how her thinking blanked out for a minute when she tried to remind David of all the things they had, because they didn't really have much of anything you could stand and look at, just as she had said—except each other. That was enough for Abby.

Apparently David didn't think so, because he said sourly, "Jist leave me be. I don't wanta talk."

As she left, defeated by his attitude, he said, his voice very quiet and kind of gruff, "Hey, Ab."

She turned around and he was surveying her with a glimmer of his old grin—eyes squinting, his cheek bulging with the chew, and he was shaking his head. "Don't never try none of this stuff. It stinks, and it's makin' me sick as two dawgs."

Abby knew then they were still friends. Maybe he would be okay after all. He looked white, and grabbed his middle as he retched, turned away from Abby and leaned against the chicken house.

It was later that evening that the shiny black Ford Couplet drove up in front of the Eason place. This time Mr. Tolsey was alone. Papa's face sobered quickly. When he answered the door there was only a half-hearted nod, a subdued greeting, and no invitation to come in. "Can I do somethin' for you?" Papa asked sarcastically.

Looking around Papa, Abby could see Mr. Tolsey, dapper in his black pinstripe suit and a stiff felt hat with high rounded crown. He removed the derby and cleared his throat. "Yes. I'd like to speak with David for just a moment if I may."

Papa hesitated, started to say something, then paused and announced, "David ain't in the house jist right now."

Abby knew he was down at the chicken house getting rid of the chewing tobacco in his digestive track.

Lucy wriggled into the doorway beside Papa and said importantly, "He's down at the cowlot, Papa."

Papa's hand rested lightly on Lucy's shoulder and he said firmly, "Git on back out of the way, Lucy Belle." Lucy quickly did as she was told.

Mama was busily packing away the last bit of food from supper into a pasteboard box, but Abby could see she was straining to hear what was being said at the door, as was Abby. And as Mr. Tolsey nervously straightened his jacket and cleared his throat, she knew what was coming next.

"Mr. Eason," he began hesitantly, "I understand that the subject I'm about to touch upon is a sensitive one for you, but I feel compelled once more to mention that the invitation we extended to David earlier still stands. Kathleen and I— —"

Papa didn't do anything that would indicate Mr. Tolsey's words affected him one way or the other, but he interrupted in a voice that was somehow both calm and deadly. "Mr. Tolsey, I always had a sayin' about things that could git outa hand. My sayin' is, let sleepin' dogs lay."

When Mr. Tolsey looked as though he would protest, Papa added in the same tone of voice, "I ain't never been one to start a fracas, and I ain't one to hold a grudge. And when we pull outa here come early mornin', I still wanta be able to say that I didn't leave not one enemy back here in Tecumseh, Oklahoma."

The tenseness between the two was very acute. Abby was tightly gripping the book she had been reading, and holding her breath. Mama was kneeling rigidly beside the box, her lower lip caught between her teeth.

Mr. Tolsey's hands lightly clasped either side of his jacket while he apparently considered disconcertedly the things Papa had said, and the ease in which they were said. He murmured, "I see, Mr. Eason."

"I was thinkin' maybe you would," Papa responded.

"Well," Mr. Tolsey laughed a bit, his discomfort quite obvious. He stepped back a little and reached inside his crisp jacket, pulling out a booklet. "Actually, the main reason I came . . ."

He tapped the booklet lightly against his hand, "I have a pamphlet here that I believe will be of interest—and of great value—to your son. I had mentioned it to him previously, but was unable to procure one until just this afternoon. If I could see him for a moment or two . . ."

Papa was silent for a while, then said stiffly, "I guess some of us could go fetch him."

"Let me go hunt him, Mr. Eason. That is, if you have no objection."

Papa nodded his head, and watched Mr. Tolsey walk towards the cow lot. Abby could see the set of Papa's shoulders and the grip of his hand on the door facing served as a silent protest.

Mama said softly, "He's up to no good, Travis."

Papa breathed deeply, resignedly, and didn't answer. For several moments he continued looking outside toward the pitiful loaded trailer and the faded green Chevie with the three thin mattresses strapped on top. They would leave early in the morning before folks in Tecumseh got up. Maybe they wouldn't see. He murmured in a far-away voice, "Got 'er packed down purty tight, don't we."

Then he turned back toward them. The kitchen was empty except for a stack of quilts, the two nailkegs he and Mama had sat upon earlier, and the box containing food for the next day. He grinned faintly. "Californians always said you could tell a rich Okie from a pore one cause they have two mattresses on top of the car instead of jist one. And us Easons has got three of 'em. Yep, we're way up in the world."

That was all Abby waited to hear. She slipped quietly out the back door. She simply had to know what Mr. Tolsey planned to say to David. She crept silently out around the outbuildings and positioned herself breathlessly behind the chicken house, leaning against it and trying to hear above her pounding heart.

"One has to make up his mind what he wants from life," Mr. Tolsey was saying quietly. He was leaning against the board fence and David stood facing it, one foot resting on the bottom board. In his hand was the pamphlet Mr. Tolsey had brought, and Abby strained to see it in the duskiness, but there were no words distinguishable.

"The future is ours to conquer, to mold. That's the real issue here. One has to ask himself, will I follow the path of least resistance—or will I face the current. Will I allow destiny to shape me—or will I shape destiny."

David laughed softly, "Sayin' it and livin' it's two different stories."

Mr. Tolsey smiled sympathetically. Then he sobered, saying tentatively, "Certainly I'm not advocating revolt, David. I've always been one to uphold Biblical principles in every facet of life. I know you love your parents and they want only the best for you—as they comprehend it. But—sometimes . . ."

The cattle stirred a bit in the lot and Mr. Tolsey watched them absently without finishing his thought. "Anyway," he began again, "The bulletin will give you some food for thought. You might write us a letter when you get settled in. Let us know how things are going for you."

"I guess it'll work out," David said without conviction.

"Of course it will son. It will if you make it. Just remember, if we're not prepared for the future, we're not prepared for life," Mr. Tolsey sermonized with feeling.

"Sharecroppers don't know much about that kinda philosophy," David reminded him. He was still grinning some, but in his voice was a mixture of apology and helplessness, even some resentment.

Mr. Tolsey reached out and clamped a big hand on David's shoulder briefly, and on his tanned, smoothly shaven face was etched compassion and understanding. "You'll make it, David. I know you will," he declared. The inadequacy the two felt right now must have made the words sound trite, even to Abby, but David was listening, nodding solemnly, accepting them as having come from a source of wisdom he admired. "Kathleen sends her thoughts—and her farewell," Mr. Tolsey added gently. His arm pulled David to him in an awkward, instantaneous embrace, then both stepped back soberly.

They shook hands. If Abby ever had any questions about the relationship between David and Mr. Tolsey, they melted away at that moment. She knew David cared for the Tolseys genuinely, and they for him. David looked as though he was leaving a revered friend. Mr. Tolsey's face grimaced as he tried to flash a confident smile at the young man he obviously admired. Uneasiness and an emotion strangely like jealousy stirred within Abby for a bit. It was for Papa's sake, mostly, for she felt sure that a line that had been rather blurred before was now identified. David's loyalty was divided between two people. Two ways of life. Two directions. He was deeply confused.

When Mr. Tolsey turned and walked away, David turned to lean against the fence, absently tapping the booklet he held against the top board. When they heard the Ford Couplet start up and pull away, David's shoulders at first straightened, then wilted as he sort of melted against the fence, his long arms draping over the top rail, tired, unsure about tomorrow. Abby knew it was time to retreat and leave David with his thoughts. She slipped noiselessly back around to the house, knowing if David knew she had been eavesdropping she would never hear the last of it.

Chapter Nine

THEY WERE UP before daylight after spending the night on pallets on the floor of the empty shack. They ate breakfast of cold biscuits and syrup. The last of the milk was blinky, but they drank it anyway and were glad to have it. There would be no more fresh milk until they were settled in the new place.

It was still dark when Papa closed the door on the tarpaper shack in Pottawatomie County that had been their home for two years. To Abby, the slam caused a sinking feeling of finality, but a tiny stir of excitement of what was ahead as well. A new beginning. Who knew what the next days and months and years held? The next place might be the very one where they would find a way to settle down forever and manage to buy their own farm and be treated like other farmers.

And at the new place she would try to start using better grammar. She had tried it before, this softening of the vowels and the pronounciation of g's and the like, but had not succeeded for longer than a day or so. This time she included Lucy in her idea.

For starters, they had decided, they would stop saying 'ain't.' And instead of 'can I' they would say 'may I.' Of course, grammar wasn't the big factor that caused sharecroppers to stand out in a crowd (most Okies dropped a 'g' now and then) but it was part of it, and the only part Abby knew of that she could change without involving money.

In the car Lucy was half-asleep and whimpering for a drink. Even though they had just loaded up and started the engine, Papa got her a drink from the canvas water bag that was tied to the front of the car on every journey so they would have air-cooled water to drink. Abby looked back at the lonely-looking ramshackle house which, along with the few outbuildings, was etched against the semi-darkness and then disappeared from view, probably forever.

Papa started up a hymn, as he usually did on trips. As they drove the country roads and through the still-sleeping town, then off west on State Highway 9, their voices blended together—all except David's. He seemed to be sleeping:

> To Canaan's land I'm on my way,
> Where the soul of man never dies;
> My darkest night will turn to day,
> Where the soul of man never dies . . .

It wasn't long until Lucy was fast asleep and the rest of them were lulled to silence by the steady hum and thump of tires on highway concrete. With the breeze lifting tiny strands of hair all around her face and tickling her cheeks, Abby laid her head against the seat, intending to rest her eyes. The next thing she knew, the slowing of the car awoke her. They were stopping for gas at a filling station in a little town called Tabler, east of Chickasha. The man washed their windshield and filled the car and struck up a conversation.

"Looks like you folks is loaded down."

Papa nodded, "Got 'er purty full, I reckon."

"Where ya headed—Californy?"

"Naw. We had our fill of that."

"Thirties?"

"Year or so ago."

"I run this place in the thirties when ever 'body and their dawg was a-goin'. Truckloads of people packed in like animals. Cars a-squashin' the springs flat with folks crammed in, one on top of anuther. Wife said we oughta go west, too. I said whut the devil fer? These-here folks'll be back 'side of six months, I said. I was right, by and large. They starved out and got runned out. I watched 'em leave and I watched 'em coming back. They left in high spirits and heads up and they come back tuck-tailed 'thout no spirits, for the most part. Check yer oil?"

"Oil's okay."

The man paused briefly with the rag wadded against the window glass. "Never did say where you folks was headed."

"Over by the state line. Erick."

"Erick. I been there. It's a clean little town. You croppers?"

Papa nodded.

"Naw, the thirties—dirty-thirties—them was tryin' days. Folks come in a-wantin' a ten cent loaf of bread for a nickle. A-beggin' gas, some of 'em. Pullin' stuff outa the truck and askin' how much I'd give fer it. I had that-there back room full of stuff I didn't need. Some of it's still a-settin' there. Looks like you got a low back tire."

They pumped some air into the tire and when Papa paid for the gas he splurged a nickle on a package of Juicy Fruit. Mama tore the sticks of gum in half as usual, and Lucy wheedled as she licked the sweet off the inside of her wrapper, "Why cain't we have a whole stick once't?"

"A half's more than you had, and enough for a body," Mama said firmly. "You might want some tomorrow, too." She added, "Besides, I got a surprise for later on."

It was a mistake to mention a treat to Lucy without telling what the treat was because she couldn't rest and wouldn't allow anybody else to rest until she found out. Mama tried to get her off by having her count the box cars on a freight train that was lumbering along the tracks besides them for a while. Then she sang about the thousand-legged worm, the way she had when they were all much younger:

> "Said the thousand legged worm
>   as he gave a little squirm,
> "Has anybody seen a leg of mine?
>   If it cain't be found
> I'll have to hop around
>   on the other nine hundred ninety-nine!"

When it appeared Lucy would not be sidetracked, Mama finally brought a Karo syrup bucket out from under the seat and opened it to show them what was inside.

"Pun'kin seeds!" Lucy squealed. "How many can we have, Mama?"

"Git a handful apiece," Mama said generously, holding the bucket over the back of the seat.

"David's hand's bigger'n mine," Lucy complained. "He can hold more."

"Stomach's bigger, too, I imagine," Mama said matter-of-factly.

"Only thing bigger on Lucy's her mouth," David commented.

"Like a pig's eye," Lucy snorted. "Like a fish in a pickle dish."

"That'll do," Mama said without looking around. "Be careful where you put your gum."

Abby had saved her wrapper so she carefully rewrapped hers and put it in her dress pocket. David stuck his to the back of his hand, and Lucy had Mama hold hers. The next several minutes were spent cracking the seeds open with their teeth and extracting the slender, nutty insides that tasted almost like the pecans Papa sometimes bought at Christmastime.

Last fall when they had canned pumpkin, it had been Abby's and Lucy's job to pick all the seeds out of the mass of pulp that Mama scooped out of the center of the pumpkins, rinse them off, then spread them on top of the chicken house to dry. The ones not needed for planting would be saved for special treats such as today.

"Mama, David spit a hull on me!" Lucy announced dramatically, marring the melody of the tires singing on the pavement.

"Accident," David said calmly.

"Was not!"

"Lucy," Abby chided. "Don't be so touchy."

"Well, it was icky . . ."

"There won't be no fightin'," Mama said over her shoulder. "Look yonder," she added. "We're a-passin' White Bread Creek. Your Papa had an uncle that lived right by White Bread Creek once't."

"Crazy name," Lucy commented.

Abby looked at it closely as they passed by. The small stream cut through the red gully and was flanked by stones and budding shinnery, and gave no clue whatever as to how it had received its unusual name. Papa was saying something about how it flowed into Sugar Creek when it was running in the spring. When the rains stopped, so did the stream. His uncle used to go to nearby White Bread School when he was in his teens and he always told about the times White Bread flooded plumb out of its banks and how he got to miss school several times because of it.

"Them Caddo Indians had a stomp-ground close by, too," Papa said. "Still do, in fact. Uncle Roy used to go down there at night in the summer and them Indians'd be a-beatin' drums and hollerin' and singin' all covered in feathers on their heads and backs and arms and the wimmen in buckskin dresses, and he said it was a sight. Him and some other kids joined in the dancin' and them Indians, they was jist proud to have 'em, he said."

"Who taught him to Indian dance?" Lucy wanted to know.

"Why, it was simple, the way they did it, he said. They jist got in a circle, single file, and jist jumped and contorted in time of the drums and singin'."

"Kinda like that time Lucy had the red ants after her, I bet," Abby grinned.

"Well, you wouldn't of been laughin' if it was you," Lucy said defensively.

"Yeah, but you would of," David said dryly.

"I wouldn't laugh at nobody with ants on 'em!" Lucy maintained indignantly. "It's *you. You're* the one that laughs at people, actin' like you're the big king of the mountain or somethin'. Like you're better'n the president—"

"I said there won't be no fightin'," Mama interrupted firmly.

"We got a long trip ahead," Papa said, looking up in the mirror at them. "Did I ever tell you young'uns about the farmer that wanted harmony between his two short-fused barn cats?" He had told them, of course, but it had been a long time so he asked, "What do you think he did?"

Usually David would come up with some clever answer, but he remained silent now, still cracking pumpkin seeds, and Lucy spoke up with interest, "Shot 'em with birdshot?"

"Nope," Papa said. "He tied their tails together. Then he had a lot of unity, but he sure didn't have much harmony!"

Papa winked in the mirror at Abby. "Now, there's a lot of unity in a thirty-seven Chevy, bein's it's a mite close, but what we're gonna need's some harmony. And it's gonna take us all a-workin', not jist part of us."

Lucy sighed deeply. "It'd be easy to have harmony if it wasn't for David."

Everyone laughed, even David, a little, and for a while at least, harmony inside the Chevy traveling down Highway 9 was a reality.

By noon, with the Oklahoma sun bearing down unmercifully for late April, not only were the passengers in the car getting hot but the car was over-heating as well. Papa pulled over to the side of the road and checked it, finding the radiator had apparently developed a leak.

Going around to the back and poking around in the trailer, he asked Mama, "How far down do you reckon them milk jars are?"

Mama stuck her head out the window. "Look in the back left-hand corner."

Papa located the gallon jars after some shifting of boxes and he and David began to trek a quarter-mile or so to get water from the Washita River, of which they had been catching glimpses since passing Anadarko. They took extra jars for water they would need for the radiator later on.

While they were gone, Mama and Abby spread the red-checkered oil cloth and laid out cornbread and potato cakes and fried chicken, and poured tin cups full of water from the canvas water bag. Lucy was ready to eat the minute everything was ready, not agreeing with Mama that they should wait for Papa and David.

"Della Sue Payne and them jist digs in whether their Papa's there, or not," she retorted.

"Waitin's good for a body's patience," Mama said firmly, waving flies away from the food.

"I already got a lotta patience," Lucy argued.

As Lucy wandered over to a small incline and stood shading her eyes and frowning across a field of shinnery toward the Washita, Abby grinned and said secretly to Mama, "She's got a lotta patience cause she don't never use none of it!"

"She's got that Eason streak in her," Mama allowed. "A-wantin' stuff *now*, and not waitin' till due season. She'll have to learn."

While they were eating a little later, Papa told them how the Washita was a chief western tributary to Red River and came meandering right out of Texas (a geography lesson poorly disguised). He had played in the Washita as a boy when they lived down by Lindsay, he said.

"She's got a lotta water in her now, but I seen the time she was dry as a peanut hull a-roastin' in the oven. It was 1913—and Oklahoma was havin' her first full-fledged drought since gittin' to be a state. I was jist five then, but I can remember walkin' across the old Washita and not seein' a drop of water nowheres. Then in the twenties, just a handful of years later, we had all that floodin'. They said up around Oklahoma City and Tulsa you near had to have a rowboat to go after your mail in! Then come the thirties, and —well, ever'body knows about the thirties."

"How come ya'll didn't go to California in the thirties like ever'body else?" Abby asked, nibbling daintily at the crisp edges of her potato cake.

"Well," Papa said, "we was kinda in a bind, and not jist money-wise. Your Mama, she was in the fam'ly way in thirty-one and a trip would of been too hard, with her sick and all."

"What was she sick about?" Lucy asked innocently.

"About nine months," Papa laughed, looking toward Mama, who was shaking her head in a quiet warning.

"Then David come along," Papa said. "And we barely got turned around and Mama, she was in the fam'ly way again. There musta been somethin' in the water up around Tishomingo."

Papa was still grinning toward Mama who was turning pink. "Who-all needs somethin' more to drink?" she asked, reaching for the canvas bag. "And there's more chicken."

"Can I have the last potato cake?" Lucy asked.

"May I?" Abby reminded her.

Lucy's eyes flashed indignantly. "I asked first!"

Abby giggled. "Take it, for all I care. I'm full anyways." She doubted Lucy and good grammar would ever mix anyway.

After dinner, Papa stretched out for a nap with the excuse the car might not be cooled down quite enough yet. Mama and Abby tidied up, then Mama kept the flies shooed off Papa while Abby and Lucy, barefoot now, searched for pretty stones. David sat leaning against a big, barren cottonwood tree with a faraway look in his eyes.

After a while, Abby went and sat under the tree too, pulling on the leather oxford shoes that were getting so they pinched her toes. She hadn't told Mama yet because that would mean two or three more dollars for a new pair. "What're you doin'?" she asked David.

"What's it look like?"

She dug her fingers into the red soil and picked up a handful, sifting it out into a tiny mountain. "I bet Erick'll be the best place we ever lived," she said encouragingly, feeling another sudden spark of hope. "The farm's bigger, Papa said."

David shrugged. "Just more work."

"And more money."

"Yeah. If."

She knew what David meant. If there was rain, but not too much rain. If there was sun, but not too much sun. If there weren't bugs or worms or burning winds or hail. If they could stay ahead of the weeds. If cotton prices held up. If . . .

"Time to go children," Mama called.

Fitted inside the narrow Chevy again, Papa began telling jokes. He told the one about the farmer's wife that wanted to celebrate their twenty-five years of marriage by cooking their best hen for supper. To which the farmer replied, "Why do you want to punish a pore chicken for somethin' that happened twenty-five years ago?"

"Now, look out, Mister" Mama warned, laughing. "You'll git my dander up with them kinda jokes."

"What did the little moron bury his wife under the floor for?" Lucy asked.

"I don't know, but he better had a reason that'd stand up in court," Papa remarked.

"So's he could sing 'I'm Walkin' the Floor Over You'!" Lucy said jubilantly.

"Once an old man went to church while the preacher was in the middle of his sermon," Abby put in. "He asked the man beside him, 'How long has he been preaching'?' The man answered, 'About 28 years.' The old man reckoned, 'I guess I'll stay. He should be about through!' "

David stated dryly, "That joke's so old the first time I heard it the Dead Sea wasn't even sick yet." And he and Abby looked at each other and laughed a bit, along with the rest of the family.

When the Easons took a trip, unlike the feuding barn cats Papa told about, they seldom had unity only, but harmony as well. It was that closeness that made the hard times bearable and the good times enjoyable, not just in across-country moves, but in everyday life. As they rolled on down the highway, Abby found herself looking ahead, if not eagerly, then at least ambitiously, to their new life in Erick as Wade Collins' new sharecroppers.

Chapter Ten

THE COUNTRYSIDE was changing from hills and valleys and bottom land to higher, flatter country with occasional rolling hills. Papa said they would be gradually getting a little higher above sea level as they traveled west and Lucy thought that meant they would see the ocean, which called for some choice remarks from David, which then called for some admonishing from Mama and a mild reminder of the unified barn cats from Papa.

Papa began another song:

> Sowin' in the mornin', sowin' seeds of kindness,
> Sowin' in the noontide, and the dewy eves,
> Waitin' for the harvest, and the time of reapin',
> We shall come rejoicin', bringin' in the sheaves.

"What did they want to bring in the cheese for?" Lucy interrupted.

David rolled his eyes in disbelief and Mama smiled back at them. "Not cheese, Lucy Belle, sheaves. You know how in the fall your Papa bundles up the feed—the kafir corn and the like. Some people calls it sheaves. Now, in the song the sheaves is representin' souls saved . . ."

When Lucy was at last satisfied with the explanation, Papa continued:

> Sowin' in the sunshine, sowin' in the shadows,
> Fearin' neither clouds nor winter's chillin' breeze
> By and by the harvest and the labor ended,
> We shall come rejoicin', bringin' in the—"

Suddenly there was a loud pop. The car began weaving crazily while Lucy clung to Abby, and Abby to the back of the front seat, and Papa fought the steering wheel. Finally the car was under control and he brought it to a stop just off the road.

Abby's knees felt weak and rubbery and she slumped thankfully against the seat back. Everybody looked at each other and Mama said shakily, "All's well that ends well, my Mama used to say."

Papa sounded unconcerned as he said, "Yep. And David, looks like you and me has us a flat to change. Ever'body out!"

Later, at Cordell, where they were getting gas, Papa had to buy a new tube, carefully extracting a bill to pay for it from the few in his slim, well-worn billfold. The other tube had been patched so many times it looked like a patchwork quilt anyway, he joked to David after the man had taken the money. It was a wonder it hadn't blown out a longtime ago. David didn't say much, just helped where he was needed, stuffing the new tube inside the old casing and pumping air into it. Abby couldn't help noticing the tire was showing cord as bad as the spare and for a moment she wondered how they could go on without money to buy a tire.

Lucy was watching a tall, skinny rail of a woman dressed in bright green pedal pushers and straw sandals and a floppy brimmed hat to match. The woman selected a Bit-o-Honey candy bar then opened the lid to the pop cooler and lifted out a dripping cold Delaware Punch.

"Wisht we could have a pop," Lucy whispered loudly to Abby, causing the woman to glance their way, looking down her long nose at them in undisguised distaste.

"Water's healthier anyways," Abby reasoned, very conscious of her cloddish oxfords and heavy brown gabardine dress that was getting too short. It seemed no matter how she tried, she always looked the part of a sharecropper—even when she occasionally didn't feel the part.

"Yeah, but it ain't half as good."

"It's *not* half as good," Abby said, giving the grammar attempt one more try.

"I know it," Lucy shrugged. "That's what I said."

On the road again, Abby studied the changing countryside with interest. There were shinnery patches everywhere, tinted a fresh green by newly opening leaf buds that would continue to unfurl and grow to lengths ranging from a baby's hand to a man's. Later in the spring and summer the various shades of purple of the meadow violet and the red of Indian blankets would constitute a gay pattern not unlike the cotton print Abby had admired one Saturday at Drinkwater's Drygoods in Tecumseh.

Interspersed with the shinnery were plots of turned ground, flat-broke by moldboarding or deeply ridged by listing back in February or March. At present most fields were sitting silent and empty of machinery, waiting, Papa said, for the ground to warm sufficiently so that when the seed was planted it would swell and burst and bring the plant forth.

That was the miracle of a seed, Papa had told them before. You could let it set off in the dry someplace for a hundred years, he said, and it wouldn't sprout or even change one iota. But expose it to light and moisture and all the king's horses and all the king's men couldn't keep it from sprouting. Mama always added that nobody but God would have figured that one out.

And even now the farm near Erick was waiting to be re-listed in order to be prepared to receive the seed. Then would come the go-deviling and the never-ending hoeing. Papa and David would do all the machine work while Mama and Abby and Lucy set the house in order and put in the garden. Later the entire family would join together in the fields, wielding hoes and making blisters on winter-softened hands.

From the front seat now, Papa was beginning a mind-building game. "I'm thinkin' of the name of a country that starts with a G."

"Germany," Abby guessed.

"Georgia," Lucy said, causing David to look as though he could fall over in a dead faint at such stupidity.

The country was Guatemala and Abby guessed it so it was her turn. They had worked through several rounds and it was Lucy's turn—because the family had an unspoken agreement that there would always be at least one easy answer for her benefit—when the car began wobbling just a little again. This time the flat was on the trailer and it was leaned over to one side with Grandma's rocker perched at a haphazard angle.

"If that don't beat a hen a-peckin'," Papa declared. Still he didn't seem overly concerned. He and David merely switched the tires again and threw the flat one into the trunk to be fixed later. "Looks like she's seen her last days," Papa said of the tire. "Maybe we can make it on in with the spare."

They ate a snack, the last of the chicken and cornbread, without tarrying too long. Papa said a trip that should have taken a little over half a day was apt to take all day and half the night at the rate they were going. Of course, a body had to expect a flat once in a while, or a boiling radiator, he allowed.

After they were back in the car he turned on the radio to the Chuckwagon Gang Singers and Mama got out a waxed bread sack of dried apricots for them to munch on. Shortly after, Lucy was asleep against Abby's shoulder, still clutching some of the dried fruit. Abby shifted her around until she was leaning on the seat instead, and leaned back herself, listening drowsily to the hum of tires, along with the rhythmic thump each time they passed over a crack left between sections of concrete, and the lively singing on the radio:

> "I have turned my back on Egypt
> With its bondage and despair
> And by faith, oh land of Canaan,
> I'm determined to be there.
> Naught of earth shall ever harm me,
> I am happy on my way,
> For I'm bound for the land of Canaan
> Some sweet day."

Abby woke with a start as Papa announced cheerfully, "Well, looks like we made it!"

She looked out and saw the sign that said: Erick Population 1591, set back toward a tree row that extended for about a half-mile along the highway. Just ahead she could see the first houses, and a motor court called The Deluxe. Papa had said not long ago how that there were getting to be motor courts (sometimes called motels, a strange word that was perhaps a cross between motor and hotel) all over the United States nowadays. People could stop anytime of the day or night and pay some money and spend the night in little rooms that contained only a bed and bureau, then be on their way the next day. You didn't even have to make the bed, he said, because they paid someone to come in and do it for you. Mama said it sounded like the height of laziness to her, and she wouldn't give you two cents to sleep in a strange bed like that, one that didn't at least belong to a relative or a good friend. Because, if for no other reason, what about bed bugs?

"Motor courts don't have such," Papa had said, but Mama had remained unconvinced.

"We gonna live in town?" Lucy asked now, looking around sleepily and incredulously.

Mama laughed and exclaimed, "Child, what would a farmer want to be livin' in town for?" and Papa explained to get to Wade Collins' place, you had to go through Erick and out on 30 highway for two or three miles toward Mayfield.

Erick seemed to be a lively place and they all craned their necks, trying to see what businesses were in operation. Some people craned back at them, apparently interested that the Easons were a three-mattress family instead of two. There was a cafe called Cal's and a Corner Drug and a store called Bonebrake's Hardware.

"They've got a showhouse," Abby told David, who was looking around despondently. The advertisement said they would soon show "The Farmer's Daughter," with Loretta Young, and there were pictures and posters plastered all around. A small booth with a glass window made an island in the center and there was already a lady on the inside. She would take people's money and give out little stubs of paper that proved they had actually paid when the ticket man came along at intermission to gather them up.

Once on his birthday, David had gone to the Pine Theater in Tecumseh with Winburn Tolsey and his wife and he had told Abby and Lucy about it: the darkness in there, the popcorn and loud music, the people bigger'n life on the screen down front, talking and moving around as though they were there in person. Mama thought it was a shame and disgrace the way people in the United States paid out good money for such frivolities, but Papa had overruled and told David he could go that once. It had cost a dime (and the Tolseys even more) and so had the popcorn, David said. Of course,

Winburn Tolsey had stipulated from the first that he would foot the bill. Perhaps even back then they had been formulating a secret plan for David.

"That'll come in handy," David answered now, quite sarcastically, "For all the rich dudes."

"They've got two banks," Papa was saying from the front. The banks faced each other and one was called The First National and one was called The Farmer's National.

"Lotta good that does the Easons," Mama said cheerfully, but somewhat dryly.

"One of these days we'll walk in one of them banks and put some money in it," Papa predicted.

"Hogwarsh," Mama answered, but then she laughed in order to show she wasn't out to hurt anybody's feelings.

A few minutes out of town they turned down a sandy little sectionline road for a mile or so then turned on another to the right, then back east again. In a clearing not too far from the road set yet another tarpaper shack, the old barn and lots further on, a windmill and two or three small outbuildings. And everywhere there was sand. Little ridges of it almost covering weeds, long stretches of it where fields would be planted, whipped out spots of it in the dooryard, piles of it around fence posts.

"Here she is," Papa said. "Wade Collins said in his letter he'd have 'er cleaned out and ready to move into. That's more'n I can say for most landlords we've had. Ever'body grab a handful, now."

Travel weary, they climbed out, stretching and yawning, receiving whatever Papa placed in their outstretched arms. Then they trudged through the weeds and sand, up the broken steps and pushed open a slightly rickety door into the four walls of a front room, the peeling wallpaper a dull brown with huge equally dull pink flowers, and the usual blackened floors. A mouse scurried toward them in confusion, then skidded and darted the other way, disappearing into the wall. Abby stepped over closer to Papa.

"Our own home again," he said cheerfully.

"Jist let me git some curtains up, and some pitchers on the wall," Mama added. "And set me some mousetraps."

About nightfall, before they had had a chance to finish getting the house aright, they had a visitor. He was a youngish man with that aura of fatigue about him that croppers get when they put more into the land than they get back. He had tiny wrinkles in a sun-bronzed face, the thinning hair was grey at the temples and his shoulders stooped. In an arm he had a gallon jar of milk and on his face was a hesitant smile.

"I heered Wade Collins was a-gittin' new croppers. I knowed yall'd be without milk, come the mornin'." He added self-consciously, "I'm called Tots Caulifield."

Papa shook hands with him and invited him to come in. He stepped just inside the door, nodding respectfully and shyly toward Mama, explaining he didn't have time to set. "We're movin' on ourself," he said. "Things is packed and ready. My little lady, she's in the fam'ly way again—beggin' your pardon, ma'm—and didn't feel up to comin' and sayin' howdy. We got three young'uns a'ready, stairsteps about this high," measuring off three scant steps.

"Tell her our howdys," Mama said. She reached for an empty jar from a box. "I'll send this back with you. Fresh milk'll be mighty welcome. Wisht we had somethin' to pay you folks back with." She looked around, a bit helplessly it seemed, at the boxes still sitting on the floor.

Tots shook his head adamantly, "Wouldn't take it if you did. Jist wanted to be neighborly and make myself acquainted afore we pull out tomorry."

"Where you folks headed?" Papa asked.

"We ain't rightly sure. I got a brother up Altus way, and Nita Faye—she's got a cousin over by Cheyenne. They might know of work. Ya see . . . " He shifted his weight, putting one hand on the doorknob and with one foot propped over the other Abby could see the soles of his work boots were almost nonexistent, even in worse shape than the upper part. "Old Deryl Sheppard—he was my landlord—he's been blowed out one time too many. Bank wouldn't go no further with him. Jist shut him off. Lost ever'thing but the home place and barely hangin' onto that by the skin of his teeth."

"Puts a feller in a bind," Papa sympathized.

"You dad-gum right," Tots said, for a moment letting the anxiety show on his face, then he covered it with a brief smile, revealing a missing tooth. "We been that-a-way before, though. How 'bout yourself?"

"It's life," Papa agreed.

"Yeah, old Deryl Sheppard, he's in a bad way, hisself," Tots said. He twisted the knob and opened the door, holding the empty jar under one arm. "One of my young'uns is a-squallin' with boils. That's another reason Nita Faye didn't come on down. She's been a-holdin' that young'un most all day. The only way she can git easy is to lay over her Mama's shoulder. They's two of them boils on her back."

"Boils can be a sight," Papa sympathized.

"I had a cousin used to have carbuncles all the time," Mama put in. "He drunk a lotta whiskey and never no water and he had bad blood to boot."

"We been a'givin' her raisins," Tots said. "Bought

a pound down at the store. It ain't pured up her blood yet, though."

"A good bait of beef liver'd help," Mama advised.

"A good bait of beef liver'd help a lotta things," Tots agreed, and they all laughed a little with the mutual understanding that life didn't always hand a body exactly what he craved.

Tots chuckled softly, then said wistfully and apologetically, "The other girls, they been a-wantin' some of them raisins and we give 'em three-four apiece, but we said, no, that's all, cause Billy Faye's got to have them raisins to pure up her blood. And the pore little buggers. One of 'em, she says, why cain't we have our blood pured up, too?" He shook his head sadly at the memory. "We put fat'back on them boils but it ain't drawed out the heads yet."

"That fat'll do it," Papa said. "It might take a while."

"Well . . . I giss I'm a-hinderin' you folks . . ."

There were mild protests, and Mama added, "If we had the stove filled up with kerosene I'd boil us some coffee. None of us ain't had time to git it filled up yet."

"Movin's a chore," Tots said. "I'd ruther take a beatin'."

"It's the dewberry thumps," Papa agreed. "Maybe this'll be our last 'un. But, then, we thought that before . . ."

Tots shifted the empty jar to the other arm and twisted at the doorknob again. He wasn't quite ready to go. He was clearly troubled and had found temporary comfort in the presence of others. "Naw," he said vaguely, picking briefly at a callous on one work-weathered hand. "We jist seen you folks drive by with your car loaded down and all. Nita Faye, she said I bet that's ole Wade Collins' croppers. We saw the direction you turned and all. We knowed yall'd be without milk. Nita Faye, she said, we got tonight's milkin'. Ain't no way we'll need it all, with us a-pullin' out, and all."

"We're much obliged to you," Papa said again. "What's breakfast without a good bait of cow-juice to warsh it down?" He chuckled a little hesitantly, wanting Tots to know he respected his right to ignore the humor if he felt so inclined.

Tots gave a token laugh of his own, saying how his young'uns could kill off a half-gallon in one setting. But his mind was clearly elsewhere, no doubt on boils and the predicament awaiting him tomorrow and the next day and even the next, as he sought a means to survive.

"Well, I'll git on . . ."

"Luck to you and your bunch findin' another place," Papa said.

"Yeah." Tots smiled faintly. "I giss if they wasn't but two kinds of luck I wouldn't have none." He turned back a last time, his smile gone, his face gaunt and shadowed both because of the darkness outside around him, and some indefinable threat of darkness inside him. "It's kinda like writin' your name in the water. It don't make much never-mind if you do or if you don't." And he was gone.

And even after he was out of sight, the atmosphere seemed heavy with Tots Caulifield's uneasiness. Even though Papa and Mama bantered back and forth some as the beds were set up and essentials tended to, the heaviness remained. Maybe it was because for just a few moments they had been confronted once again with the uncertainty croppers live with. If the natural elements didn't get them, then other circumstances often did.

Getting ready for bed a little later—all the face and feet washing and rummaging in boxes for night clothes and combing out braids, right down to the blowing out of the lamp—they were each preoccupied with their own thoughts. Life, the man had reminded them, is like writing your name in the water. It didn't make much never-mind if you did, or if you didn't. Didn't make much impression, he meant, of course. Didn't count for much. The world went right on, without taking note that you had passed by.

Abby pulled the frayed sheet around her and tried to forget the despair in Tots Caulifield's eyes. Beside her Lucy was asleep already, had been since the moment her head hit the pillow. David, in the corner, on his bed until they could get him a little room built, was tossing, sighing deep, restless. From the back room, Papa and Mama talked in hushed murmurs.

All of them here together in a tarpaper shack near a little town called Erick, located in Beckham County, Oklahoma. The Easons were here, willing to begin a new phase in their life. A new life no different than the old one. Only the name of the town and the people would be any different.

Chapter Eleven

SPRINGTIME DRAWS A farmer into the fields for long, hard hours—stirring the earth with his plows while nature caresses it with warmth and rain.

In field after field around Erick, the tractors and listers were busy, crawling slowly, leaving swaths of dark, moist soil behind them. It was the same soil, Papa had told them before, that had received the seed for the centuries since Indians first crossed the natural land bridge that was once between the continents, or later paddled their kayaks across the open waters of the Bering Strait and finally made their way to the place that would be called Oklahoma.

Back then the land had mostly been prairie except in places the Red man planted corn, beans and squash. Today it produced cotton and grain sorghums and wheat. The cotton would be gathered and ginned with the fiber being sold and shipped to textile mills as far away as England or France or the New England states, or even as close to home as Sand Springs. The seed would be used for the feeding of cattle with some saved for next year's planting, or sold to a cottonseed oil mill and made into cooking oil or soaps or cosmetics for use by those with financial means.

Such luxury! The Easons and croppers like them used hog lard for cooking, made their own soap from grease and lye, and Mama was convinced cosmetics were used only by hussies—and who had twenty-nine cents to throw away on a lipstick?

The wheat would be harvested and sent to mills at Yukon or Enid, or transported by ship to Europe or Asia. The sorghums (milo, kafir corn and similar grains) were either sold as money crops or bundled and stacked to be used for feeding livestock during the winter.

And just as sure as seeds grow, the weeds come. From spring until late summer a war is waged against weeds, the weapons being a hoe and file and a jug of well water, and what Mama sometimes called "main-strength and awkwardness."

The war is fought from dawn to dark, and refought in bed at night with recurring dreams of swinging a hoe in a never-ending jungle of weeds and Johnson grass. There are casualties—blisters on the hands until callouses form, the aching of over-taxed muscles and early in the summer, the smarting of sunburn to which raw potato might be applied before bedtime. Clean faces in the morning become weathered with field silt until by evening the eyes and lungs are full of it (especially on a windy day), and the mouth is ringed by it and it grits between the teeth.

Pleasant day-dreams or thinking games had always been an escape for the Easons, but in the spring of '47 outside influences interfered. There was the lack of rain, which was not excessively unusual for western Oklahoma, but was critical now because of no winter moisture. There was the early arrival of the heat. There was the fact that Wade Collins' land had been used too hard for too long resulting in a dishearteningly sparse stand of cotton.

"Crop rotation might be the answer," he had mused to Papa late one evening out by the road where Papa, Abby and Lucy were putting in a new post on which to perch the mailbox after the old one had collapsed. "The Soil Conservation Service has been sending out brochures. They did a world of good over in McIntosh County in the late thirties, testing soil, advising about crop varieties that build it up. Next year, we'll see . . ."

Then there was David's bewildering attitude. Occasionally he seemed to be snapping out of it and becoming himself again. More often, he seemed to personally hold a grudge against them all, especially Papa, and seemed to take satisfaction in not allowing anyone to forget it. Not by words, but by his silence.

No one mentioned the breach, except for the one night when Papa casually stepped out on the sagging front porch as David was on the way to his sleeping room and almost offhandedly and very gently reprimanded him for his attitude. David had listened in silence and nodded, going on his way, and for a few days at least, it seemed he might have put out a greater effort to be one of them, only to slip away again.

Because they were naturally optimistic about such things, they merely waited in patient anxiety for the breach to heal itself, as a cripple with a broken leg endures it with long-suffering, understanding that he will again be whole one day. For everyone knows neither broken bones nor breaches last forever.

Mama stuck her head in the door of the new place that had been theirs for a month. "Papa wants you kids to see all the lightnin' bugs out here."

Abby laid down the coverless prose and poetry book she had been reading in the ring of light around the kerosene lamp and Lucy jumped up from where she had been playing paper dolls. David sat unmoving in the shadows, hunch-shouldered against the wall, his long, slender legs folded, and staring moodily as he had been since supper. Beside him lay the small pamphlet Mr. Tolsey had given him before they left Tecumseh. Abby had often wondered about it, but had never mentioned it because David was never in the mood for discussing anymore.

"You comin', David?" she asked.

"I've seen lightnin' bugs before."

Mama and Papa were sitting under the elm tree on the slat back chairs they had taken outside from the supper table. Mama was churning cream in a half-gallon jar and Papa was whittling out a butter paddle from a chunk of wood he'd picked up somewhere. The little flat paddle David had made for Mama a few years before had been lost in the shuffle of moving and since then she had been using a spoon to press the milk out of the finished butter and to work the salt into it. Her hint to David that she needed another had gone unheeded.

Papa pointed toward the shinnery knoll that was almost in their front yard. There seemed to be hundreds of tiny, glittering lights, disappearing and then reappearing like those amazing flashing signs they had seen in Los Angeles the one time they had gone there. It was a beautiful and intriguing nighttime scene.

"How come they's so many?" Lucy breathed.

"Jist a new hatch growed off, I reckon," Mama said. "'Ever' few nights it seems like we have a whole slew of some different kind of varmit. It was miller bugs the other night, remember?"

"Your Gran'pa used to say lightnin' bugs was God's little lanterns," Papa reminisced. "He said they was huntin' pore souls that didn't have no light inside of 'em. No *Licht*, Gran'ma called it. Ever'body oughta have a light, he said. He was sentimental and easy-affected that way, your Gran'pa was."

"Put him in his grave before his time, too," Mama declared, sounding slightly annoyed, though she had scarcely even known Grandpa back then since it was before she and Papa got sweet on each other. "Always them notions of doin' things in a big way. Didn't have a lick of education, hisself, but always a-wantin' more schoolin' for his boys, even when there wasn't no money. Even when there wasn't no cause. Ever'body knows schoolin' don't make a farmer. Should of been content with his lot and the lot of 'em all, but he couldn't, someway."

"Aw, Mama," Papa said easily, "A feller cain't help dreamin' a little."

Mama scoffed, "When he should of buckled down and kept his boys under wraps, he didn't even do that. Them high and mighty notions rubbed off on them and ever'thing got outa hand after that. Your Papa'd be alive today if he'd of got it straight in his head from the start that sometimes dreams are better off forgot."

Papa winked at Abby. "I b'lieve Mama's got enough spunk she could fill Brother Whitten's pulpit come Sunday. Course, she'd have to take a text if she did."

"You know ever' word I'm a-sayin' is the truth!" Mama exclaimed, taking up her churning again. But she laughed a little so Papa would know she wasn't angry.

Abby laughed, too, but she didn't like to think about what Mama was saying about Grandpa. It sounded too much like Papa and David. They were both easily affected, sensitive, as Grandpa had been, the type that could very possibly pine away over some unreachable dream. Putting that thought away from her as highly improbable, Abby studied for a moment on something Papa had said. "I bet you could use lightnin' bugs for a real lantern," she said, seeing it in her mind. "You could put 'em in a Mason jar with a lid on."

"You're always one with the notions, Abby-girl," Papa said, and the moonlight revealed a little glimmer of pride in his blue eyes. "But that one's a'ready been thought of. Them that lives over in other lands sometimes gathers 'em in bottles and carries 'em in forests and such. I read it in the World Book as a boy."

Papa was always telling about something he saw in the World Book. When he was little some lady had given them a whole set of out-dated ones, minus the R volume that had been lost, and that had been his only reading material other than school books and the Bible. To this day, he said, if you asked him to tell you some about any word that began with an R he was up salt creek without a paddle, just plumb dense-headed and couldn't give you a single fact. Abby and David used to talk about how they wished they could see—and read—just one World Book, never mind a whole set.

"Let's try it," Lucy said eagerly, and scooted away to get a jar.

The fireflies were easy for Lucy to catch—Abby wouldn't touch them with a ten-foot pole—and soon there was a jarful of them flitting around and giving off intermittent glows. With a wire they fastened the jar to a branch of the elm tree where Papa and Mama sat.

"Those city folks got nothin' on us," Mama gloated. "We got our own brand of 'lectricity."

"When're we gittin' real 'lectricity, Papa?" Abby wondered absently, watching the glow of the fireflies.

"Someday," Papa said, looking at the fireflies too, but as though he weren't seeing them. "Someday when old Wade Collins or whoever is our landlord decides to break loose with a dollar."

"We could jist git it ourself," Abby suggested hopefully. Ever since the first time she had been in a house at night that had electricity with light reaching every corner so one could read as well as in the daytime, she had secretly longed for electric lights for her family. To say nothing of the electric ice boxes that froze little blocks of ice for the tea and kept the milk as cold as the back room in winter.

Papa shook his head and bent over his whittling again, squinting in the half-light of the moon. "The house ain't worth wirin', nohow. Besides, it's Wade Collins' place to do it. It's his house."

Abby pondered that for a moment. Of course she knew the houses in which they lived never belonged to them. It hadn't seemed significant until now. It suddenly bothered her to think that David had been right. They really didn't have much they could stand back and look at.

She looked at the house in the dull light of the moon, a tarpaper shack, like all the rest. A shack that had been built without a foundation so that the corners sagged badly now from the unceasing Oklahoma wind whipping the sand out from under the concrete blocks on which it perched.

It had three rooms, though. Most of the others had only two. Usually she and Lucy had to sleep in the corner of the kitchen. This one had a kitchen and a separate front room where she and Lucy slept. Then there was the tiny lean-to that was Papa's and Mama's bedroom. David, of course, had his little box-like cubby that Papa always built for him since he became thirteen.

The yard was sand, and had shinnery roots sticking up in all sorts of skinny, grotesque shapes, some of them like snakes rearing up their heads. There was no grass, just some stickers and a few sunflowers and careless weeds, and one lonely, spiny bear grass that Papa said was a liliaceous-type plant. That made it remotely kin to the lily of the valley spoken of in the Good Book, so Papa said to treat it with respect.

They could have kept it all hoed down (except for the bear grass, of course) only there was not much energy left after hoeing cotton all day. The cotton was hardly knee-high to a grasshopper, but the weeds were already coming on even though there had only been the one inadequate rain just after planting. That was the amazing thing about weeds, Abby often thought. They could make a crop when nothing else could. The lack of rain didn't stunt them. Too much rain never washed them out the way it did crops. Hail and other calamities didn't phase them, either.

In fact, there was really not much energy left for anything after a hard day in the field. At night they were exhausted and just came in and dunked off in the horsetank to get rid of the field dust and ate whatever was left over from dinner and went to bed. Except once in a while, on a night like this, when they felt up to whiling away some time.

Being a sharecropper was hard and Abby was realizing that more and more. Thirty year old women often looked forty or fifty with leather skin and stooped shoulders. Men that should have been in their prime became grizzled and bowed over under the pressures of trying to see their family survive. Men like Tots Caulifield—and a multitude of others.

It was easy to understand why Grandpa had played out so early in life because it happened all the time. The only thing worse that Abby could remember was following the fruit in California. The camps and the filth and the cursing and fighting and drinking and being called fruit tramps at school by haughty Californians. Demanding straw bosses, treating them like children who didn't have the wits to know an over-ripe from a flat when it came to peas, nor a bruised peach from a green one. It was another, harsher world, a world that the Easons hadn't anticipated, and hadn't even tried to fit into after being confronted by it.

As Papa always said, "Travis Eason's bunch may be a lowly lot in the eyes of the world, sharecroppin' and what-have-you, but that ain't no excuse for draggin' your belly down on the ground instead of standin' tall and lookin' people in the eye. Travis Eason's bunch'd rather be honest and law-abidin' and civilized than to be rich or famous or good-lookin'. Of course, there ain't no law that says we cain't be as good-lookin' as the next feller, and we can work to'ard those other things for later on!"

Like civilized people, the Easons went to church, too, when Mama felt up to it—all except Papa. He never did, but he still read the Bible and he always said he admired the good Lord and sure thought going to church was a right fine idea. He meant to go with them, someday.

So the Easons could stand hard work as long as they could hold their heads up and were all together and had their health and the good Lord to look out for them. That's how Mama looked at it, and she mentioned it every once in awhile when some of them seemed to have a more high-flown aspiration than she considered necessary. "There you go," she might say, "tryin' to let your feet foller your mind off instead of your mind a-follerin' your feet." Certainly none of them were complaining. Except for David, and his was mostly done silently by the look in his eyes and the face that was pinched and unsmiling more and more.

Before, if he had a little time off he would be doing something profitable. Reading or whittling or making diagrams of something to build someday when he got the money. Not too far back, they would have all been playing hide-and-go-seek or freeze tag or black sheep scatter while Papa and Mama looked on, or drowning out crickets which was accomplished by pouring a pop

125

bottle of water into the cricket's hole and watching him come to the top for air. David thought he was too mature for all that now. But Wade Collins had a mare at the lot, and a new colt that David could have been fooling with. He could hardly say he was too mature for that. And, before, he would have certainly come out to see something if Papa mentioned it.

Papa was still telling about lightning bugs in his 'teaching' voice. He was saying the World Book told how it was a mix of chemicals like magnesium and oxygen that caused the glow and told how Cuban ladies sometimes tucked them into their hair for decoration, or pinned some that were called click beetles to their party gowns. Lucy was enchanted by that, but Mama said it sounded like a lot of hooey to her. Said she'd have to get pretty bad off to try and fancy herself up with bugs.

When there was a long enough silence, Abby asked quietly, "Papa, I wonder what's the matter with David." As if they didn't all know, with the probable exception of Lucy. But they had tried to pretend not to notice for long enough, hoping it would change. Something had to be done; it had to be talked about and figured out.

"Too big for his britches," Mama said immediately. Not mad, but put-out. It seems as though lately she was beginning to wonder if she could handle David, with his moods and all. "The Tolseys shouldn't of said what they did, there in the beginnin'. Not in front of him, they shouldn't. Went to his head. Give him idees that was too big for him to handle. And I'm a good mind to tell 'em so if I ever see 'em again."

"It's jist growin' pains," Papa said soothingly, examining the butter paddle's progress and taking off another sliver to smooth it up. From the tone of his voice there was no indication that he had ever felt the same about the Tolseys as Mama did—uneasy and uncertain. With them so far away now, the threat was over and done and as he always said, better to let sleeping dogs lay and not be waving a hambone under their noses. "When you're nigh seventeen you think you gotta hurry and git there and try to move the world, or somethin'."

"Was you that way?" Abby asked gravely, knowing the answer but needing to hear it audibly for her own ease of mind.

"I 'spect ever' boy is. 'Specially if he's a Eason."

Abby thought deeply for a moment. Felt a spark of hope. "When'll he git over it, do you reckon?"

"Whenever he takes a notion."

Abby sat staring at the lightning bugs winking in the darkness. God's little lanterns. Ever'body oughta have a light. A *Licht*. That was David's trouble. The move and the uncertainty over college and all the hard work and his *rauh* age had brought him to the place he just didn't have much *Licht* left in him anymore. Like Vickie Barkley, back at Tecumseh, and like Grandpa Eason during Papa's boyhood.

Hesitantly now, for fear she was probing too far, "Papa, is he gonna git to go to college?"

Papa shifted positions in his chair, running his thumb across the edge of the finished paddle. "Daughter, like always when somethin' big's in question, there's some conditions that's gotta be set by. There's money. There's smart. And there's grit. Now, outa those three, which do you think holds the most weight?"

Abby studied for a moment. "Grit."

Papa nodded, satisfied. "Did you ever see a Eason that didn't have no grit?"

"No." Unless it was David. She wasn't entirely sure of him anymore.

Papa nodded again, and from all outward appearances he was calm and assured. "David's got the smart — we all know that — and he's got the grit. I'd say that don't leave no doubt about college, then, nor anything else he sets his mind to. Wouldn't you?"

Chapter Twelve

ABBY REASONED THAT if David was short on *Licht*, he might be short of grit, for she was not for sure whether they were interchangeable. The solution should be simple: Somehow get him out of that tight, somber little world he was living in nowadays and make him see there were interesting things he was missing out on. Make him laugh.

Maybe the rest of the family could continue to let David's problem slide, but she was of a different persuasion. She could see that ignoring it was not only not healing the breach, it was possibly making it worse. As always happened when a pressing need was clearly defined, her heart burned with zeal and diligence and a multitude of ideas flowed to meet that need. David had always scoffed at her concerns over other people's predicaments. Little did he know that he had become her latest project.

She began her subtle undertaking on a sweltering Sunday afternoon, the one day in the week they were free except when crop tending was in dire straits.

"David, let's go ride Cherry," she said with just the proper amount of enthusiasm—not too much, and not too little.

"Too hot," was the disinterested response.

It was hot—unseasonably so. Lucy was sprawled on the rag rug by the bed sleeping, dressed only in her underdrawers, and little beads of sweat stood out all over her face. David was slouched down on the floor where it was the coolest against the worn linoleum, a wet towel draped over his stomach and chest, idly trying to balance a roll of tape on his long, bare toe. Abby watched for a minute from her position on the double bed. Finally the tape fell off and rolled across the block of sunlight on the floor and to the bed. She reached out a foot and sent it back to him.

"We could dunk in the tank first."

"Too hot."

"For dunkin'?"

"For anything."

"We could dig a cave, like we used to."

"I out-grew that way back there."

Abby was silent for a minute, not discouraged but merely needing new strategy. Caves had often proved David's weakness. On the rare occasion when there was time off from the field they had made some outstanding caves, digging into the side of a shinnery hill and building little campfires inside them, often begging potatoes from Mama and baking them in the coals.

Once they had even found an arrowhead, pinkish in color and chiseled from pure quartz. They had wildly surmised that some Indian had dug his own cave there and had lost the arrowhead while waiting inside. But Papa said the shinnery hills weren't there in the days of the Indians, that there was mostly grass and the shinnery took over only after white men's cattle over-grazed the land. When the grasses died out, the winds whipped the sand around, piling it up around clusters of shinnery trees, which eventually grew up through it, whereupon more sand piled around it until finally there was a hill. David kept the arrowhead in a cigar box now, along with a coyote's tooth, a piece of unused railroad flare, some fool's gold and a few chips of real marble Uncle Lewis had brought him from someplace in Sequoyah County.

"We might could dig up an arrowhead," she tried again.

"Umph," David grumbled.

"Marbles'd be fun," she continued gamely. "We could play keepers."

That was the ultimate in generosity, Abby reasoned, because she had never played a game of marbles with David that he didn't win. They usually played for 'fair' where the original owner received back his marbles no matter who won. David was soft-hearted enough that even when they played keepers, he ended up giving them back most of the time. For, as he said more than once while feigning impatience, how could he play her a game later if she never had any marbles left?

But now he merely said without emotion, "Outgrew that, too."

"Cat and Mouse?"

"Same."

Abby flared up just a little. "Sounds to me like you think you out-grew about ever'thing that's fun."

"You'll grow up someday."

"Ha! It'd take an act of Congress to get me to grow up if I hafta act like I got green grapes in my mouth the way you do."

"Might take congress, at that. I never did see such a tomboy."

Thoroughly exasperated, Abby said, "Well, let's *do* somethin'."

"Too hot."

Abby lay back on the bed, defeated for the moment. There was a little coolness against the quilt Mama had made of old sock tops long ago, and she pressed her warm cheek against it, closing her eyes. From the kitchen came the pungent, greeney smell of boiling poke greens and the musical sounds of the gurgling of them were pleasant. Mama and Papa were in there and Mama was stripping the stems off of more of the greens and putting them to soak in a pot of salt water to get the bugs and sand off. Papa was bolting spoon handles on some of the old lids. They were talking, and once in a while they laughed.

"Well, at least you don't do like Amy Lamb's ole man always did," Mama was saying. "He used to git hisself throwed in jail about twice't a month. If he didn't show up at home the kids'd jist say the law musta got after Papa again and go on about their business."

Papa sounded as though he were gloating a little, the way he did sometimes when he was funning. It was the same way David used to sound, pompous and smart-alecky, but charmingly so. "I reckon Travis Eason was cut out of a different piece of cloth than ole Dub Lamb was. The good Lord, He cut out Travis Eason and He threw away the cloth that was left and the *Schere* and all!"

Mama declared in that dry way she had when Papa was hoo-rahing her, "I 'spect that's the livin' truth! I imagine the scissors was wore out, anyways, with Him a-tryin' to trim off all the rough edges!"

Papa answered jauntily, "Woman, you got the best ole man this side of Pushmataha county, and you might as well own up to it!"

"You wouldn't be a mite high on yourself, now would you?" Mama shot back. They both laughed.

For as long as she could remember Papa's and Mama's going on at each other had been a comfortable, fixed part of life. It was an indication that all was right in the Easons' own particular world. There might be unrest and calamities elsewhere: atomic bombs being tested out there in the Pacific, national turmoil caused by past and present steel and mine workers' strikes back East, growing hostility toward the Russians, even disasters much closer to home like the terrible tornado up by Woodward back in April—the one that was written up in newspapers everywhere and that Papa heard about on the car radio the day after it happened. If you dwelled on those circumstances or other ones equally worrisome, Abby had found, you might find yourself drifting out into a world of uncertainties and fear. But the Easons were safely insulated from that with the security afforded them by their acceptance of each other; by the strong, abiding love displayed by attitude rather than kisses or hugs, and by their belief in God and country.

It seemed as though Papa and Mama didn't hoorah as much as they used to, though. Now, since the move and the doubtful state of the crops, and once the heat had gotten to everybody (temperatures already in the eighties according to Erick's weatherman, W. R. Clancy) and since David was having such a low spell.

David. Something had to be done. Abby wracked her brain lest she had overlooked any possible activity that might interest him, and tried again, rolling over to a fresh spot on the bed in order to get cooler.

"Let's do screen tests," she suggested, but failed to force much optimism into her voice. According to the Silver Screen magazine she had read at a friend's house once, real life movie actors did screen tests in order to show directors they had the ability to act out make-believe situations realistically. She and David used to do some extraordinary screen tests. Sometimes David was George Patton, giving the impassioned speech to Uncle Lewis' 45th Infantry, "Born at sea, baptized in blood, your fame shall never die." David was so realistic the first time he did it, the hair had stood up on Abby's arms (sitting there on the ground holding stick guns, she and Lucy had represented the entire 45th Division).

Other times David would be Rhett Butler in "Gone With The Wind" and would say to Abby, who was Scarlet, "Frankly, my dear, I don't give a hoot," then turn on his heel and walk arrogantly away. More than once Abby had almost rolled on the floor with laughter, David was so good at it. She liked drama the best, though, and could do a very passable scene of a lady getting a telegram saying her husband was missing in action.

But they hadn't done screen tests in a long time, and now David only gave her a look of disdain. "Kid doin's."

"Well," she said impatiently, forgetting for the moment that she was attempting to lift David's spirit instead of trying to wither it with sarcasm, "You'd be better off if you'd be more of a kid yourself, instead of actin' like a sour old gran'pa. If that means you're growed up, I don't never want to grow up."

For good measure, she stuck out her tongue in David's direction but he didn't see it, luckily. She didn't like to think of growing up, though. It seemed too confining and much too boring, and even a little frightening. At going on sixteen, she was getting dangerously close. She preferred being a tomboy and not worrying about lily-white skin and soft hair the way some girls did. Everyone said Rhonda Gregory, back at Tecumseh, rubbed lemon peel on her face every day to try and bleach out her freckles. And it was common knowledge that Mary Barfield used buttermilk on hers. Judy Green broke a raw egg into her water when she washed her hair (so her little brother, Tim, said) and put black shoe polish on her eyelashes. It was a little disgusting the things some girls did to fool everybody into thinking they were beautiful.

Flies were crawling on the ceiling and she idly counted twenty-three of them while giving David ample time to snap back from her rather scathing indictment. But David was ignoring her, concentrating on the roll of tape balanced there on his toe, even while he moved his foot experimentally back and forth. Abby watched with a mixture of growing impatience and keen interest as he got more and more proficient with his act, making all sorts of foolhardy moves that usually would have upset the tape, finally giving it a flip the way a circus clown would have. Only the tape didn't rebalance on his toe, but went rolling off to itself. Unconcerned, David closed his eyes, relaxing against the wall, rearranging his cooling towel.

Abby couldn't resist giving another jab. "I guess you're so growed up you'd ruther to set there and mildew before you'd git up and have some fun for a change."

"Ever what you think," David said dryly.

Abby sighed deeply and sat up, trying to regain her sense of duty toward David's recuperation again. "Papa could show us how to make pea shooters with clothes pins. Or we could learn to hang by our toes on the windmill crosspieces like Justin Newberry showed us that time."

"I could design my own pea shooter if I was a mind to," David mumbled sarcastically without even opening his eyes. "And Justin Newberry is either doublejointed or touched in the head, or both."

Abby smothered her retort and said enticingly, "I know where some boards are that'd make good stilts. They even got nails in 'em we could pull out to straighten and use again."

Nothing from David. He seemed to be sleeping.

"Papa heard in town people is catchin' big perch over in Turkey Creek. Ben Findsterwald caught him a catfish a foot and a half long."

Still nothing.

There was a long, thin cottonwood limb lying beside Abby that she had stripped of leaves earlier, planning to make a fishing pole out of it. She picked it up craftily and touched it to the tip of David's nose. He thought it was a fly and waved his hand to get rid of it.

Abby waited a few seconds and did it again, with the same results. Then she trailed it over his lips and he shook his head vigorously, blowing air at the fly and frowning, but still not opening his eyes. Abby went through all of it again, remarking casually, "Boy, the flies are awful today. Must be gonna rain."

David's eyes popped open suspiciously in time to grab the limb, twist it out of Abby's hands and ruthlessly break the prospective fishing pole to bits while she giggled a bit hysterically.

"You'd wart a guy plumb into his grave," he grouched. "You'd even give Will Rogers the all-overs." But he unfolded his long, slim body and got up, slowly, as though he really was an old man, and went to the door, draping his cooling towel over the screen door spring.

Abby followed him outside and they wandered down toward the lot. There wasn't a cloud in the sky and the sun was still high enough that their shadows were midgets following along behind them. Abby opened her mouth to mention it and closed it again. David wouldn't be interested, having seen the shadow-midgets almost every day of his life as he worked in the fields. The sand burned her bare feet so that she occasionally had to step into the skimpy shadow of a careless weed or sunflower for relief. A horsefly was intent upon drawing a feast from the back of her leg, but she finally slapped it unconscious and ground it into the hot sand with her heel.

At the lot David sat listlessly on the side of the horse tank while Abby smoothed Cherry's velvet coat. The colt, Cloudy, peered around from the safety of his mother's bigness and watched warily.

Abby had an inspiration. "We should try to break Cloudy, David."

"Oh, sure. Who'd git broke first, you or him? And I bet you'd git in dutch with old Wade Collins. I bet he'd pitch a fit plumb to Georgia."

"Well, I'd jist pitch one right back at him," Abby declared. Only she wouldn't of course. "There ain't—isn't—any harm in it, if we don't make him spooky."

"Git a rope, then," David said, rolling his eyes upward to show just how dumb he thought the idea was.

Abby found an old piece of frayed rope in the hay shed and held it out to David. "You do it," he said, idly skimming bits of moss out of the water and tossing them onto the ground. "I'll pick up the pieces."

First she closed the lot gate, then picked some careless weeds, nice tender ones that grew around the tank where the water ran over sometimes. Then she stood inside the lot and held them out, standing like a statue without moving. Cherry came over and snorted at the weeds and began nibbling, Cloudy close behind. But the colt stopped a safe distance away and blinked his large, beautiful dark eyes comically at Abby.

When Abby would have to move in order to go after more weeds or grass, Cloudy would wheel sharply and trot away, but always came back, getting braver each time. Once he even sniffed delicately at her hand, then snorted in fright at the unfamiliar human scent, raced crazily around the lot, kicking up his heels ferociously. Abby laughed delightedly and even David joined in some.

Then she crawled over the lot fence and sat on the horsetank, too, trailing her fingers in the water and watching slender blue horse-doctors hover then alight on little moss rafts. "Breakin' takes too long. Let's ride Cherry instead."

"You can."

"Watchin' isn't as fun as doin'."

"It *isn't*?" David mimicked, making fun of her attempt to speak better English. The resolution she had made before they left Tecumseh failed as often as not. The years of both hearing and speaking cropper variety had left its imprint deeply entrenched.

"Let's dunk, then," she said, ignoring the thrust.

"You."

Abby deliberated for a moment, felt another surge of inspiration mixed liberally with impatience, and snaked an arm out, pushing David backward.

He yelled sharply in surprise and anger and disappeared into the green water—all except his feet and legs—and was back up immediately, slicking his wet hair out of his eyes and sputtering with rage, "You sloppy-jawed baboon! I'll show you how that feels . . ."

Abby saw the look in his eyes instantly and stopped laughing, shrieking, "I won't never do it again! Honest, David! Cross my heart and hope to die."

David lunged for her and she darted away so fast her braid flew around and hit her face, and she began screaming in a kind of agonized terror and excitement. She was fast as a roadrunner being chased by a coyote, her bare feet skimming over the hot sand so rapidly there was no sensation of the scorching of them, or the jabbing of stickers. But David, with his unbelievably long legs, was even faster. When he caught her, he twisted her arm behind her back and commanded, "Walk!"

Toward the horsetank they went, Abby pleading desperately and resisting with each step. At the edge he picked her up bodily and heaved. The brief, scary sensation of sailing through the air, the back-slap as she landed, the slight shock of cool water as she went under, and especially the rush of water up her nose, were not experiences she would soon forget. The last thing she heard before going under was David's very authentic guffaws.

If she hadn't helped him recover his *Licht* entirely, then at least she could rest assured she had given it her best—and perhaps last—shot.

Chapter Thirteen

NO MATTER WHERE they lived there was always an abundance of wild fruit. In Pottawatomie County they had picked plums and grapes and currants along Squirrel Creek. In Seminole County they had picked them near the South Canadian. Down in Bryan County one year they had all the wild dewberries they could eat, and canned forty quarts besides, to be used in jams and cobblers all winter.

The North Fork of Red River lay just a few miles north of Erick, only three miles from their place on Wade Collins' land, and Papa took them there one Sunday afternoon to pick plums. David didn't want to go but Papa said that a family should do things together because that's the way the Lord ordained it. Abby heard David say under his breath, "I guess *that's* why we're all of us in the fields nearly twenty-four hours a day. I don't know about anybody else, but I'm about caught up on all this together-business."

Abby defended Papa and worried about David and his missing *Licht*. She longed for the times when he was under foot, warting Mama or talking man to man with Papa, or alternately pampering Abby and Lucy with his big-brotherliness—or cutting them down to size with his sharp wit and the mischievous glimmer in his clear, blue eyes. These days it was almost unbearably quiet in the fields and around the house. David's perplexing attitude had set him on the far side of an ever widening gulf, making him more and more untouchable, and none of them quite knew how to cope with it, let alone close it up.

It was hot at the river, even hotter than the fields because the plum thickets were down along the dunes and surrounded by cottonwoods and river willows on one side and head-high reeds on the other. Air could not possibly stir there. Perspiration quickly streamed from their faces and caused scratched arms and legs to burn and itch. Lucy was almost in tears. To add to her discomfort, she was wary of bees and wasps that were buzzing from bush to bush and plunging stingers into ripe fruit at random.

"What if I git stung?" she whined.

"You think a bee's gonna look twice't at you when he's got somethin' sweet in the bushes?" David asked irritably. He thumped at one of them, and knocked it spinning. It buzzed and fretted angrily in the sand as it attempted to regain its bearings.

"Mama, he's a-makin' 'em mad," Lucy reported worriedly.

"Don't stir 'em up," Mama said to David. And to Lucy, "If anybody gits stung we'll jist put some bleach on it and go on. I brought some jist in case."

"Cain't we quit?" Lucy begged.

"Jist as quick as the buckets is full," Mama promised.

Papa spoke up, "Bein' down here by the river reminds me of a church I knowed about that stood on the river banks. One Sunday the preacher was about to start in when this-here drunkard come in and set down. Well, that set the preacher off. He raved and he rared and he said, 'If I had all the wine and beer and whiskey in the world, I'd pour it ever' bit in the river.' " Papa paused, wiping his forehead with a square piece of old sheet that Mama had meticulously hemmed and made into a handkerchief. All eyes were on him and he grinned. "Doggone if that drunk didn't stand up and start in singin' Shall We Gather At The River!"

They all laughed except David, who continued to pick and either didn't hear or pretended not to. Sometimes Abby just wanted to pinch him. She feared he had no intentions of trying to pull himself out of the mulligrubs and was snug in inflicting a cold shoulder on those around him.

The best part of the plum-picking was the eating. Each piece of fruit looked just a little redder and a little juicier than the one before. All of them ate more than their share, but even then it didn't take long to fill the three galvanized milk buckets they had brought along. Mama and Papa poured them all out on the checkered oil cloth and started sorting. The very ripe went into one bucket, the partially ripe into another, the greenish in still another to await ripening and the wormy ones were pitched aside.

Abby listened as they talked about local croppers they had either met or heard about. There were the Davidsons down south of Wade Collins that had that retarded boy. Everyone said Ches Davidson had caused the simple-mindedness when he got drunk and beat up Nanny Davidson while she was in the family way. Apparently he had not learned his lesson because he hardly passed up a Saturday night getting lit up like a Christmas tree. And his three other boys now in their teens were fast following in their father's footsteps. Abby was sure such reputations fostered the idea that croppers were at least a step below most other individuals. She wondered—were sharecroppers a lowly sort because of their choice of livelihood, or had they made their choice of livelihood because they were a lowly sort?

Then the Barnetts, Papa noted, were not bonafide croppers, but kept themselves busy with seasonal work and managed to keep the wolves stayed off their door. Abby had heard that Ty and Levi Barnett usually went to school without shoes except in the dead of the winter. The Barnetts foraged for items at the dump ground—a practice Mama upheld because "the main difference between new and used is jist a bar of soap or a coat of paint." Her family had done the same thing when she was growing up and they had found some unbelievable goodies out there—furniture that was hardly worn, dishes with and without cracks, even boxes of clothes in pretty good condition, and once some venetian blinds with only a few slats broken or missing.

Then there were the Jones about a mile from the river. They found an abandoned house and moved in. Like the Barnetts, Clarence Jones did what seasonal work he could, and was a decent hand.

The Findsterwalds had brought the loaf of cracked wheat bread and much good will the day after the Easons moved in. They were the ones whose youngest son, Dickie, had quit school at sixteen and lied baldfaced about his age and got himself into the war—just a month after they had lost their only other boy to it. That was back in early '44. Iva Findsterwald had told them all about it one Sunday after church while they waited for Papa to come and pick them up.

Abby sat nearby, idly listening to the talk and sifting through the sand looking for empty snail shells. She found several perfect ones and many partials and carefully placed them in the pocket of her jeans to be stored later with other treasures she kept in a match box tucked in the bed springs.

The conversation then turned to the need for rain—as most conversations did eventually. "It ain't always dry in these parts," Papa said, tossing a wormy plum over his shoulder. "I was talkin' to the County Commissioner out at the road one day—Earl Hill was his name—and he was tellin' how the bridge used to warsh out once't in a while, the river'd git up so high."

"Ain't much danger today," Mama commented, glancing at the narrow trickle of water on the wide, sandy bed, her hands deftly sorting plums as she talked.

"Most years they have head rises in the spring, water five and six feet high. You gotta have a big rain between here and Amarillo to do that. I guess them head rises is what takes the bridge out. Feller named of Jim Mayfield was a-tellin' how they seen a coffin lodged on the bridge once't durin' one of them head rises. Must of warshed a grave up somewheres. The coffin was empty, though."

"That'd be a sight," Mama said, pushing her brown hair back and wiping her forehead with the back of her arm. "This heat's a sight, too."

"Course, them was the days of cornstalk bridges," Papa said. "They wasn't made outa cornstalks, mind you, but was as weak as cornstalks was. The water'd git up and out she'd go. In '23 he said it was out for ten months and the only bridge around was one up north of Shamrock, Texas."

"Ole Earl worked from sun-up to sun-down while she was out, a-pullin' folks' Model T Fords across with a team of mules and horses so they wouldn't have to make the long drive around. Water waist deep and swift and the sand quicky. He said it was somethin'. Nice-actin' man, Earl Hill."

"I'm not covetin' a rain that'd warsh out a bridge," Mama said, working the green plums out of the pile. "But I'd admire to have one that'd put some life into the cotton crop."

Papa glanced toward the long, wooden bridge nearby. "Take a good 'n to warsh out that bridge. But they say it happens purty reg'lar, n' matter how high and good they're built . . ."

David was stretched out full length under a cottonwood, moping Abby assumed. She wanted to insist he do something with them—search for empty shells of fresh-water mussels, or look for mud-Martin's nests under the bridge. Instead, she talked Lucy into wading in the shallow stream that meandered across the wide sandy bed of the river with her. They washed off the itchiness and dust and plum juice and ended up splashing each other until they were soaking wet and gasping from laughter.

They undid their braids and ran giggling through the sandy ridges and reeds and salt cedar with their hair streaming out behind them, drying in the wind. It was a nice day—a day that was a rarity for the Easons, sunlit and lazy and carefree and perfect for all of them except David, lying there like a knot on a log, alone, apart, the way a sick or wounded animal sometimes stays to himself, away from the herd.

As usual Abby tried to sort her feelings of pity and impatience for him, and as usual neither affected him much one way or the other. Even when she brought a baby mud-Martin to him that they had found lost from its nest, he merely looked, touched a tiny wing tenderly with one finger and mumbled, "Find a nest to put it back in and don't be handlin' it."

On their way home, Papa decided to stop at the Joneses. They had seen the house on the way out to the river earlier. Compared to the usual tarpaper shacks, this one fell short. Some of the windows were boarded over. Others had a seasonal covering of pasteboard punched out to allow some ventilation. The asphalt shingles on the roof were in ruins, the damaged places showing a many-layered sandwich of a variety of colors and types. A screen door hung by one hinge, flopping in the breeze, and the entire structure leaned precariously.

All of them except David walked through the sand, weeds and litter up to the broken wood step. Papa knocked.

A haggard face of a woman peered out. "Whaddaya want?" she asked, puzzled.

"We're your neighbors," Papa said, pushing his battered straw hat back a fraction from his forehead.

The woman pushed at the door cautiously and it scraped along the floor for a foot or so and stopped. She was holding a small, dirty-faced boy on her hip and from behind her on each side peered two more equally soiled faces. She asked, "Which neighbors are you?"

"Wade Collins' croppers," Papa said. "We jist wanted to stop and make acquaintances and say our howdys. Name of Eason, down south." He gestured with a grin toward Abby and Lucy. "The girls here, they been a-playing' in the river and they look like a couple of drownded muskrats."

Abby pushed at her hair wishing she had rebraided it. But it was tangled and stiff as a board with sand and wind and river water and probably would have been like braiding a horse's tail.

"I thought maybe you was the welfare," the woman said apologetically. "We're the Joneses. I'm Ludy. Clarence, he's over a-plowin'. We ain't one to work on the Lord's day, but we don't always have no say." To the youngsters still clinging to either side of her colorless, worn dress, she said sharply, "Ludy Beth, Mayzie! Git back in that house! You heard what I said before."

Bare feet scurried across the floor inside.

"They's got the sevenyear itch," Ludy explained, hoisting the little lad on her ample hip to a more secure position. "I cain't ask you folks in. It's ketchin'."

"No never-mind," Papa said. "We was jist out

pickin' plums and thought we'd stop a minute. You tried sulphur for an itch?"

"Jist Cloverine Salve is all we have. Might of been puttin' water on it, for all the good it's done."

"You git some sulphur and rub them young'uns down ever' night for three, four nights in a row and it'll do the job," Papa promised.

Mama spoke up. "You gathered any plums or made any jelly this year, Miz Jones?"

"Gracious sakes, call me Ludy," the woman exclaimed magnanimously. Then she sighed softly and shook her head. "I ain't hardly been outa this house for a month of Sundays. The kids, they been a-gittin' sick one after the other. And now they got the itch. Junior, here, he ain't got it yet. I'm a-tryin' to keep the girls away from him. That's how you git it, by touchin'. They been a-scratchin' theirself to death."

"We got some plums in the car," Mama said. "You're welcome to some of 'em."

"I ain't been a plummin' this year," Ludy said longingly.

"Abby-girl," Papa said. "Run and git one of them bucketfuls."

"I'll git somethin' to put 'em out in." Ludy disappeared then reappeared with a shoe box, which Papa dumped full.

"Me and the kids, we could jist make ourself sick eatin' on 'em," Ludy said thankfully.

"Ain't nothin' better'n wild plums," Mama answered.

Ludy shifted the hefty youngster on her hip again. "The reason I thought you folks might be the welfare or Public Health or somethin', 'cause Clarence, he heard how they jist up and took some kids away from their fam'ly down at Hollis 'cause the fam'ly couldn't keep enough vittles on the table. They ain't got no right to step in that-a-way. We're a-tryin' our best, Clarence and me, and I'll tell that to 'em if ever they come. We may not eat fancy, but we eat. We may not have a mansion, but it's a roof over our head. Now, if he was a 'beatin' on 'em and mean to 'em, I could see it."

Papa and Mama was nodding in complete agreement and sympathy. Lucy sighed impatiently and whispered to Abby, "How come we're not playin' with them little girls?"

"Maybe some other time," Abby whispered back.

"Course..." Ludy began worriedly, her voice dropping secretively, "This-here ain't our house, neither. It was jist a-settin' here, empty. But we cain't he'p it. We didn't have no place else to go jist yet."

Papa and Mama nodded again, once again sympathetic, but lacking concrete solutions.

Resuming her former thought, Ludy demanded, "And what would the gover'ment do, once't they had 'em?" Concern and determination transformed her brow and made her eyes fierce for a moment. "Would they see 'em through a nightmare or stay up with 'em durin' a sick spell? Would they kere for 'em jist like they was their own? You know they wouldn't! Clarence, he said jist don't let nobody on the place if they look like the gover'ment." She laughed a little, sheepishly. "Course, I don't know what the gover'ment looks like, and how I'd keep 'em staved off. I imagine they drive a big shiny car." Her gaze swept over the faded green Chevie parked in front.

"And wear a fedory hat," Papa grinned. In her mind, Abby saw Winburn Tolsey in his black hat and pinstripe suit, and she concluded that she would rather face something the government could come up with than the insidious thing that Mr. Tolsey had propagated.

"And carry a walkin' stick," Mama put in. "I seen one that did that once't—remember, Travis, in Californy where they was givin' out them free typhoid shots and makin' ever'body take 'em?"

"Course, the gover'ment can be a good thing," Papa allowed. "But sometimes they git to expandin' and they expand right in on top of a feller if he don't watch out."

They all laughed and agreed.

"I wisht I could have you folks in, but I cain't," Ludy said. "It's jist one of them things." She glanced at Abby and Lucy. "You got some purty girls."

"Well, we're proud of 'em," Papa said, and the pride showed for a bit as he tousled Lucy's tangled hair and passed a hand over Abby's shoulder. "We'd best git on, anyways. We got chores to see to. If you folks ever need anything, holler. We're not two miles away. Come and visit and take a meal with us."

Ludy nodded, and gazed out across the pastures and fields and said without conviction, "If we ever git straightened out. If it ain't the virus, it's this confounded itch."

In the car, Abby closed her eyes against the breeze coming in the window. It had been a good day, despite the hardship at the Joneses that was not so disturbing as it was thought-provoking. They seemed to be well-fed and reasonably close-knit; that was the main thing. She wished she had thought to give the little girls some snail shells to play with, but they had the plums. They would enjoy those.

"I'll git this ripest bunch on to boil first off," Mama was saying from the front seat. "They oughta make sixteen cups, at least. That's a lot of jam and jelly time you mix in the sugar." She added, "I'll have to buy some more sugar this week."

"We might oughta put some in the dug-out to ripen

along slow," Papa answered. "And maybe try dryin' some."

"Sugar's high," Mama said. "Even on sale it's ninety-nine cents. We got enough for one batch, though."

"One batch better do us this time," Papa said. "Till times gits better."

Chapter Fourteen

"THEM JACK RABBITS is eatin' the corn and peas faster'n Wade Collins can git a stand," Papa said to Mama, as he poured another bucket of water into the boiler on the stove.

Bent over the rubboard scrubbing a stain out of Lucy's good school blouse, Mama didn't pause nor look up. "What Wade Collins needs is a chicken wire fence. Or a hound dog to chase 'em off," she said.

"Cost a purty penny to fence that big a field," Papa said.

"If it was winter we could dress a dozen or two of 'em and hang 'em on the north end of the house," Mama went on, wringing the blouse out and pulling another one up out of the water. Her hands were puffy and bleached and the fingers shriveled like raisins at the tips, but it was not a condition about which to take much note. It was an affliction that had come each wash day since she was a girl growing up and would continue until death or frailty prevented it in the future. "My Papa used to do that. Kept rabbit meat all winter long that-a-way—ground it for sausage and used it for stew. I imagine your bunch did the same. A good bait of fried rabbit'd be good."

"Too late for slaughterin'," Papa said. "They're havin' young'uns now, right and left. Be tough as bullhide, anyways. If you're a-cravin' rabbit meat, you want cotton-tails, not jack rabbits. And you want 'em in winter, not summer."

"Somebody better git a gun out there and thin 'em out," Mama declared, rubbing a collar vigorously with soap. "We got to have a garden some way."

"Ole Wade Collins has been runnin' 'em down in his pick-up."

Mama looked up, startled. "I never saw the beat of some people."

Papa chuckled. "Saw him out there on the back sixty, givin' 'er the gas and flushin' 'em outa the bushes. Had some guy with him. Heard 'em laughin' all the way over to where I was a-fencin'."

"Never growed up, sounds like," Mama said. "Wastin' gas for frolic, when some of us barely has . . ." Her voice trailed and she tossed another wrung-out item into the blueing water.

"People like him has their frolic at the cost of good sense sometimes," Papa said blandly. "How much more water do you need?"

Mama straightened up, one hand pressing into her back. "That oughta do me. Abby-girl, is that starch done? I forgot to gather up David's dirty clothes. Do that, then come and hang out this basketful. Tell Lucy Belle to come and help. Now, mind, git a rag and wipe the clothesline good. These sand storms. . ." Her voice faded away again and she bent back over the sudsy water. "Travis, did you ask Wade Collins about another cow?"

Papa nodded as he stepped outside. "He's got another comin' fresh in a week or two. We'll jist have to do without milk and butter till then."

Abby turned the burner out from under the starch she had been stirring, put on a lid to prevent a scum from forming, and went to David's sleeping room. She didn't go in there often, and she looked around now to see what was new, if anything. On top of the apple crate shelf was a tall narrow container that looked for all the world like a wine bottle. She stared at it in concern and dismay for a few seconds, thinking David surely wouldn't stoop to drinking—even if he had chewed tobacco that one time—and if he did he surely wouldn't leave it in plain sight.

With apprehension, she reached for it and opened it, frowning and sniffing, wondering whether or not to taste it. If didn't smell at all the way she imagined wine would smell. Suddenly something dawned on her and she laughed aloud with relief. This must have been what David had concocted one day when Mama and Papa were at town.

She had smelled some spicy odor coming from the kitchen and had found David in there busily working with some ingredients. He finally told her what was boiling so briskly in the pan—hair oil, wood alcohol, leaves of peppermint that grew in clusters at one end of the house, and a cinnamon stick that he'd probably saved since Christmas—but no amount of wheedling would make him tell what it was for.

She remembered that Sunday as Papa was driving them to church, smelling that same cinnamon-minty aroma that seemed to be emanating from David's direction. Mama had suspiciously asked Lucy if she had slipped some cookies out of the house and Lucy said she sure hadn't and David hadn't said a word, just kept looking across the country side.

David and his homemade cologne! She set the bottle back in place, making sure it went exactly on top of the little dust-free circle from whence she had taken it. It wouldn't do for him to know she had snooped.

She reached under the bed and pulled out the pasteboard box that held his dirty clothes. As she did so, the little booklet he had pored over so many times, slid out, and she opened it curiously. "University of Oklahoma Bulletin," it stated at the top of the page.

She pondered over bits at random. It made for dull

reading, but the pages gave the appearance of being handled repeatedly. Some parts were underlined. She read some of them:

"A budget of $400 will enable a student to spend a semester at the university, living comfortably. Some students live on less. However, due consideration should be given to health, and sufficient food and a comfortable room should be provided for in the budget. General university fees are $20 to $48 a semester on a basis of $4 per credit hour—"

An unexpected sound outside made Abby jump and hastily push the booklet back under David's bed, even though she knew he was out in the fields. He and Papa had been taking turns with the go-devil, trying to stave off some of the weeds ahead of the hoes.

There was something else under the bed and her hand closed around it, drawing it out. It was a baking powder can that rattled as though it had money in it. There was a slot cut into the lid and taped to the side was a paper on which was scrawled, "College Money."

She pried the lid off and poured the coins on the bed. Four nickles, one dime and thirteen pennies. She picked them up one by one, working and kneading them in her hand, delighting in the unusual feel of a handful of money.

It was then that David stepped inside. She whirled in fright, her braid coming around and slapping her in the face. "I—I thought you was plowin'."

"What are you doing in here?" David demanded.

"N-nothin'. Mama sent me to git your dirty clothes. And—I found this."

"Well, I'd be beholden if you'd leave my money be."

Fumbling hurriedly, Abby replaced the coins. She couldn't keep from asking, "Where'd it come from, David?"

"My business," he said sourly.

Used to they would occasionally get a penny on Saturday, or sometimes even a nickle. Abby recalled now that while she and Lucy were always busily sucking on penny candy or licking at an ice cream cone, David never seemed to be eating on anything. Even as far back as a year or two he had apparently been saving for college.

"I—I could help you save," she said, suddenly awed again by David's unusually fierce determination.

"I'd like to know how," he said curtly. "It's been a long time since we got anything."

That was true. They hadn't had even a single penny to spend since weeks before leaving Tecumseh. "If we do git somethin'," Abby added hopefully.

But David was shaking his head. "It's not gonna work, anyways."

"But if we do git a nickle sometime..." Abby persisted, only briefly allowing herself to think of that cold, creamy vanilla ice cream that she was as much as saying good-bye to if she kept this commitment. "If we do . . ."

David grunted, "If we do git a nickle, me and you both every week for a year, how much do you think that's gonna come to? Five dollars and twenty cents, is how much. How many years do you think it'd take to git enough for one semester of college? Seventy-seven, is all."

Abby sighed, experiencing some of David's hopelessness. If only he didn't care so much. If only cropping was a little more profitable. If only Winburn Tolsoy . . .

She shut off that thought and said inadequately, "Papa'll think of somethin'."

David sank down on the edge of his bed in his

patched, too-short pants and the worn shirt that was too thin for patching and would soon land in the ragbag. He said bitterly, "I'm gonna take this forty-three cents I've got and buy a hamburger and a pop and forgit it."

Abby knew he wouldn't, though. She gathered his bundle of laundry in her arms and wondered anxiously just what he would do.

"Wade Collins says he'll give you kids fifty cents apiece to pick up shinnery roots for a couple or three hours Sunday afternoon," Papa said at the supper table. "And he said we could have the roots to burn for winter, to boot."

Abby looked at David quickly, thinking of the money they could add to his can. But he was scowling a little. "That's our only time off."

"Do we haf-to?" Lucy whined.

"Jist two or three hours," Abby encouraged them. "It wouldn't seem like any time, hardly."

"Then you do it," David mumbled, scraping up the last of his beans.

It turned out they all three did it. Papa didn't think it would be a good idea to turn down the landlord, especially if he was willing to pay out good money. So, dressed in their oldest clothes and wearing cotton-snapping gloves that had the fingers worn through, they all three trooped over to Wade Collins' right after Sunday dinner.

To Abby's horror, Connie Collins was out there in the yard waiting, dressed daintily in jeans, a pink shirt and pink tennis shoes. Her hair was like a pale golden cloud about her shoulders. Abby had seen Connie a few times at church and she was always surrounded by pastel-frocked girls who alternately giggled behind their snowy white gloves, or sat snootily surveying the preacher and congregation. Abby always felt like cringing when the scrutinizing gazes were turned her way, yet she always managed to act as though she were so intently interested in the sermon or the song service or the announcements that she had no idea she was being sized up—and likely being disapproved of.

"Hi, Abby," Connie greeted her, as though they were old friends. "Isn't this maddening? I was going to do my nails and Daddy came up with this simply outrageous idea that I should learn to pull my share of the load, as he calls it." She flashed a dazzling smile up at David. "Hi."

David nodded, barely, and muttered, "Howdy," and climbed up on the tractor where Wade Collins proceeded to give him last minute instructions Abby wished he would act a little friendlier, smile or something. It never had been his nature to be hostile, especially around a landlord or a pretty girl. Today he was confronted with both and he was acting as though his teeth had been set on edge by green grapes again. She knew he was painfully aware of his ragamuffin appearance. He never could stand for anybody outside the family to see him with even a hair out of place, let alone in worn out clothes. Especially a girl as pretty as Connie. It could be that seeing her had thrown him into a stew and he was trying not to let it show.

Abby had seen him looking at her a few times at church, as though he were secretly eyeing a Lincoln Continental or the Tolsey's Ford Couplet, but he always remained aloof, not just from Connie, but from them all. It was as though he had left his old personality back at Tecumseh, back at the hands of Winburn Tolsey, and had picked up a new, bewildering one that allowed no indulgence in pleasantries—let alone frivolities. He was more and more a stranger, David was, a foreigner that none of them knew nor understood.

As for Connie, Abby had seen her giving David many a sidelong glance and once she had whispered behind her white glove to Gina and Lisa Hugg, "It should be a pure sin for the sharecropper's son to be that good-looking!"

And now she was acting as though sharecroppers weren't at all beneath her dignity, laughing and chattering as she and Abby and Lucy rode on the bumpy wagon that would take them to the field.

"Why didn't you wear your old clothes?" Lucy asked her, fascinated, it seemed, by the pink tennis shoes.

Connie's laughter tinkled gaily, "These are my old clothes."

"They don't have no holes in 'em," Lucy said in solemn awe.

Connie was looking at David, sitting straight and tall on the tractor seat, strands of his tan-colored hair lifting with the breeze, and didn't hear Lucy. "Will your brother be in high school, Abby?"

Abby nodded. "He'll be a senior."

"Oh! So will I! I think that's marvelous!" And Connie's soft pink lips curved into another smile, her pearly teeth perfect, her green eyes deeply speculative.

At the edge of the field David stopped the tractor and stood silently surveying the impossible hodge-podge of shinnery roots sticking up out of the freshly turned earth. Connie stood beside him, her shoulder gently brushing his arm. "Isn't it horrible? Daddy had it deep-plowed—I think that's what he called it—and it's impossible to plant anything with that awful tangle of roots everywhere."

"We might as well git to work," David said without

looking at her. "We ain't—" He caught himself and mumbled quickly, "We aren't going to get through if we don't."

Abby smiled smugly to herself. If Connie Collins had so much influence on David that he could suddenly become language-sensitive, then she could probably bring him permanently up out of the doldrums without half trying. And judging by the adoring look on her face, she had some sort of similar goal in mind already.

"I should have worn some gloves," Connie chattered. She held out her hands and all of them looked at the perfectly smooth skin, the pink-tinted, flawless nails. "I won't have any fingernails left!"

"You can wear my gloves," David offered, then he remembered the holes. "But they'd be too big." He turned away to start to work.

"Oh, I don't mind," Connie smiled, her hand lingering on his arm briefly. "That is, if you don't mind."

David shrugged and handed her the gloves which were obviously several sizes too large. She pulled them on, a forefinger protruding out a worn spot on each hand and they all laughed, even David, who at last allowed himself to look into Connie's face.

After that David's unnatural reticence vanished. When a root was stuck deep and tight and defied the girls' efforts, he ripped it loose for them, his slender, yet well-muscled arms rippling with strength developed from years of grueling manual labor.

This generally elicited a comment from Connie. "Your brother's so strong, Abby," she might say just loudly enough for David to hear, yet quietly enough to make him think the words were not for his benefit.

It wasn't long until they were all bantering and laughing as though Connie were a part of the family. Everything was funny to them; the perspiration dripping off noses, the time Abby pulled on a root with such force that she sat down quite abruptly when it gave, when the tortoise Lucy picked up promptly dampened the front of her shirt. When Connie found a baby rabbit, she and David looked at it together, standing very close, not looking at each other, but very aware of what was happening between the two of them.

By the time they were finished, the wagon was piled high with roots and Connie Collins' pink tennis shoes and shirt were coated with damp, brown soil, and she was as dirty as David, Lucy and Abby.

"Aren't we awful?" Connie giggled, brushing at her shirt. "Mother will die. Simply die. She was horrified when Daddy suggested I help, anyway."

"How come?" Lucy wondered.

"It doesn't take much to horrify Mother," Connie answered. They all laughed and she and David exchanged eye contact briefly.

Unloading the roots behind the house would take at least thirty minutes, but Connie insisted on coming and helping and there was more laughing, an unbelievable lot. Abby's hopes and expectations for David's complete recovery were at an all-time high.

When they were through, Lucy suggested brightly, "Connie, you oughta come in and we could git a drink. Mama might even let us make some tea, or somethin'."

Oddly, Connie's smile faded instantly. "Oh." She looked down, pulling a little at David's big gloves. "I'd better get on, I think."

"It wouldn't take very long," Lucy said hopefully.

"Well—not today, Lucy."

"You oughta come and spend the night with Abby sometime," Lucy said, her deep blue eyes glowing hopefully. "You could sleep with Abby, and I could sleep on a pallet of quilts. We might could pop some popcorn and tell ghost stories. We'd have all sorts of fun, wouldn't we, Abby?"

Abby nodded and smiled a little, embarrassed to think of Connie's sleeping in her bed with the patched sheets and frayed cover.

"Why don'tcha—tonight?" Lucy prodded excitedly.

"Oh, I can't. . ." Connie seemed ready to end the conversation and commented brightly, looking at the pile of shinnery roots, "We picked up quite a load, didn't we?" She smiled toward David, but he was looking the other way, oddly avoiding her gaze.

"Please?" Lucy begged. "We could play games and ever'thing."

"Lucy," Abby said firmly, "Connie might some other time."

"When?" Lucy demanded.

Connie's face became as pink as her fingernails. She looked down again, "Mother doesn't let me do—much visiting. Usually."

The revelation made Abby feel odd, let down and awkwardly conspicuous—ashamed. She didn't dare look at David. He probably caught Connie's revelation before she had. He had more at stake.

They were sharecroppers, Connie had said in so many words. Even someone like Connie could laugh and have fun with croppers under limited circumstances, but could not become close friends. Even though she was totally enamored by David, Connie was trying to explain without actually mouthing the words, that the relationship could go this far, and no further.

"Why not?" innocent Lucy asked again. "I've seen you go home with other girls from church."

"Lucy—" Abby cautioned once more.

"I—well, Mother—" Connie sputtered.

"We could have fun," Lucy persisted.

David was standing stiffly to one side of the tractor. He didn't look up, and his voice sounded hard. "Give it up, Lucy Belle. Don'tcha know rich folks don't pass the time of day with the likes of us, except when they have to?" Then he looked point-blank at Connie and added, "And sometimes even when you think maybe one of them might be sorry for the way they acted at first, they show they're really not. They show they got one face for public and one face for private—and us croppers better remember which side of the line we fit on."

"It isn't like that, David," Connie protested. "This isn't the same thing at all."

"David didn't mean it that way," Abby said quickly.

David was still looking at Connie grimly, and it was painful to see the change in the way he viewed her right now in comparison to a few minutes before. "Are you ridin' or walkin'? If you're not afraid somebody'll come along the road and think you're a cropper, you might as well ride."

"I'm not afraid of that at all," Connie said indignantly, hands on hips. "If you must know, mother strictly forbade me to go into a sharecropper's house a long time ago because—well, because sometimes they have lice-and-things." Her face flamed brightly. "There! You just had to know! It isn't my fault she's like that!"

"What's lice-and-things?" Lucy asked curiously.

"It's okay," Abby said, humiliated, yet sorry for Connie at the same time.

"I'm going," David said abruptly. "You ready?"

"Yes." There were tears in Connie's eyes. "Abby, I had fun, anyway."

She was holding David's gloves and she handed them to him. "Thank you," she said quietly, her gaze sweeping over his hands, rough and scratched, even bleeding a little in one place where a splintered stob had scraped the back. She reached out spontaneously and touched the place gently with her smooth, pink-tipped finger. "I'm sorry. I should have brought my own gloves. I—"

David turned, shrugging off her sympathy.

"David—couldn't we talk for a minute?"

"Everything's been said," David answered curtly, without looking at her. "I forgot for a while, but I won't forgit again."

"But—"

He climbed silently onto the tractor, starting it with the new-fangled electric starter that would have been sure to fascinate him all over again any other time but right now.

Connie got into the wagon, her face wet with tears. Above the roar of the engine she said, "Abby, can we be friends? I don't care what mother says. I care, but—"

Abby nodded affirmatively as the tractor and wagon lurched away.

"What's lice-and-things?" Lucy asked again, a bit impatiently, but Abby didn't even have the heart to answer.

Chapter Fifteen

IT WASN'T OFTEN they got to go to town. Papa took the cream late one Saturday afternoon, and was going to pick up chicken feed. They went with him.

Connie Collins and her mother were in town in their new Studebaker car and they waved gaily as though the Easons were good friends. At church Mrs. Collins always nodded a quick greeting without lingering to pass the time of day. She didn't want to risk lice being transferred, Abby decided.

Papa let David out in front of Hood's Drug, winking and saying jovially, "I'm glad standin' on the corner watchin' the girls go by is still free, Davy boy!"

David shrugged as though girls weren't on his mind. Papa gave him a nickle to spend, and Abby wondered as they drove away whether David would buy a sparkling-water fountain drink or put the money in his college can. Probably in the can, as the two of them had the dollar earned by picking up roots. Lucy had planned feverishly about what to buy with her fifty cent piece, carrying it with her everywhere, even to the field—even after Mama told her to put it up and keep it put up. She ended up losing it and had shed a gallon of tears since then.

Abby and Lucy got out at the cream station, which was next door to the laundry. It was just like all other such places they had been to—the sour cream smell overwhelming at first, but somehow really not that offensive; and the board floor was oiled and black.

Abby watched as Mrs. Abla tested the butterfat. This would determine how much it was worth. First she poured some of it into a long, narrow bottle and with an eyedropper, dripped a few drops of acid into it. Then she put it into an electric machine which had a gauge on it, and turned on a motor. Within seconds the butterfat had come to the top where it was measured with a gauge.

Afterwards she poured all the cream into large cans sitting at the back and handed Papa some dollar bills which he carefully folded and put in his pocket to give to Wade Collins. The Easons took out their share in milk.

Outside, glancing into the busy, noisy laundry next door and getting a warm whiff of the soap and bleach, Abby said, "I wish we could bring our dirty clothes to the warsh-house instead of—" She stopped and laughed a little. "But I guess as long as we got a rub board we better be glad."

"It costs fifty cents an hour to warsh in there," Mama exclaimed.

"Some day we'll have our own warshin' machine," Papa predicted.

Lucy stared. "You mean one in our house that sloshes back and forth with the little rollers that turns, and all?"

"That's the wringers," Papa said. "So you don't have to twist the clothes up in your hands to squeeze out the water. No more blisters and no more rub boards."

"That'll be the day," Mama said cheerfully, knowing it would probably never be.

"I'd even go so far," Papa predicted, "To say one of these days a body'll walk into a store and won't even be able to *buy* a rub board, much less use one."

Mama shook her head at that and said dryly, "Now you're dreamin' again," and they all laughed.

Down the street north was Bennett's Ice Cream Factory and the smells coming from it were vaguely like the ones at the cream station—stale milk and oiled floors and some pleasant aroma that perhaps was a blend of chrome fixtures warmed by the touch of hands, and tapioca starch cones and fruit flavored sundaes. As they walked by, Abby glanced through the wide screen door at the people sitting at the black counter on three-legged stools and licking ice cream cones. Her mouth watered and her insides were suddenly, desperately thirsty for something cold, which caused her to think of the nickle Papa had given David. A nickle would buy a double-dip, the big sign said. But a nickle was a lot of money. Papa couldn't really afford to give David one, but he likely did it to try and make up for what David had to give up back in Tecumseh. Abby looked away from the store and was glad Lucy hadn't realized they had just walked by an ice cream store.

Ches Davidson's boy, the retarded one, was standing in front of Funderburg's Meat Market. Papa asked him how he was and he answered quite normally, "I'm a-doin' jist fine." Then he watched them with the vacant, childish expression he always had when they passed in the car on their way to town, and as they opened the door he added, "I seen a man in a groad-rader yestiddy. It was Joe Hendrix, I think."

Papa paused and responded as though Ches Jr. was adult and sane, "What was he up to?"

"Oh, he was a-smoothin' up the dirt. A-smoothin' up the bumps, and all. A-makin' the roads nice."

"Well, they shore need it," Papa said. Then he lifted a hand in farewell. "You take care now, Junior. Ya hear?"

Paying at the cash register inside was Ches Davidson and his wife Pearl. "Why, there's my neighbor! How're ye, neighbor?"

"Middlin'-to-good," Papa said, matching Ches Davidson's tone.

"How're ye likin' this heat?"

"Ain't too bad if you can stay in the house with a coolin' towel and a breeze from the south window," Papa replied.

"Sho nuff!" Ches's boisterous laugh filled the little store. "I tole my old lady here, I said, Pearl honey, you git yourse'f a job in town and then yer old man, he won't haf to kill hisself a-croppin'! Why we near had a tear-up over it!"

"These wimmen, they got their own idees," Papa grinned.

Pearl and Mama smiled at each other shyly. "I been a-aimin' to come up and make myself acquainted," Pearl said. "You got a garden up yet?"

"What the rabbits left, we have," Mama said. "Them rabbits is a sight this year."

Ches Davidson was drifting away. "Well, you folks drop over somtimes and we'll chew the fat and maybe take a snort or two." A wink, greatly exaggerated. "My ole lady, she'll likely whup me now, when she gits me home. She's one of them teetotaller's. She don't like the stuff, and don't like nobody that does . . ."

When they were out of hearing, Mama told Papa under her breath, "I can tell you right now, I don't take to his ways." She was studying her list, and murmured, "We better not git much. But we're plumb outa flour . . ."

They passed slowly down each aisle looking at things stacked there nicely. There were colorful packages of Jello and Koolade and cans of peaches and apricots and even milk in cans called Milnot. Lucy was handling items at random. "Wisht we had some of this, Mama."

"Lands sakes, child, what do we want with canned milk? We got us a cow!"

"Some of this?"

"We can our own apricots. And got some dried, too. Now, don't handle the stuff."

"We don't never git to buy nothin' outa cans. If I had my fifty cent piece . . ."

"Well, that's cause you got a Mama that sees to her bunch," Papa said mildly. "The way Mama's is s'posed to. She ain't got a lazy bone in her body, Mama ain't, and that's the way the good Lord intended it."

"Well," Lucy sighed, "I wisht she jist had one lazy bone. Jist one. Then maybe we could buy some of these-here little beet pickles, or somethin'. . ."

When they got to the check out counter there was only flour, corn meal and baking powder and a small box of Lipton's tea. As he was paying, though, Papa picked up two peppermint sticks and Lucy could hardly contain herself, causing the store lady to give her an indulgent smile and make some laughing remark to Papa and Mama.

Outside, Abby chided her quietly, "You shouldn't act like you don't never git candy or nothin'."

"Well, we don't," Lucy said innocently, busily sucking the stick to a point on one end. "What am I s'posed to do, jist stand there?"

"Well, I guess that's askin' too much," Abby said a bit dryly.

Across town at Turner Grain and Elevator for feed, Lucy stationed herself in front of the gumball machine. "Wisht we could git some gum," she said to Abby. "If I had my fifty cent piece. . ."

"You're always a-wishin'," Abby said. "Jist be glad we got peppermint sticks. Besides, it hasn't been long since we had a half-stick. A few days ago, remember?"

"I swallered it," Lucy said glumly.

"I have some at home," Abby said suddenly feeling mischievously inclined. "You can have it."

"I can?"

"Sure. It's ABC gum."

"What flavor is it?" Lucy asked, getting excited.

"Oh, ABC gum is sort of all the same flavor."

"What color's the wrapper?"

"ABC gum don't come in wrappers."

"Well, where is it?"

"On the bed rail."

"Can I have it soon as we git home?"

Abby finally let a giggle escape. "Don't you git it? ABC gum—already-been-chewed gum!"

Lucy's mouth twisted a little as she tried to comprehend. "That don't even make sense," she said.

"Well, sure it does. . ." And the next ten minutes were spent trying to explain the joke. Abby sometimes wondered why she even bothered with Lucy when it came to pulling jokes.

When they drove by Marquis Hatchery, Papa mentioned the baby chickens and turkeys that were there. Naturally Lucy begged to go see, but Papa said there wasn't time. "David's prob'ly a-wonderin' where we are," he said.

David wasn't in the drugstore, though, nor on the bench outside. They had to walk the streets and look inside several places before they found him in the pool hall. Mama had a pure fit when she found out.

"I don't see no harm in it," David explained. "I didn't shoot no pool myself."

"There's people cussin' in there," Mama declared. "And prob'ly drinkin' and no-tellin' what all."

"The sign said no drinkin' and no bettin' and no cussin'," David said.

Mama's voice became a little calmer. "I've never been in a place like that in my life. I jist don't want my young'uns in there."

"Girls don't care if they go in there, or not," David said, getting argumentative. It seemed to Abby his stubborn streak was growing wider all the time, and would possibly someday overcome him. "I don't see no harm—"

"No arguin' with the boss," Papa broke in easily. "Anyways, the mainest thing is, we didn't know where you was. When we let you out one place you need to be there when we git back. It needs to be understood ahead of time if you're goin' somewheres else. That's the mainest thing."

"Yessir," David mumbled.

"Now, what I wanta know is, did you see any purty girls?"

"Not really."

"I bet there's some around," Papa encouraged. "They'll be showin' up come fall when school starts. Now, me, I first set sight on your Mama when I wasn't much oldern' you are."

"Now, Travis," Mama reprimanded gently. "David's got a long time at home yet."

"We saw Connie Collins twice't more'n you did," Lucy told David importantly.

"Whaddaya want, a medal?" he asked recklessly.

"Now, she's a purty girl," Mama said. "But stuck up, if you ask me."

For David's sake Abby offered, "She's not really stuck up. It's jist she—" She had to think fast, "—she's already got friends and all."

"Jist true to her raisin'," Mama said frankly.

Later, when Abby was feeding the chickens and David was getting ready to milk, she got a chance to ask if he had seen Connie in the drug store. When they had driven by on the way to the feed store, Abby had caught a glimpse of her going in there.

David only shrugged, emptying bran into a five-gallon bucket.

"Well, did you, or not?"

"I guess so, if it's any of your bees-wax."

"Did you git close enough to say hi?" Abby wanted to know.

"I got close enough to say anything I wanted to say," David said.

"What did you say, then?"

"Nothin'."

"Nothin'! Did she say anything?"

"She would of."

"If she would of, why didn't she?"

"I walked off."

"Well, that's silly," Abby scolded. "You act like her bein' born wearin' a silk garter's a fed'ral offense."

"I know when I been looked down on."

"I think you're making a whole patch of peas out a one little hill. I think you're goin' around with your feelin's stickin' out like a bunch of warts and jist a-darin' somebody to touch one of 'em. She can't help how her mother is, anyways."

"Yeah, and you don't know but half the story."

"What *is* the story, if there is one?"

"My business."

Abby made an impatient sound. "I bet you already spoiled your chances with her, the way you been actin'."

"My chances was already spoiled with her from the day I was born," David said moodily, slapping bran dust off his pants. "There's a line drew between us and them, and don't say you haven't noticed it."

It was true, of course. "Well," Abby said lamely,

"You jist showed her you got a hat higher'n hers, and I don't think it's right."

"Her own brand of medicine," David said, and got the bucket of bran and the empty milk bucket and headed for the milking stalls.

Chapter Sixteen

ON THE FOURTH of July, the town's churches, along with the Chamber of Commerce, had planned a late afternoon fellowship and singing with a food spread for everyone. Afterwards there would be a fireworks display. Papa was going, even though he had never gotten around to going to the church house with them yet. Mama said it would be alright because it was for the whole town, anyway, and not just the church folks.

The announcements posted downtown and in the newspaper and even from the pulpits said they were also planning contests with prizes: the fattest baby, the sourest man, the oldest couple, the best singer, and the biggest liar. David looked at Lucy and said dryly that he knew who could win the fat-baby contest. Papa winked at Lucy and said he was pretty sure he could win a prize whether anybody else did or not. Mama allowed as how she knew which one it would be and Papa said he was humbled at her unusual confidence in his singing. Then he practiced a little on them, crooning and swaggering,

> "Five foot two, eyes of blue,
> Could she, could she, could she coo!
> Has anybody seen my gal?"

The ad in the *Beckham County Democrat* said there would be a contest especially for the farmers: the longest stalk of corn, the best stalk of cotton, and the largest Irish potato. The Easons' potatoes were hardly cracking the ground yet, but Abby dug a few anyway. Papa said they would easy fit in a tea cup and maybe she'd better try the stalk of corn, instead. Walking through the corn patch and looking over the peas and corn the rabbits had left, Abby found stalks all the way from a foot tall to her height of just over five feet. Back in Tecumseh, she had seen corn that grew to ten feet. The cotton was no better. Papa said the tight land farmers south of town had the advantage there and maybe she ought to enter the singing contest in his place.

"Yeah, that'd be smooth," David said in a drawl more like he used to, "When she tries to hit them high notes at church, them high notes start tryin' to hit back!"

The food, fun and fellowship, Mama said, was the mainest thing, like Brother Whitten said at church. A body didn't have to enter contests to have fun and visit and eat. The whole idea was for folks to get to know each other better and maybe get their minds off crops and taxes and strikes and the economy in general.

They skipped the cotton patch the afternoon of the Fourth and David pretended it almost threw him into a state of shock. They dressed chickens and cooked instead. Mama made lightbread and opened some of her chow-chow and the last jar of pickled peaches. Abby talked her into enough sugar for cookies, even though Mama warned that the scant quart jar they had would be all they'd buy till times got better. Sugar was a ridiculous eleven or twelve cents a pound, she said, unless it was on sale.

While all the cooking and water carrying was going on, each one had his turn in the galvanized wash tub in the back room. When Lucy had to carry a bucket of water because the others were busy, she was highly insulted and began her habit of wishing again. "Wisht we had runnin' water like people in town does."

And Papa answered, "Why, we got runnin' water, Lucy Belle. When we need water I jist send one of you kids runnin' after it!"

While Mama and Abby laughed, Lucy maintained

stoutly, "When I git big I'm a-gonna have water that gushes outa pipes when you turn the handle."

"Well, I bet you do," Papa said mildly. "I bet we all do one of these days."

Abby braided Lucy's hair into two braids, then her own into a long one down her back, as usual. Then she tied the ends with bright ribbons they had gotten for Christmas one year, after first pressing the wrinkles out with the flat iron.

Dressing in the heavy brown frock Mama had made her out of one of Aunt Myrtle's skirts, Abby thought again of the dotted swiss and taffeta like Connie Collins and some of the other girls usually wore to church. In the winter, some of them probably even had velvet. The back row always looked like a gay flower garden with the dazzling white of hats with veils and feathers and make-believe flowers and the gloves and the various pastel colors of the dresses. Very pale pinks and greens and yellow and blues. Abby hadn't been invited to sit on the back row and didn't expect to; nor did she even want to—very much. She would have been as out of place there as a crude, careless weed in a patch of daisies.

David looked nice in the almost-white shirt Mama made from two flour sacks and his one good pair of pants that was only a little bit too short. Abby wanted to tease him about the likelihood of his seeing Connie Collins at the picnic, but she knew better than to mention it. She could only hope David didn't keep cold-shouldering Connie.

It seemed almost the whole town turned out for the picnic—Methodists and Baptists and Pentecostals and Nazarenes, and even some reprobates, Mama figured. The main festivities were centered in the park, but the baseball field was across the road and caught the overflow. There were horseshoes— "Well, ole dead-eye finally got himself a ringer! First one I ever saw pitched over-handed!" and croquet—"Dead ball, I say!" Some children were lagging for turns in anticipation of a marble game—"Slip! I get another try!" "Yeah, I know you! You call slips if you don't go halfway to China!" Others were involved in impromptu bouts of roughhousing—"Joe Palooka goes into the fourth round! Pow!"

    Abby watched all of it in interested silence, twisting thoughtfully at her worn purse strap, feeling a part of the activity even in her impassive state of mind. It was easier to observe than to risk rejection. Most croppers (except, perhaps, for Papa and David) lacked the confidence it took to thrust themselves into situations or conversations, especially those already in progress.

    She and Mama began setting dishes out of their pasteboard picnic box. Besides the chicken and lightbread and cookies, there were boiled eggs, fresh tomatoes and mild banana peppers, and the last three cucumbers rescued from fast-wilting vines. They had also brought salt and pepper shakers (Mama's good porcelain ones given to her by Aunt Myrtle and used only for special occasions) and a bowl of pale yellow cow butter decorated with spoon-imprinted daisy petals, as well as the dozen rejected potatoes that Abby had later scrubbed and boiled with the jackets on.

    "You kids oughta go find somethin' to play," Mama suggested, slicing bread with deft strokes of the butcher knife. "Ain't that Wade Collins' girl over there, Abby? By that table with them other girls?"

    Abby looked, and it was indeed Connie, dressed fit to kill in a beautiful mint green dotted swiss scattered over with pink and yellow flowers. She had on white sandals and when she turned away, Abby saw she also had on sheer silk stockings with the darker seams perfectly straight down the backs of her legs and ankles.

"That's her," Abby said, "But she's busy."

"We're too skeered to do anything," Lucy said, hanging on to Mama's good print dress with one hand.

"Now git back a little or you'll make me cut somebody," Mama said, and Lucy moved back a half-step and continued to glance furtively around at all the mind-boggling activities.

Brother Whitten came by for a moment and visited. "I'll declare, those girls are growing up just since I first met them, Sister Eason. You certainly have a nice, well-behaved family."

"Thank you," Mama said, shy pride shining in her deep blue eyes. "They sure 'nough grow up in a hurry."

"We have four of our own, you know. All grown and married . . . ."

A nearby voice called tauntingly, "Liar, liar, pants on fire!" and an earnest scuffle ensued between two boys Abby recognized from church, rolling red-faced in the dusty grass.

Brother Whitten looked on for a moment and in departing he winked at Abby, commenting with a smile, "Looks like a sermon on turning the other cheek is in order for Sunday!"

Papa and three other men were under a tree close by discussing weather and crops and who was 'laid by' and who wasn't, and the benefits of crop rotation and terracing in order to reduce soil erosion and depletion. Abby sat at the table and listened to them and all the other sounds, the slam of mallet against ball, and horseshoes clinking against stakes, the good-natured jesting and the flaring of young tempers, and Mama and Iva Findsterwald (from down the road south, and who made such delicious cracked wheat bread) exchanging greetings and small talk.

The men's conversation then turned to politics, first labor versus management, and how the president had handled last year's auto and steel strikes, then to the astounding $8½ million gift of John D. Rockefeller Jr. to help out the United Nations, and then to John L. Lewis' coal strikes and how they were as much an annual ritual as the first sighting of a groundhog by Oklahomans.

"Anyhow, the miners sure cottoned to him. They say in the homes of most miners there's two pictures hanging: the Virgin Mary and ole John L. Lewis."

"You heard what he said about the American Federation of Labor, didn't you? He said, 'The AFL has no head; its neck just growed up and haired over'. . ."

And from the marble game, "He keeps a-histin' and I ain't a-gonna play if he's a-gonna hist!"

"Well, take your dear old marbles and high-tail it outa here, then."

"Well, you're a-cheatin'."

Now the men were discussing the dam that had recently been built across the North Fork of Red River north of Altus, forming the Altus-Lugert Lake. One man was telling how there were three main canals and hundreds of small ones so that farmers all around Altus could begin irrigating their crops. Toying with the white porcelain salt shaker, Abby wondered idly what it would be like to see water flowing out over your crops, all the water they needed so that they would grow and grow and produce and produce and bring in money that would pay the bills and buy a farm and a house—not a big one—and there would be money left over for David's college.

"Abby-girl," Mama said, handing her a knife. "If you and Lucy ain't gonna go have fun, slice the cucumbers. Now, taste of the end to make sure it ain't bitter. This dry weather . . ."

Abby peeled and half-listened to Mama and Iva Findsterwald chatting about the price of coffee—45 cents a pound, like buyin' gold dust—and sugar, 99 cents on sale down at Pucketts—too precious to eat, ought to set it on a shelf and admire it. More interesting was the talk drifting over from Papa and the men under the tree.

"—calling it the Truman Doctrine," one big, scarlet-faced man was saying. "I'd say more like the devil's doctrine. I'm tellin' you, that 400 million's comin' outa *our* pockets."

"What it boils down to," another man—tall, skinny and intense—protested, "is two choices: free or Communist. Can we stand by and let 'em take over Greece? I say no."

Papa had been telling the family that very thing after reading some newspapers Wade Collins brought down after he was through with them. Abby had read some of them herself. Now Papa put in, "If Greece falls, Turkey's next."

Abby always marveled at how Papa could fit into almost any group, strangers included, and speak opinions and exchange ideas without being intimidated by someone who might have more money than he did. The only man in that group that he knew was Ben Findsterwald, a fellow cropper.

"Abby, gimme a cucumber," Lucy said, sighing dejectedly, and looking around. Abby handed her one slice and ate one, herself, still listening to the men.

Ben Findsterwald was agreeing with Papa. "Truman hisself said it. Then the middle east. It's like a cancer spreadin'."

The skinny man added, "And I say it's the duty of

the United States to stave off the Russians over there the same as we would if they was steppin' their feet right here in Erick."

"Sure, by George," the big man said, taking out a pouch of Bull Durham and cigarette papers, "when a man's got a two hunnerd dollar land payment comin' due December one, what's 400 million dollars? Shucks, I ain't got the first dollar to'ard neither one!"

All of them laughed, agreeing. Of course, Papa had never had a land payment due in his life and probably neither had Ben Findsterwald, but they could well imagine what it would be like.

"Look at it this way," continued the skinny man, not willing to let the matter be closed so easily, "Uncle Sam spent 341 billion toward winnin' the second war. And this 400 million Truman's askin' for—why that just amount to one-tenth of one percent of what we spent on the war."

"Why, you must have done a heap of calculatin' to come up with that figure, Pete," the big man said, and everyone laughed again, good-naturedly.

"Came out in a speech to Congress," Pete admitted. "But it makes sense, by Ned. What I'm gettin' at is we could well be stavin' off another country's fall—and eventually another war. A third war. Look at it that way."

Then they were all stating opinions at once.

"I tell you, the government's gettin' too big—"

"Greece has got to keep her independence—"

"Truman pointed out another thing," Pete said, coming out on top of the conversation once more. "Total'tarian regimes are brought on by want and deprivation. They spread because of poverty. A hungry man will grab at straws even if they're attached to the commies on the other end."

Abby sliced cucumbers meticulously, tasting a sliver off each end to test for bitterness, thinking a lot of evils were brought about by want and deprivation. If David had money for college, the Easons' main problem would be solved, with everyone content again.

"Now hens," Mama was telling Iva Findsterwald and another lady, "they're a-selling for 28 cents a pound. Travis heard it over the radio yesterday, over KTJS. Wisht I had an extry dozen to sell."

"One of my hens has gone to eatin' her own aigs," Iva said. "I'm a-puttin' pot-ash in the water and it ain't stopped her yet."

"I'd add a little salt, too," Mama said.

Ben Findsterwald, under the tree, was gesturing for emphasis, "And besides, the commies has got no right—"

"If Truman thinks the little man can help shell out 400 million, he better think again . . ."

Lucy, leaning despondently with her elbows on the picnic table, sighed. "We oughta not jist set here, Abby. Let's go over to where them people is across the road. Maybe we can watch somebody doin' somethin'."

The marble players were still having their problems as Lucy and Abby began the trek across the park. "That ain't legal, smoothin' the ground. You lose a turn."

"I didn't smooth it. There was a rock in the way."

"That ain't legal, neither, movin' a rock . . . ."

There were clusters of men standing about, thoughtfully staying clear of marbles and croquet and horseshoes, all deep in discussion. Abby and Lucy threaded their way through and fragments of various conversations stood out, revealing the common man's concerns and motives and expectations.

"The way I see it, crosswind plowin' is the answer to wind erosion."

"Before the war a dollar was worth a dollar. Today it's worth 65 cents."

"I was always laid by before the Fourth, but this year . . ."

"I knew ole Truman would finally admit he made a mistake, reviving the OPA."

"—ad in the *Greer County Republican* a-tryin' to draw people into Erick. 'Twas 1902 or 3, I recollect. 'We ain't got no bollweevils in our cotton,' it said, 'and we ain't got no green bugs in the wheat, and we ain't got no grasshoppers nowheres'. Jiminy! I wish they could take a walk through my cotton field right about now."

The two girls crossed the grassy bar ditch and continued on to the baseball field, probably more conscious of themselves—their looks and their shyness—than were others. Not many of the people looked like sharecroppers, but that wasn't surprising. Most sharecroppers didn't mingle with city folks for one of three reasons; either they were too calloused to care, or they cared but felt too much out of place, or they simply couldn't spare the time away from the crops. Papa said the Easons knew their place and knew how to be abased when necessary but he didn't think it hurt to abound once in awhile either, and if the crops couldn't wait one day, then they were too far gone, anyways.

Some kids were playing softball in the corner and a few people were sitting on rough board bleachers watching. Abby headed there, for lack of a definite destination. David was sitting there alone, looking toward the game but not at it. Abby didn't sit beside him, knowing how it would rankle him to be saddled with sisters, but sat a little way back and pretended to get interested in the game herself.

"Why didn't we git some of that lemonade in the big crock?" Lucy wanted to know.

"We should of," Abby said. "We will in a minute."

Out of the corner of her eye she saw someone approaching David. It was Connie, and she plopped down beside him as though that was her place. If he was surprised, he didn't show it, but just kept looking at the boy who was at bat and kept fanning the ball.

"I think you're being tacky," Abbie could hear Connie say accusingly.

"Ever what you think," came David's clipped reply.

"You won't give me a chance to explain things, will you? I don't even think you **want** to understand."

"Croppers are kinda dense."

Suddenly Lucy caught sight of the two and exclaimed excitedly, "Connie Collins is talkin' to David!"

Abby shushed her quickly.

"Let's go over there."

"No," Abby said, clutching Lucy's arm in case she tried to dart away. "They might jist wanta talk."

"Well, we could talk, too."

"Hush, Lucy. Look at that guy runnin' for second base. He's as fast as a cheetah ever thought about, I bet."

At last Lucy became engrossed in the game and Abby went shamelessly back to her eavesdropping, hoping she hadn't missed anything important.

"I'd like to know why you're so touchy," Connie was saying, looking very perplexed. Her pink lips were pursed prettily and one hand was resting lightly on David's arm.

"I got a lot to be touchy about," David came back. He leaned forward, moving his arm away from Connie's touch and leaning his elbows on his legs and his chin on his hands so Abby was afraid at first she might not be able to hear anymore.

"Like what?"

"If you don't know, then you won't never."

"I don't understand."

"Like fun, you don't."

Connie kept looking at him but he never looked at her and apparently didn't intend to. She finally said, "That day in the field you acted as though—well, that you had forgiven—and forgotten."

"Maybe I had. For a minute, till you started puttin' on your airs again. I ain't makin' the same mistake twice't."

"But that wasn't my fault! Mother—"

"Don't go blaming nobody but yourself."

Connie burst out softly, "You just can't stand me, can you?"

"I guess I cain't stand what you stand for," David answered.

"And what's that?"

"Uppity-bunk," David said, tight-lipped.

"I'm not like that!"

"I've seen you on your high horse a-plenty."

Connie looked good and mad. "You have not!"

David shrugged and began concentrating on the game as though he were through discussing.

Connie gave his shoulder a little shake in order to get his attention. "You asked for it, treating me the way you did that first day at church."

"I treated you?" David asked, grimly incredulous. "It was you that treated me." Then he added abruptly, "I don't even wanta talk about it."

Connie leaped up, her skirts billowing in a lovely cloud about her, her hands on her hips. "Well, I don't want to talk anymore either. Ever." Then she flounced away, very much back on her high horse, though Abby didn't blame her after the way David had treated her, acting as though his entire life situation were somehow her fault.

She could hardly stand for Connie to go under those conditions and David couldn't either, judging from the way he looked after her so miserably. She wanted to go shake him, but there really wasn't much use when David had his mind set about a thing.

While they were eating a little later, the chicken delicious, the lightbread only slightly dried from the breezes, a girl about Abby's age brought her plate over and asked if she could sit with her and Lucy. "I don't know a soul," she confided.

"Don't you live here?" Abby asked, salting her cucumbers and tomatoes. The girl didn't exactly look like a sharecropper but she didn't look like what David called uppity-bunk either. She looked like someone you could be comfortable with.

"I'm staying the week with my aunt," the girl said. "She made something for the picnic that my uncle likes called pizza. He ate it overseas, during the war. Do you want a bite?"

Abby looked dubiously at the wafer-thin slice of red, pie-like substance and took the bite the girl broke off. The dough seemed tasteless and the spicy-tomatoey taste was overwhelming.

"How do you like it?"

"Well," Abby said hesitantly, then continued with her usual honesty, "I think they shoulda kept it overseas." Then she giggled, and the girl giggled with her, and Lucy, with fresh tomato juice running down her chin, laughed with them.

After that, the day was more fun because Abby and Leah walked around together, chattering and laughing and drinking lemonade, with Lucy close behind.

The contests gave much cause for hilarity, with all

those entering each category lined up on a makeshift stage. Papa didn't enter after all, naturally, but they all got a kick out of the ribbing and carrying on by the other contestants. The best singer did a rendition of *Skip To My Lou*, while standing on his hands. There was a tie for the biggest liar. Wade Collins told the story of his windy neighbor asking to borrow the crosscut saw so he could cut into a right nice 300 pound watermelon he had grown. To which Wade Collins replied, "Sorry, my wife was using it to cut up a cucumber she grew and broke it!" The other winner stated self-righteously, "A lie has never crossed these lips, and never will."

Abby didn't know any of the farmers who won with samples of their crops, but she couldn't keep from feeling a little covetousness when she saw one of the prizes was a certificate from the Dixie that was worth a pair of Levi's of any size. Papa or David either one, could have certainly used a new pair of Levi's.

The sun was going down when a prestigious-looking man in a blue serge suit—probably a minister from one of the other churches—called everyone together for the singing, after which the fireworks would be displayed.

Abby and Leah sat on the grass and Lucy squeezed in between them and all the voices blended together in Rock of Ages. Across the crowd, David was still alone and unhappy. Several layers of people away sat Connie, also alone and miserable. Abby thought, a bit impatiently, that at least they would make a good pair if they ever did get together because they both sure knew how to give cold shoulders and wear high-hats.

Chapter Seventeen

THE WHOLE FAMILY was hoeing in the pea patch down south of the house late one afternoon when Wade Collins came driving up in the new Studebaker, along with Mrs. Collins and Connie. Mama seemed uncertain as to what her position should be—hostess or hired help. If Mrs. Collins had been a fellow cropper, Mama would have stopped her work and leaned on the car door and visited about pickle-making or gardens or whether carbolin oil or creosote dip was better for getting rid of mites in the chicken house.

As it was she only nodded to Mrs. Collins and continued her hoeing, stiff and unnatural, while Papa and Wade Collins discussed the weather and crops. And while Connie and David carefully avoided eye contact, with Connie looking down, or out across the road, and David staring at his row, chopping with steady deliberation.

"We oughta go talk to Connie," Lucy whispered to Abby.

"We're supposed to be workin'," Abby reminded her. With Connie so solemn there would be nothing to say. That day in the field when Connie had fit in so perfectly now seemed like a fantasy that never really was. Kind of like the comedy David told them he saw at the showhouse that time. Things happened in there that you weren't even supposed to believe, he said, like a coyote getting run over by a truck or hit with a sledge hammer and popping back up as good as new. Comedies might be interesting or funny, but they weren't life, apparently—and unfortunately, neither was Connie Collins.

"She don't have nobody to talk to," Lucy said.

"She can talk to her mother."

Lucy looked incredulous. "What would she want to talk to her mother for?"

Abby laughed a little and started to say, what would she want to talk to *us* for, but that would have made Connie out a villain, so she just said, "Let's git to work and try to finish our rows out."

"Papa ain't."

"He's a-talkin'."

"Well, I'm a-lookin'."

"Well, look then," Abby said.

As he was about to drive away, Wade Collins suddenly remembered he had come for an express purpose, and handed a bundle of newspapers out the window, as well as a letter.

"Don't know why this was addressed like that," he told Papa. "Somebody that wasn't sure of David's whereabouts, I reckon."

Papa said he was much obliged and the Studebaker took off in a little cloud of dust and fumes and Papa stood looking down at the letter, his face tightening a little. He looked over at David. "It's for you. Addressed care of Wade Collins."

David accepted the letter in silence, scanned the envelope and started to push it into his pants pocket without reading it.

"Maybe you better open it," Papa said.

David wanted to protest, the look on his face said he did, but then he shrugged and ripped it open. The whole family watched him read the letter, except Papa, who began his chopping again.

"Who's it from?" Mama asked when David finally finished and began re-folding the paper.

"Mr. Tolsey."

Mama stared, instantly suspicious. "What'd he want?"

Papa had stopped chopping now, and was motionless, waiting for the answer. David breathed deeply and his look told them he would answer only because he had to, and he crammed the letter into his pocket. "Same as he always wanted."

Mama passed a hand over her perspiring face, and she murmured, "I do vow."

"Well, he don't never give up," Papa said in his hard voice. "Well, I'm a-gonna write to him myself. I'm a-gonna tell him out clear and straight—"

"I can answer my own letter," David interrupted, tight-lipped.

Papa clipped off a careless weed with his hoe. "I know you can," he said, his voice at once controlled. "But I don't think he's listenin' to you. I coddled him along before, and he didn't listen to coddlin', neither, looks like. Looks like all he understands is a foot put down, and that's what I aim to do."

"He jist mostly wanted to tell me about his new car, anyways," David persisted. "He got him a Cadillac, instead of a Lincoln Continental Cabriolet."

Papa leaned on his hoe, his face dark with suspicion even more disturbing than before. "What's he want with a new car, when he's got that fancy old'n? What's he gonna do with that old'n, anyways?"

David gestured feebly and mumbled reluctantly, "He—he said he'd give it to me, if—"

The expression on Papa's face must have stopped David. But Papa said nothing, began hoeing again in a silence that was somehow ominous, and everyone returned to work, too. The crabgrass was thick as hair in around the peas and corn, and the watermelon and pumpkin vines. It was hard to get it all without scraping out a good plant in the process.

"Like this, Lucy Belle," Mama said for the umpteenth time, and demonstrated how to ease the crabgrass out with the corner of the hoe and leave the plant intact.

"It's too hard," Lucy complained. "And the gnats is a-buzzin' in my ears and a-gittin' in my nose. I breathed one already jist now."

"It's the weather," Mama said. "It means a rain."

"We could use a good rain," Abby said, mostly because everyone seemed uncomfortable and she didn't want a silence to begin growing. She wasn't always good at keeping busy conversations going but at times like this it seemed essential to try. "I heard somebody say at the doin's Saturday that they didn't git no moisture in the winter."

"A good rain is what we need," said Mama, who could keep busy conversations going and meandering indefinitely. "Travis, you think it might rain? The gnats is out, and all."

Papa glanced at the sky, back to the Southwest because that was where the rains would come from when they did get ready. "It might," he said.

"I can answer my own letter," David said humbly. "Mr. Tolsey—he didn't mean no harm."

"I know he didn't," Papa said, his voice reined in, still very controlled. "But he's did harm anyways. He's did a lotta harm."

"I don't see what you don't like him for," David said, with only a hint of accusation.

Abby gripped her hoe handle, hurting with Papa and David both, yet still scraping out the crabgrass and pushing dirt back in around the plant to hold it straight against the onslaught of future winds.

Papa's voice was still amazingly steadied, "It ain't a question of likin'," he said. "It's a question of havin' my own flesh and blood yanked outa my house with money and schoolin' and fancy cars bein' the bait and me bein' made to look like a culprit if I don't go along with it. A culprit that don't have no feelings or no reasonin'. Well, I think he should of had more feelings then to come a-bargin' in and tryin' to take over without talkin' to me in private first. I think he over-stepped his bounds. And he's a-gonna know it after I git that letter wrote. He's a-gonna know it for sure."

And later, after bedtime, when Mama and Papa did most of their serious discussing, Papa talked about it some more. The walls were thin, just one-by-twelves stood side by side and held together with crosspieces at the top and bottom and then covered with the heavy, dull wallpaper. You could hear every word or sound between them, even those times when you were trying not to.

"I don't know," Papa said quietly and heavily. "Maybe I was wrong back there in the beginnin'. D'you think I was wrong, Maudie? Not lettin' him, when he wanted to so bad? D'you think maybe I was just bein' bull-headed?"

Mama murmured firmly, "No, I don't. You did the only thing you could. Folks ain't supposed to hand out their kids to this'n and that'n. I couldn't of rested easy not havin' no say in his raisin', and not knowin' what was goin' on. Him up at Tecumseh and us down here. Never seein' him, or nothin'. Besides, we need David in the fields, he knows that as well as anybody."

"And it wouldn't of been right, the girls not havin' all that stuff David would of had," Papa said, still trying to convince himself. "Fancy vittles and fancy cars and a radio, and a big, fancy house."

Mama sighed tiredly, and without much hope. "It was Winburn Tolsey started it all. David was jist a boy sixteen, havin' fun teasin' the socks off of ever'body. Winburn Tolsey set his mind on things too heavy and too big."

"I ain't one to hold grudges," Papa said. "And I'll git over this one. And even when I was a boy I wasn't never one to wanta hit nobody. But when I read who that letter was from—when I saw that name up there in the corner . . ."

The bed springs shrieked and groaned as one of them changed positions. In the bed with Lucy, Abby's mind was tired with trying to figure out everything so that it would have a happy ending, the way books always did. David's situation was one of the few she had ever come across that literally seemed to have no solution.

"And then when he said that about the car . . ." Papa's voice trailed again, and there was an uneasy silence broken only by the shrill song of a cricket and the night-creaking of the house as the day's heat left it. "You know how he is about cars and such."

Mama said vaguely, "If it hadn't of been for Winburn Tolsey."

"I'll write him tomorrow, first thing," Papa promised. "I'll lay it out straight." He breathed heavily and added, "But it's like the fox a-gittin' sight of the hen house. Ain't nothin' ever the same after that. Ain't no satisfaction to be had, knowin' what's jist over the fence . . ."

One Sunday afternoon Abby approached David again while everyone else was napping. She was compelled to do it after watching him and Connie at church throwing all those haughty but forlorn looks back and forth when they thought the other one wasn't watching.

"David, how come you're still actin' that way toward Connie?"

"Take her down a notch, what else?" he answered grimly, lying back with his bare back against the cool floor.

It was a wonder David kept answering all her prying questions about Connie. That proved to Abby that he secretly wanted to talk about her, so she ventured further. "What does she need to be took down for?"

"You blind, or somethin'? And deaf?"

"Well, you're saying she's high and mighty, I guess. I think you're being high and mighty as much as her."

"I don't see how you conjured that up."

"Ever'time she tries to talk you cut her down like you're a mowin' machine."

David barely raised one eyebrow and didn't answer.

Abby tried to get back into "The Legend of Sleepy Hollow" in her prose and poetry book, figuring she had pushed her luck far enough. But in a few minutes she just had to add, "It's jist as bad for you to high-hat her as it is for her to high-hat you."

"I'd admire to think it was that simple," David said bitterly. He was staring at the ceiling without considering the flies that were crawling up there. His mind was into deep thoughts, whether of Connie or other perplexities, Abby was unsure. Papa had mailed the letter to Winburn Tolsey and had tried to win David back ever since with remarks meant to interest him or make him smile, and to gently tug him back into the family circle. David remained distant but polite. So polite it was painful to them all and the lines in Papa's forehead had deepened considerably with this newest stumbling stone, this continued worry that was even more potent than the concern about rain or strikes or the direction of the government.

"What're you talkin' about?" Abby asked.

David's voice was as caustic as the lye Mama used in her soap making. "Do you think a girl like her is going to be seen dead with somebody like me with his pants too short and his shoes half wore out—even if she did decide she liked me?"

"You'll git some new pants before school starts if money holds out," Abby encouraged. She wanted to add that clothes surely wouldn't matter that much to Connie, but she knew they would.

"It's the whole general idea," he said tightly.

Lucy snorted and made sleeping sounds and Abby got up and waved a fly away from her mouth. Little drops of sweat were standing on her face, some of them merging to form tiny rivulets that trickled down off her nose and onto the rag rug where she was lying. Abby waved her book a few times to fan a breeze and it lifted stands of Lucy's hair and kept the flies at a distance.

"The least you could do," Abby said to David quietly, so as not to disturb Lucy, "You could be a gentleman whether she's a lady or not. Papa and Mama taught you to. You never treated anybody else this way I ever remember. Even that time Chad and Mike Norman acted the way they did, you took it half-way calm and you and them ended up bein' friends."

David breathed deeply, staring unseeingly at the flies on the ceiling again, and Abby watched him with keen interest. For once he looked as though he thought she might be saying something that made sense. Then he shook his head and muttered, "There's not no future in it."

"I'm not talkin' about that," Abby explained patiently, going back to her place on the bed. "If she was ugly as a mud fence, you'd have the same obligation."

"If she was ugly all of this wouldn't of happened

in the first place and it wouldn't make no difference, anyways." David said.

"Well, listen at you!" Abby said. She had never seen David so dense headed in her life. Boys apparently lost all reasoning power when faced with a pretty girl. She had seen other boys fall prey but until now, she had always remained convinced that David had more sense.

"We live in two different worlds, Connie and me," he said bleakly.

"Well, where's the rule that says the doors can't be opened up where people can go in and out to either world?" Abby demanded.

"You'll learn," was all David said, and Abby suddenly felt some of his hopelessness. She said softly, "David, I think someday it'll all be over." She was not speaking only of Connie now, but all of it—the hardships, education, discriminations, the problems within the family, the frustrations of so often being considered society's underdog. "The good Lord usually sees fit if we jist don't give up."

David said nothing, but kept rubbing the sparse patch of blondish whiskers across his jaw with long brown fingers the way Papa always did when he was thinking especially deep.

"A person's got to keep his backbone," Abby said. "Like they said Grandpa used to say when they first came over from Germany. The way Papa put it was, if a person could keep a level head attached to a strong backbone he had over half the battle won."

"Yeah, but he didn't do it," David said dolefully.

"But—he *would* of," Abby insisted. "If he—" Not having known him personally, she was unsure just what Grandpa had lacked that caused him to break and then never be able to come out of it. It had to be that he lost his faith, his *Licht*, and was never able to regain it. She felt a stirring of fear as she had a few times before, because David's inability to snap out of his depression and recapture his *Licht* could lead him into precarious paths further on down the line.

"We gotta keep trustin'," she tried again, and wished she had a way with words that could help her explain everything she was feeling. But the words would not come, though she sought silently and anxiously for them for a minute, and David seemed ready to shut her out, closing his eyes and turning his face away from her.

Quickly, she threw in a last thought, "Grandpa didn't *have* to give up."

"Maybe he did, and maybe he didn't," David murmured, as though the subject was already closed. Then he added moodily, "Maybe he couldn't help it."

Abby's heart contracted in apprehension at David's calm assertion and the apprehension manifested itself in a new burst of impatience, "You're crazy outa-your-head if you think a body can't fight his way outa things —with the Lord's help."

"I guess," David agreed sarcastically.

To Abby it was almost a relief to hear the sarcasm rather than the languid acceptance of defeat that had been present earlier. She pushed on, as though goading him would bring back some life, "What did Connie say that could be so bad you treat her like a piece of wore-out shoe leather?"

No answer.

"Musta been purty bad," she said somewhat loudly, leaning off the bed and as near his ear as possible in order to make her point.

David frowned, covering the ear with one hand, and muttered a blunt imputation, "Nuisance. Worryment."

"I think she got her bluff in early," Abby added.

David rolled over and sat up, looking as though she

had almost pushed her luck too far. Then he became listless again, saying with only a hint of grimness, "I'm fed up with girls, anyways. If you could git that through your skull, I'd be obliged. And as much as I'm fed up with regular girls, I'm a dozen more times fed up with one Connie Collins. So try to let that soak into your brain, if you've got one."

"I think you like her anyways," Abby said daringly, either because she was a little fed up herself, or because she was still trying to see if David had some sort of spark inside him that she might be able to ignite. Instinctively, she tensed, ready to leap up and run for her life if need be.

But David didn't even answer. He got up, brushing the grittiness off his back, and wandered outside. When Abby went to the window to look out, he was leaning against the elm tree with what Papa used to call a dying calf expression on his face. She wondered if he was thinking more of girls or sharecropping or college or even of Winburn Tolsey's Ford Couplet which but by fate could be his. Not that it mattered, perhaps. At present—suddenly—one seemed almost as hopeless as the other.

Chapter Eighteen

RAIN, OR THE lack of it, was the main topic of conversation from the feed store to the church.

They had waited for the spring rains in vain, except for a scattered shower here and there. Pete Calley (Ben Findsterwald's landlord) showed two-tenths in his gauge once when three miles away at Wade Collins, he was joking that he got a half-inch (the drops were a half-inch apart).

Farmers sat in Cal's Cafe and smoked and drank coffee and talked about the weather. "The weather is definitely separating the men from the boys," they all agreed. No one was sure what it meant, though.

Clarence and Ludy Jones, the poor couple with the three little tykes out north of town, would be the next to go, some said. They certainly weren't the first to succumb to drought, and they wouldn't be the last. How could you live like that, those more fortunate asked each other, with holes in the floor letting in the rats and holes in the ceiling letting in showers of dust? One consolation—no need to worry about rain coming in.

And talk of the Joneses always prompted mention of the young cropper commonly referred to as Tot's something-or-other. He never stood a chance, they said. There was not much way for a young fellow to get in and stay without family hands old enough to put in a day's work. That very thing had put many a man out in the cold. The old saying that a cropper's wife needs to produce half-grown off-spring instead of babies was sure enough true.

With the conversational ball rolling in that particular direction, it was usually pointed out that at least Deryl Sheppard still had his homeplace, and he didn't have a young family to worry about. Two plusses. But it was too bad the banks couldn't have gone with him one more year, they always added. At this point, the talk would usually shift to the subject of those in banking—those who had to watch their p's and q's, what with federal examiners breathing down their necks.

It was no longer sound business to borrow on a handshake or a shoulder-clap as it had been in the past. But it was unanimously concluded by those brooding over cooling cups of coffee that it was the federal people who were without hearts—bankers were merely pawns. They had to have a signature on a dotted line. It was just that simple. And it was the general agreement that these days taking a pen in hand and applying it to the bottom of one of those duplicate papers was a little like signing a personal death warrant.

When it was learned for a fact that the Joneses were moving on, the Easons dropped by and paid their last respects. Mama took them a syrup can full of dried apricots and Papa offered a strong arm to help load the car when they were ready to go (for there was no trailer to be had in which their few sticks of furniture might be loaded and Papa's offer of his two-wheeled trailer was quietly and firmly refused. ''Fer the simple reason,'' Clarence Jones said matter-of-factly, ''We likely won't never be in this part of the country again and you'll need it fer your next move.''). The furniture would be left behind. Probably couldn't have held up under another move anyways, Papa told Mama on the way home.

So on a Sunday afternoon the women packed the small items and the men loaded the mattresses and a pair of bedsprings on top of the old car and the other necessities into the turtle and back seat. Abby and Lucy kept the youngsters occupied by playing with them under the cottonwood tree near the front door. The itch was a thing of the past but it kept Abby busy keeping Junior's runny nose cleaned with a rag supplied by Ludy.

Mayzie and Ludy Beth shared a baby-doll, a rubber one with only one arm and with the painted-on eyes almost worn off so that the scratched and worn face stared at them blankly.

"What's your baby's name?" Abby asked.

"Gertie," Mayzie said.

"She's sick, lawsie me," Ludy Beth offered, sighing.

"What's the matter with her?"

"She's got the confounded itch."

After everything was finished, the grownups stood by the car talking. The former light joshing and hoo-rahing were put aside now, and with a few well-chosen words, Papa offered his condolences.

Clarence accepted in silence, his weather-worn face solemn. Then, "I giss we're headed fer Arkansas. My people down by Durant is on welfare and I don't want none of that. I stay as fer away from the gover'ment as I can git."

"Clarence, he ain't one fer handouts," Ludy said, pride showing in her eyes.

"They git a welfare rope around yer neck and they li'ble to hang you. They li'ble to think they can step in and have their say about too many other things." He glanced automatically around at his three little tots, the little girls on either side of Abby and the baby in her arms.

"Any work in Arkansas?" Papa asked.

"Chickens," Clarence said, removing his battered straw hat and scratching his blondish hair. "I giss I'll he'p Ludy's Pa with the chickens. Down there they raise them chickens by the hunnerds."

"It's jist that Clarence, he's partial to dirt farmin'," Ludy added. "They's jist somethin' about growin' things in the ground."

"Aw, Ludy, jist anything to make a livin'," Clarence protested mildly. "I ain't really that choosey."

"A body cain't help having his druthers, though," Papa said.

"If it'd rain," Mama said, glancing without optimism at the skimpy dry weather clouds in a pale blue sky.

"Well, the old-timers say it don't rain at night in July, and seldom in the day," Clarence added. "And this year it didn't rain in June, neither."

"We got that one little shower as I recall," Ludy said.

"And if it rains in August, who's gonna keer by then? It's too late fer the cotton. You need them early rains fer cotton and we jist didn't get no early rains."

"A good rain in August'd he'p a little," Ludy contradicted softly. "It'd he'p the crops a little, and ever'body's feelin's a heap more."

Clarence grinned some. "These here wimmen. They always got to have the last say."

Papa grinned back, giving Mama's shoulder a quick squeeze. "What gits me is they're nearly always right!"

Clarence's smile faded into deep thoughtfulness. "I was jist a'wantin' so bad to git settled in a place and stay there afore Ludy Beth starts to school. She'll be startin' to school come fall. I wanted her to maybe start to school in one place and still be a'goin there five or ten years from now. Them was my plans at first. Erick's a fine town, got all them there churches. We was gonna start in a'goin' to one of them churches, that big red brick'n with all them there steps a'goin' up."

"Well, Clarence," Ludy sympathized, "They's churches and schools and other towns in Arkansas or Oklahoma. They's been bigger miracles happen than that."

"We'll see," Clarence answered, replacing his straw hat and breathing deep. "We'll see, I giss . . . ."

As the Easons drove away, Abby looked back and Clarence and Ludy Jones and their little family were still standing, watching. She waved and they waved. There was something sad back there, and Abby watched them intently until they were obscured by the shinnery and hackberry growing along the roadside.

"We'd jist as well be trying to hoe all of the Great Plains," David said, his face pinched and dusty and sweat-streaked.

More and more he was becoming outspoken with his complaints. He was leaning on his hoe and looking down at the scrubby little cotton plants, the leaves already drooping in the mid-morning sun, and then out across row after row of cotton that could scarcely be seen for all the grasses and weeds.

"What has to be, has to be," Mama said, without looking up. The bottom of her faded bonnet moved in the torrid wind, her shirt—one of Papa's old ones, and long-sleeved so her arms wouldn't burn— was flopping, too. She chopped, dug, and scraped ceaselessly in the dry, powdery dirt. Abby often marveled at how long Mama could go without even once looking up.

The Johnson grass must be uncovered and pulled out of the ground with the corner of the hoe because its roots went deep, snaking out in all directions, spreading, spreading if you left even one little pale, innocent looking root joint. The careless weeds, some of them almost as thick as Papa's wrist, had to be hit below the ground, too. Otherwise they would stubbornly revive and begin to branch out again. They were so tough Abby's hoe would bounce off if she didn't go beneath to the tender part.

"I'm ready to tell ole Wade Collins to take his cotton field and chop it hisself," David said sourly. "What's it gonna make, anyways, with all the grasshoppers?"

A big one landed on Abby's arm, its hideous, scratching feet clinging to her shirt and even digging through to touch her skin, and she shook it off in a little shudder of horror. Bugs—any kind—she hated and would never get used to, even if she worked in the fields for the remainder of her life. Her dislike of them was legendary in the family. David used to make remarks about it. "Ole Ab could prob'ly hit all the high notes in God Bless America if that'd happen at jist the right time," he once said admiringly (this had been when she found a centipede in her shoe one morning). Or he would chase her screaming through the house with a cricket or some other such creature until Papa would smilingly call a halt to such torture.

"And if it wasn't for the grasshoppers, what's it gonna make without some rain?" David's present tirade continued to Mama's back, because she was well on down her two rows already.

"Catch your row up, David," was all she said, still not looking up.

Chop, dig, scrape. The tinny sound of the hoe against the weeds and dirt. The sun, white and hot, burning their backs. Grasshoppers flying, singing through the air, landing on their clothes, hair, creeping up pants legs. Crawling on the outside rows of the cotton, chomping their little jaws until the leaves were all full of holes, and finally nothing much was left but a stem. To Abby, the puzzle was why didn't they eat the weeds instead of the cotton?

"And even if it rains, there's the boll weevils that'll

come," David said, whacking vehemently with his hoe at whatever was in his path, half chopping the weeds so that later they would sprout out at ground level and it would be to do all over again. "And what the boll weevils leave, ole Wade Collins gits most of. We're out here killing ourself and he's in the house running his swamp-cooler and drinkin' lemonade with ice cubes in it."

Mama finally straightened up, one hand supporting the small of her back where the leaning-over ache was always the worst. One hand using the long tail of Papa's shirt to wipe the dripping perspiration from her forehead and over her nose. "You're not cuttin' your weeds under the ground good," she said. She looked grim, with her flushed face, the whiteness rimming her mouth, the tired eyes. "And I won't hear no more gripin'. Gripin' won't change the weather and it won't kill the grasshoppers. It won't put us under a cooler and it ain't goin' to give us no lemonade with ice cubes. Gripin' won't do nothing, and that's that." And because lately David seemed to have the attitude Papa was to blame for everything, she added, "Your Papa's doin' all he knows to do. The weather ain't his fault, or nobody else's."

"If you ask me, he should go out in the oilfields," David growled. "Make some decent money there."

"I said there won't be no more gripin'," Mama said again, raising her voice. She turned back to her work.

"If he did we'd jist see him twice a month," Abby explained softly, a bit indignantly.

David shrugged. "Better than breakin' our back for twenty-five cents worth of cotton. We could move there, too. They have oil camps, you know."

"Sure they do," Abby said, "But . . ."

"We've moved everywhere else in the United States," David interrupted her peevishly, "and lived in pea camps and Okievilles in California. I'd say an oilfield camp wouldn't be a whale of a lot different to people like us."

"... the oilfield camps is full and all the jobs took," Abby finished. Everybody was talking about it, including the newsman on K-TJS. David knew it, certainly, but it seemed his disturbing new nature required him to pluck and pull at every loose string as if he were vainly trying to unravel the circumstances that were twined about him and squeezing off his hopes and aspirations.

"If you ask me, he's not doin' his family right," David continued flatly. "He needs to think about that once in a while."

"He's doin' his best, David," Abby said defensively. "You know he is."

"Where's Papa now?" Lucy whined. Compared to her long hoe and the ragged, too-big shirt of David's that she wore, she looked little and helpless, and wretchedly hot.

"As if you didn't know," David said irritably, slapping a blister bug off his pant leg and ramming it into the dirt viciously with the heel of his worn shoe.

"Papa's gone lookin' for a job," Mama said quietly over her shoulder.

It wasn't news to any of them, nor did it offer any hope. Papa had gone looking for jobs twice now, since the news reports over K-TJS began giving out forecasts of a long-term drought and dirt-cheap cotton. "Dirty Thirties style," Ben Findsterwald had predicted pessimistically one day in the road (croppers visited more in the roads than in homes, it seemed to Abby, sitting there for a few brief moments with windows rolled down, an arm slung comfortably over the door, and the motors idling). "Not no moisture in the air. I remember that feelin'. Your skin gits drawed like parchment, your lips chap and peel, your throat's dry as the teacher's chalk board . . . ."

Papa had begun listening to the news once in a while over the car radio and sometimes they all went out there (except David) and listened and talked about what they heard. Big in Oklahoma news was Governor Roy J. Turner's economy programs that actually seemed to be working, and his tollroad proposal. Nationwide, there was the president's warning of coming inflation and his enlargement of the plan they were calling The Truman Doctrine. Coal boss John L. Lewis' latest escapade was mentioned (another strike for higher pay, naturally). Locally, there was not much news except for job shortages and the prediction that the annual rainfall would be down considerably from the twenty-three inch average.

"Wade Collins hisself said I oughta find somethin' to tide us over," Papa said one night, flipping off the car radio with finality and frowning unseeingly into the darkness. "Work the crop on the side. He's a regular kind of man, ole Wade Collins is, when he wants to be . . . ."

But work—any kind—was hard to come by. Papa said the reason was that back in '45 when the war was over, industry had had to shift down to peacetime operations which had put some men out of work. Add to that the fact that all those army men getting back home and into the mainstream of civilian life required additional jobs—to say nothing of the strikes that kept sending people from the east out to the west hunting for steady work. That put everything in a bind all the way around. Ben Findsterwald's boy, Dickie, never had found a steady job since his stint overseas. Of course, as Iva

Findsterwald said herself, that was partly his fault—restless as he was and all.

Sharecroppers, as well as a multitude of others, were running scared, Ben Findsterwald claimed one day in the road. And it had been brought home to them already by Clarence and Ludy Jones' predicament, and Deryl Sheppard's and Tots Caulifield's before that.

And last night, over the clatter of dishes she had been washing at the time, Abby had heard Mama and Papa discussing jobs again. He would go look again today, all the way over to Elk City. Only he'd heard Armour's, an enterprising chicken-plucking, butter-making place, didn't need any more hands, nor did Kelley's, nor any of the regular places of business. Shell Oil was a frenzy of activity everyone was saying, finding that rich oilfield as they did, and he would try there, too. Elk City would be a far piece to drive, but he had exhausted all possibilities in Erick and in Sayre. He had been everywhere including the syrup-making factory—Springdale Food Company, all with no success.

Abby sighed wearily, glancing back at her row. At least it gave her a quiet sense of accomplishment when she looked behind her and saw the Johnson grass and careless weeds and crab grass lying battered and beaten on the ground, already wilted in the glaring sun.

David was staring desolately ahead, leaning on his hoe handle.

"David," she said hopefully, flopping her braid up and down with one hand to cool the back of her neck, "if you look back once in a while at what you've already done, instead of so much at what's to come yet—"

"It's there, whether you're lookin' or not," David muttered.

Abby tackled a big patch of Johnson grass and began analyzing David's situation. It was more complex than she had first thought and she could see now that she was helpless to change it. The reasons for his hopelessness and crankiness were myriad.

It was the heat. The kind of heat that sucked at a person's strength until there was almost no reserve left for standing and facing life.

It was being in the fields all day, day after day, fighting the heat, as well as the grasshoppers and blister bugs and weeds, when by a little twist of circumstances, he could have been lolling in Winburn Tolsey's library, rich with all those books. It was liking Connie Collins even while giving her the cold shoulder in order to show her a sharecropper is nobody's door mat. It was being almost seventeen and not owning anything but the clothes on his back and the few folded in his apple crate shelf on the wall of his sleeping room. And, worst of all, it was not having any reason to believe that the future could ever be any different than the present.

Abby was understanding more and more about what Papa had begun calling the "sharecropper's dilemma." He had mentioned it again last night, an unusual viciousness marking his words, no doubt because he was thinking of his own children this time, especially David. "You share crop," he had said at the supper table, "because you don't have no education to do nothin' else, and no money to strike out on your own. And you don't have no education or means to do nothin' else cause sharecropping don't leave no time nor produce no extry money." Papa should know, being a third generation sharecropper. Once a cropper, always a cropper, was what people said—only it had never seemed to bother him before.

Because David's plight seemed to be the central point of Papa's revelation, sometimes Abby almost wished he had let David stay back at Tecumseh where his dream could so easily be realized. Why not let him go even yet? But when the desperation subsided and she recovered her senses, she was always appalled and frightened that she could even consider such a thing.

"Papa's comin'!" Lucy screamed. She flung her hoe and raced wildly toward the narrow dirt road where billows of dust rose high enough to cloud the sun, and were coming nearer.

The rest of them dropped their hoes wordlessly. Abby felt a dread and hope mix up inside her chest and cause it to start quivering. Papa might have found a job. There might be a reason to hope their situation could ease up some, and that David . . .

She anxiously studied Papa's face as he climbed out of the car. It was hard to tell. He was smiling a little. But his eyes. No, there was no job. She could tell now.

He held out a brown paper sack to Lucy. She looked inside and squealed, "Big Hunks! A Big Hunk candy bar for everyone of us!"

But Abby was watching Mama and Papa, the look that passed between them. It was a look that registered uneasiness and some kind of secret, wordless communication. Then Papa turned back to the car. "Doggone, I slap-dab forgot!"

He drew out four bottles of Royal Crown Cola, still shiny wet from the icy water in the pop cooler, and Abby swallowed hungrily. A Big Hunk with its chewy white taffy and crunchy roasted peanuts, and a searingly cold Royal Crown Cola—both together, at the same time! She couldn't remember ever having them like that before.

No one asked about the job. Lucy was too little to care. David was too bitter, and Abby and Mama both knew without asking. They sat down in the shade of the car on the hot, dusty ground, each savoring quietly every bit of the feast Papa had bought in town—with money, Abby knew, that could—and should—have bought groceries for the table.

Chapter Nineteen

LATE ONE EVENING just after supper, there was a knock at the door and it was Connie Collins, of all people. Papa stood politely, as he always did in the presence of ladies, and from over at the table Mama said, "Will you come in?"

Abby found her voice by then, and stood back a little in case Connie wasn't afraid of lice anymore and decided to come in. "We—was jist gittin' the dishes done."

"We still got some taters left," Lucy added generously, "if you're hungry."

Connie was smiling sweetly, very striking in her black jodhpurs and shiny pink western shirt. Her pale gold hair swished softly about her shoulders as she looked from one of them to another. "I can't come in just yet. I only came over to ride Cherry—if I can talk someone into saddling her for me." She glanced at David, who had been guardedly watching her, but looked quickly back down at the old padlock and key he had been fiddling with.

"David'll be glad to," Papa said. "Won't you, David?"

"I'll git my shirt," David said. After dunking the field dust off before supper, he had not bothered to finish dressing.

Because there seemed to be nothing to say, all of them watched David go over to the double bed where his clean shirt still lay folded. He was swaggering a little, and his lean, muscular tanned back and arms rippled impressively as he pulled on the shirt and began buttoning it.

"I didn't know you could ride a horse," Abby said, to make conversation.

"Oh, I can't really," Connie smiled dazzlingly, still watching David. "I hoped you—or David—could teach me."

"I don't know how too good," Abby apologized.

"David's good at it," Papa said. "He'll be glad to tell you how, I imagine."

"David can ride with one hand tied behind his back," Lucy said.

Down at the lot, Connie chattered gaily as she had when they had all picked up roots together, and as though she and David hadn't gotten into it at the Fourth of July celebration. David saddled and bridled Cherry and led her out of the barn and into the lot. Connie was peering in between the boards. "Oh, do I have to come in there? I thought maybe—"

"You don't wanta give her a chance to run away, do you?" David asked. He added in a slightly sarcastic drawl, "I guess we shoulda rolled out a carpet in here."

"But, she isn't going to run away, is she?"

"Only if she bucks you off," David replied with exaggerated patience.

Connie's pretty green eyes widened. "Does she buck?"

"Only if she's not used to you," David answered. He turned then, talking to the mare, hiding a sudden little smile that only Abby could see from her position on the fence. "Bein's she's your property, I doubt she'll do anything."

"But, I've never been on her in my life. She doesn't *know* she's my property."

"Well, come on and I'll help you up," David said. "I don't think there's a horse in the country that'd buck off a Collins."

"Now you're being catty," Connie said, looking hurt. But she slipped through the boards and David helped her get a foot in the stirrup and put his hands around her trim waistline to help her up.

"I'm too heavy for you," Connie protested.

"Like a feather," David scoffed.

In the saddle, Connie looked down, frightened. "She's pretty tall, isn't she?" she said.

"Jist relax," David said, relaxing a little himself because, for the first time, Connie was more on his level since he was being the expert.

"D-don't turn loose, David," Connie exclaimed as Cherry stomped her foot to get rid of flies.

David grinned and muttered to Abby and Lucy, "Stand back. No tellin' what Cherry'll do."

Cherry stood there, as Abby knew she would. Cherry wouldn't buck if you put a firecracker under her. Connie's teeth were beginning to chatter. "I think I want off."

"Well, a little buckin' never was anything to git excited about," David said. "Here, I'll lead her around till you git used to it."

They began circling the lot at a snail's pace, carefully skirting the west edge where the overflowing water tank had made a big puddle. David was swaggering some, alternately encouraging Connie and warning her to be careful. Abby thought David was carrying it too far, lording it over Connie in order to pay her back for things that really weren't her fault, anyway. Connie couldn't help being born on the upper end of the scale from a sharecropper. She would tell that to David later.

"She's a good rider, Connie is," Lucy said admiringly. "I bet she can do most anything, don't you Abby?"

"Probably," Abby said. Everything except getting

David to like her, and the horse riding might be a break through. David seemed to be enjoying it and was apparently more ready than he had been for weeks to forgive Connie for her former injustices, real or imagined, toward him.

"H-how am I doing, Abby?" Connie asked once, as they came by.

"Real good," Abby said. "But don't worry. Cherry's not gonna—"

"Ab," David interrupted, "I wouldn't talk too much around a nervous horse." And looking up at Connie, "Are you ready to try it a little faster?" he asked.

"I'm not sure, David—"

"Hold on tight," he said, increasing the pace. Connie gasped slightly and David tossed Abby a grin.

"David," Abby said. "She's not used to it. Be careful . . ."

But David wasn't listening. He was encouraging Connie, "You'll be riding them barrels for Beutler Brother's rodeo over at Elk City if you keep this up."

"Really, David?"

Around the lot they went, with David and Cherry both beginning to trot a little. Connie was looking more sure of herself now, buoyed up by David's praise, and turned once to wave at Abby and Lucy, which was possibly why she lost her seat and began sliding to the side. Or, maybe it was because David made too sharp a turn to avoid the water hole. At any rate, it was a terrible place to have a fall and Abby watched in horrified silence as Connie screamed and landed with a splat into the mud.

Lucy was almost beside herself with concern. So, it seemed, was David. In a frenzy he bellowed, "Whoa" at Cherry, and the mare glanced at him questioningly, since by that time she was already standing still. Then he darted around, wading straight into the mud to help Connie up, but she was already storming out of the squishy stuff before he could even reach her.

"You!" she sputtered angrily at David. "You did that on purpose!"

"Look out who you're accusin'," he said, his sympathetic expression fading away.

"You got closer and closer to that awful mudhole," Connie ranted, "And faster and faster—"

"It was *you* that let go and turned around to look at Abby and Lucy," David shot back. "Wavin', showin' off—"

"Showing off!"

Abby felt sorry for Connie. She looked so odd, covered from head to toe with smelly mud. It was even in her hair, and rich, dirty water was dripping down onto her once-beautiful shirt. At the same time, in a slightly hysterical way, the entire episode was somehow a little amusing with Connie attempting to remain dignified under impossible circumstances.

David was over his first concern, and even the brief show of anger at being wrongfully accused, and was beginning to see the humor too, but was managing to keep it mostly to himself, looking Connie up and down the way she and other girls did when anyone new came into church.

"You could pass for a dirt dobber's nest," he said approvingly, his light blue eyes squinting into the beginning of a friendly smile. Then he offered, "Come on over to the horse tank and I'll douse you off with a bucket."

Connie gasped angrily, "You wouldn't dare!"

David laughed a little, not quite sure of himself. "Well, what do you want me to do?"

"I want you to stop laughing!"

"Who's laughin'?" David shrugged, then in spite

of himself he laughed again, this time with more humor.

"See there," Connie accused hotly.

"Well, I wish you could look in a mirror—" David replied.

"My hair is ruined!" Connie shouted. "And you don't even care!"

"Why, your hair's washable, ain't it?" David asked, laughing some more.

"Stop that!" Connie commanded shrilly, stomping one squishy foot and raising a little puff of corral dust in the process.

But David couldn't seem to help it, or wouldn't, whereupon as Abby and Lucy watched mesmerized, Connie marched over to him and slapped him full across the face, leaving a muddy handprint.

David sobered instantly, an angry glint in his blue eyes. His fist doubled instinctively to strike back. "Why you . . ." he growled, bracing for another blow that did not come.

"I've never been so humiliated in my entire life," Connie cried in a rage. "And all you can do is make fun."

"Maybe it's good for a body bein' on the wrong side of the fence for once in his life," David stated bluntly. "Maybe he oughta stay there awhile and learn how it is to be looked at and talked about and laughed over."

Connie was listening in silence now, David's words stunning her. He continued with growing anger. "Maybe then he'd git in his mind how the other half feels, like they're jist half-human or something. Like they're dimwits that don't have any feelin's or no ideas of their own, or don't need nothin' except somethin' to fill up their bellies and never mind what their head wants."

David didn't normally offer his opinion so freely, especially if it might be a hindrance to someone. He stopped now, abruptly, and when he added his last thought it was part an apology, part a plea for understanding, but still with a fraction of defiance. Abby could tell he was shaking on the inside with all he was feeling. "Maybe gettin' a taste of good cowlot mud'll be good for a Collins. Maybe it'll open up a Collins' eyes."

Connie found her voice then, and screeched in disbelief, "Then you *did* do it on purpose!"

"I didn't say that," David answered, shrugging in defeat. "But maybe I should of."

"Oh!" Connie looked more furious than ever. "Don't ever speak to me again, David. Not ever, ever!" And she slipped through the fence and marched away.

"Connie," Abby called anxiously, but Connie didn't seem to hear. Abby hurried over to David, with Lucy close behind. "You should go tell her you're sorry, David."

David looked at first as though he was about to hurry after her, but then he didn't. "She slapped me," he said, as though he still didn't believe it. "I never been slapped that hard in my life."

Lucy thrust her face up to David's chest. "Well, I'm glad she did! I wisht she'd a done it twice't."

David didn't seem to hear. He brushed her aside with one arm and wiped absently at the muddy print on his face, still watching Connie heading for home.

Chapter Twenty

IT CAME TO the point that the cotton was wilted from the previous day's onslaught of heat when they came out to the field at daybreak. Abby knew that meant the roots were eating from the plant instead of from the soil simply because there was no other nourishment. It had happened in the thirties, people said, but Abby was too young to recall it.

Though he was noticeably silent about it this time, Papa had mentioned in times past that the unnatural self-consumption of the plant was like a body constantly drawing strength from inside himself instead of some outside source, namely the Lord. He said a body's natural resources might last him a while, but when the going got to the rock bottom, the spirit needed to be tapped into something bigger and stronger than himself. Otherwise it was in danger of withering and dying.

They chopped anyway, as toilers of the land always had and always would. A farmer did not walk away from an ailing field. He did what he could, slaying the enemy weeds that were sucking moisture from much deeper down than the cotton. Pushing soil up around the cotton plants with his hoe—'dirting' it—so that if there was any moisture left at all, it would not escape by evaporation. Abby was finding out firsthand now that you work the fields, but you never place hope in them.

The winds increased, hot dry winds that raised the dust all the way into the heavens and made the days appear less bright. After a few weeks, everything was dusky and eery. They were in the fields on Saturday when Abby noticed the sun was like a hazy red disk.

She called it to Papa's attention and he took note of it for a moment, leaning on his hoe handle and mopping at his face with his homemade handkerchief a bit absently. It was as though he were not considering the appearance of the sun so much as the conditions that caused the appearance.

"Like in the thirties," he said almost to himself, raising his hoe and clipping off a weed wth a practised deftness that required no thought, "We didn't hardly see the light of day one time for nigh a week." Then perhaps thinking he might have inadvertently caused some concern, he added, "Course, I don't expect it'll ever happen again, now that most people's learned to keep a cover on the land."

"Sometimes you can't git a cover on it, though," Abby said, thinking of several fields around, especially of the quarter-section a few miles away that belonged to Jim Hagerman. Because Hagerman had failed to get a stand of wheat the fall before, his deep-plowed field had moved the entire winter, he had told Papa. An effort to put in cotton had also not succeeded, and the winds had rutted out small craters and valleys and piled sand up in the fence rows, even covering much of the fence posts and wire. The road on that section line, as well as a few others, were no longer passable. Earl Hill, the county commissioner, had put up 'Road Closed' signs because they couldn't get in with a crew to clear the roads until the rains came. In the meantime, that was Hagerman's and several other farms' topsoil that was hovering in the air and reddening the sun's rays.

"It ain't like it was back then," Papa assured her. "Dirt was a rollin' in from New Mexico and Colorado and Kansas, buryin' us alive. 300 million tons of it in one day, I heard. That was back when they said we was all one big spread-out dustbowl. People's educated theirself about the land since then, what with the Soil Conservation Service and a good dose of common sense."

They chopped in silence for a few minutes and Papa added in an apparent effort to buoy their spirits, even chuckling a little. "We didn't git it verified exactly, but once durin' that time we heard a feller from New Mexico was suein' a farmer up around Guymon. Claimed the farmer had half his best farm land and he was wantin' it back. Well, the Okie, he filed a counter suit after awhile, cause about the time he got his crops in they all blew back to New Mexico! Never did hear who come out."

The restrained laughter lifted up into the hazy, dusty air and was gone. Hoes scraped dully against dust-laden weeds, raising stifling puffs all around them. Blister bugs, grasshoppers and dust. Cotton plants in the throes of suffering, and dust. Heat that scorched backs and arms and heads—and dust. Uneasiness that could choke and bind and threaten as much as the dust, and because of it.

"Papa," Abby said in a small voice. "Are we goin' back to California?"

Everyone stopped dead still, as though an invisible switch had been thrown, while they waited for the answer. Papa glanced at each of them, thinking thoughts they did not have time to interpret. He shook his head. Mama began the chopping motion again, automatically causing the others to follow suit.

"Nope. We're gonna tough it out," Papa said. "Everybody needs to git it through their heads we're gonna make it." They were straightforward words, yet Papa was speaking them very gently as though he was soothing a group of play-worn children. "We don't know the meaning of the word 'quit,' if'n the Easons don't. And California ain't got nothin' I ever wanta see again."

He kept watching them for a minute, his big hands, hard and shiny with callouses on the insides, sun-browned and strong on the outsides, gripping his hoe handle. His voice went on, calm, almost unemotional, "Mama, we got any of them Elberta peaches left in the cellar?"

Mama pushed at her bonnet and wiped at her sweaty forehead. "We got two or three jars left."

"We got some whuppin' cream?"

"About enough for a makin', if it ain't spoiled."

They chopped on, wondering what Papa was leading up to. He continued on in that easy, non-excitable way. "Does anybody here feel up to a game of checkers?"

"I do!" Lucy cried, throwing down her hoe decisively, her streaked and sweating face glowing with sudden interest.

"Only you lost two of the black ones some way," David reminded her with more resentment than that misdemeanor warranted.

"I didn't neither. They jist rolled under the bed, is all."

"Why didn't you git 'em, then?"

"Cause it was dark under there, and there coulda been a mouse."

"No mind," Papa said. "We can use bottle caps if they're lost."

"Travis, if you got something on your mind, speak it out," Mama said, beginning to smile a bit, her eyes peering questionably, even a bit warily, from inside the shade of her bonnet.

"When we git to the end of these rows," Papa said, "We're gonna lay down these hoes and make a beeline for the house. We're gonna whup up some cream and smother it over a big bowl of yeller Elberta peaches. We're gonna have a game or two of checkers, winners take winners. We might even read some poems, "When Malindy Sings" or "Casey At The Bat" or "Paul

Revere's Ride." Papa's voice was still easy, almost without emotion, but there was for a brief moment, a look out of his eyes that was curious. It was a look of recklessness, of a vague defiance. "Wade Collins cain't begrudge us a half-day outa the fields. We put in our time. More than put it in, as a matter of fact."

"I'm ready now," Lucy said. "Do we hafta finish our rows? My hoe's agittin' dull and the handle's loose. I think it's fixin' to break."

"Pick up your hoe, Lucy Belle," Mama said.

Lucy picked it up, sighing. "Can we play some Hide the Thimble?"

"I expect we can," Papa said. His squinted blue eyes were looking out across the field now, not seeing it. "There's more to life than breakin' backs and sweatin'. When a feller forgits that, he's in danger of breakin' his spirit. He's got to keep that in mind." He rubbed at his jaw for a minute and added, "He's got to keep that in mind while the dust is movin' and the cotton's burnin'."

The cotton, listless and heavy under the weight of dust and the rays of torturing sun, stretched row upon row. Cotton that was capable of putting fear and a smattering of anger into a grown man—fear for his family and what would become of them, and anger against natural setbacks and obstacles and even against landlords who might—or might not—give a thought to the plight of his croppers. And deeper down, a frustration against men like Winburn Tolsey, who could offer your boy the sun and the moon—and a Ford Couplet—while his own Papa could offer only hard work and long hours and practically no pleasant bread at all, maybe a bowl of yellow Elberta peaches and whipped cream, or a half-stick of gum. Boys don't always count a home and love and a parent's sweat or tears as privileges. It was natural for boys to look lightly past sweat and tears and become blinded by imagined possibilities and Ford Couplets with leather tops.

They were preoccupied with their own thoughts as they worked their way slowly toward the end of the row. Even the thought of a celebration of sorts did not ease the unidentified fear that hovered about them and made them apprehensive. They piled the hoes and file and water jug into the '37 Chevie. Papa began telling them, with a perfectly straight face and a hint of the old teasing glint in his eyes, about the time in the thirties that a farmer reported seeing a prairie dog vainly trying to dig a hole in the dust, ten feet up in the air.

"I don't think he could of did it," Lucy said.

They laughed a little even while the silty field dust fogged and boiled around the moving car, causing them to have to roll up the car windows. Briefly, Abby thougth of the little air coolers people were buying nowadays to hang on the car window. David had told her all about them, how they kept the inside of a car at a temperature almost like a spring day. Wade Collins had one for their Studebaker and the pickup both. And Winburn Tolsey surely had one in the Ford Couplet and very likely another for his new Cadillac.

Papa was reminiscing, "Did I ever tell ya'll about the man that went down to Oklahoma City to buy a new Ford in an extra-heavy dust storm back when your Mama and me was a lot younger?"

Mama said not over a half-dozen times, but Papa went on anyway, knowing she was joshing, "They said the car was the purtiest blue you ever saw, but none of us down at Tishomingo could of swore to it, cause by the time he got home the car wasn't any color a'tall. Sandblasted that purty blue paint plumb off, don'tcha see . . ."

Chapter Twenty-one

A NEW CONCERN came into being, very subtly and gradually. No one talked about it, but it grew steadily in the backs of all their minds, picked up through some strange process of osmosis that exists within the structure of close-knit families.

As one day slid into another and there was not much change in the weather, the money situation, nor anything, really, it became more apparent that David would not be going to college. He very possibly would not be going to high school either next year.

It happened all the time to common laborers and, as such, might not have been a situation about which to take more than casual note. But Abby had an awful feeling that for someone like David, it would be a last straw sort of condition.

She found Mama alone in the house late on Sunday evening and approached her with the problem. The suspense of not being certain drove her to it, and not even her pounding heart and quaky voice could hold her back.

"Mama, how come it's got to be David that skips?"

There. She had finally done it—had brought it out into the open where they could talk it over and maybe work something out. Circumstances were never quite so scary if you could just examine them together with someone else who was concerned.

Mama looked at her briefly then concentrated on the stocking she was darning. "Git me another spool of black thread, Abby-girl."

Abby got the thread. She prodded, "Mama . . ."

"Skips what?" Mama said vaguely, measuring off a length of thread.

"School." She could barely get the word out.

Mama threaded the needle silently and knotted the thread while Abby waited with eternal patience.

"A lotta reasons," Mama said finally. "A lotta reasons, but I'm jist trustin' the good Lord . . ." Her voice faded away and she slipped her hand inside another sock and set to work. "It ain't a set fact yet, anyways," she added, but without conviction.

"What reasons?" Abby persisted.

"He's the oldest, child. And he's a boy and can turn out more work. And he don't have no clothes that fit. I never did see a boy who growed so fast."

"If he cain't go, I don't want to go either," Abby said.

Mama looked up and shook her head as if to say she was hard pressed to understand that kind of reasoning. "It won't hurt David none to stay out. He's done had more schoolin' than most of us. It's jist a year likely, anyways. A year's not much compared to a whole lifetime."

But a year would seem like a lifetime to David, intent as he was on learning. And it was a known fact that if a cropper's kid laid out one year of school he was through learning. Abby wanted to say that, but she didn't. She thought of something else he would detest if he *did* make it back. "He'd be in my grade next year, Mama. He couldn't stand that, and it's not fair. It's not fair for him not to get to go—"

"We've got to think of us all," Mama argued. "Not jist one in the fam'ly. We got to live some way, Abby. That's what it all boils down to."

"We can all stay out in early winter like we always do," Abby persisted, deep concern making her stubborn. "We can git the cotton out quicker than ever, since there won't be much of it. Then we could buy David jist one pair of jeans. That's all he'd really have to have, Mama. Jist one pair that we could warsh at night, maybe on Wednesdays and Saturdays. I'd warsh 'em myself, Mama."

"David's pants ain't the half of it," Mama said, her chin set. "After we git out Wade Collins' cotton, Papa and David's gonna have to hire out and help some others git theirs out, or maybe work at the gin or haul off cotton down to Altus. They got to git some work while it's there. We got to have somethin' to see us out the winter."

"But when the cotton's all done could he go to school?"

"When the cotton's all done it'll be February. School'd near be over."

"But when Wade Collins sells the cotton—"

Mama's patience was suddenly worn thin. "Abby, cotton that brought fifty cents a pound last year ain't gonna bring twenty-five this year. That's already settled accordin' to market reports. Cotton ain't gonna see us through this time. We been a-buyin' groceries down at Puckett's on credit, as well as coal oil and chicken feed at Turner's. The car's got to have some work. We cain't keep askin' for credit and not never payin'. We'll be lucky if . . ." Her voice trailed again and the needle worked in and out the frayed heel, bringing the worn part together deftly, the nimble fingers pulling and working and manipulating, making the darned place remain flat so it wouldn't rub a blister on Papa's foot.

Abby watched for a minute. She clenched her fists together, thinking of the college book and the baking powder can with a dollar and forty three cents in it. "What about David's college?"

Mama had been really angry so few times that Abby was almost shocked to see the way she looked for a moment, her mouth in a tight, grim line, her eyes harsh and flashing. "He's got to git them far-fetched notions outa his head. It ain't natural, in the first place."

"But if Winburn Tolsey still wants him—"

Mama cut in, her eyes still bright with anger, "It's Winburn Tolsey that started all them idees in the first place. It's all his fault. David's got to git his feet down here on the ground again, or things is a-fixin' to go haywire. They might-near are, anyways. He's got to put ever-thing outa his head except stavin' the wolves off from the door. We all got to."

There was a silence and Mama seemed to wilt. She whispered, "We got to trust the Lord or things is fixin' to come apart. Papa—he'd ruther take a beatin' as to keep David outa school. I think he'd might-near ruther to lose an arm. But—he don't have no choice, Abby. The way things is."

Abby swallowed at the hurting in her throat and gave it one more try for David's sake. "He can't help it if he wants to go to college worse than anything else."

Mama fumbled at her lapful of socks and darning supplies, and got up. Then, as though forgetting what it was she had intended to do, she sat down again, arranging things and measuring off some more thread.

"Mama," Abby whispered. "I don't think he can stand it, not goin' to school."

Mama wiped quickly at her eyes and gripped the sock to her chest for a moment. Her voice sounded strange, as though it was full of hurting. "I know it, Abby-girl. That's what's a-worryin' me so much."

And as Abby turned away, she saw tears drop down on Papa's socks.

Mama was cutting hot corn bread, putting a big chunk on each of their plates of black-eyed peas, and there were tiny clouds of steam going up all around. "Travis, why couldn't we jist raise some chickens or turkeys like old Fagin Garner and them does?" she asked.

It was a casual sounding question in order not to raise curiosity, because not one of them was willing yet to come before the entire family and admit they knew how serious the money crisis was becoming. Somehow it was easier to side step it or dodge it or merely to pretend it didn't exist.

"I'd already considered that," Papa said as he cut his cornbread open to butter. "Garner got into chickens in a big way and a half dozen more people did too. Ever'body jumps in that-a-way because the prices is good like they was last year. And what happens? Brings the prices to rock-bottom. Poultry ain't gonna be worth a doodly-womp by time they git growed off. Old Fagin Garner's a-fixin' to see some hard times, hisself, if he's dependin' very much on them turkeys to git by."

No one said anything, but ate in silence. Abby wracked her brain, trying to think of some way they could make money.

Papa continued, "Besides, where'd we put 'em—in David's sleepin' room?" He shot a glance across the table as though he hoped that might put a smile on David's long face. But David only shrugged.

"You gotta have buildin's," Papa said, sounding put-out suddenly. Not put-out at any of them, but at circumstances, the way he was that day in the cotton field. The way he was a little more all the time. It worried Abby because anger had never been Papa's way, yet at the same time she understood. They were about to get boxed in for lack of resources, with no plausible way to turn, and the natural reaction if you weren't very careful would be to get mad simply because there wasn't a solution. "You gotta have property to put the buildin's on. You gotta have brooders for heat when they're young, and feeders and waterers. You gotta be able to buy feed right along till they're growed off without seein' any returns. Other words, you gotta have some mighty close friends down to the First National Bank."

So turkeys and chickens were not the answer. But Abby had thought of something. She said cautiously, in case her idea wasn't worth much, "Why don't we go out and pick poke greens and take 'em to town to sell? Lots of folks like poke greens, and they're growin' free along the roads. And there's still wild plums and grapes at the river."

Reaching for a green onion from the plate, Papa studied for a minute. "Not a bad notion," he said.

"Oh sure," David scoffed at Abby. "You think people's gonna pay for somethin' they could git for nothin'?"

Abby shrank a little from David's scorn. "I was thinkin' of folks that don't wanta take time to go out and pick."

"Yeah," David went on, "I guess we could go pickin' instead of eatin' meals. Or instead of sleepin', bein's that's the only time we git off."

"That'll do, David," Mama said a bit absently, as though she, too, was thinking deep and trying to study out an answer.

Abby thought of something else. " We could take in ironin', me and Mama could. And Lucy."

"Well, I cain't iron nothin' but han'kerchiefs," Lucy pointed out.

Papa said thoughtfully, "That's a fine notion, too. Except'n Mama's might-near got her hands full with field work and cookin'."

Lucy spoke up again, anxious to be a part of the

discussion, "Once't at school we read about some foreign ladies that growed their hair long then cut it off and sold it for money." She glanced at the long braid hanging down Abby's back as though measuring it. "Abby's got enough, I bet."

Everyone laughed a little except David, who was methodically chunking cornbread down into his glass of milk with a spoon and said dryly, "I wonder what the market value'd be on sun-bleached, wind-blowed prairie straw?"

"I wouldn't have short hair if it'd please the president," Abby assured everyone. Papa always said you could tell when a girl was becoming a growed-up young lady because they always cut off their braids and ponytails. Ever since then she had been vaguely suspicious of girls who suddenly turned up at school or church with shortened hair. Even more so when the new hair-do seemed to trigger a chain reaction: painted fingernails, earbobs, high heels, fluttering lashes, swinging hips that were perhaps a result of backs being thrown out of kilter by shoes with three inch tall heels.

She stared across the room unseeingly, trying to think. "If we jist had some extry cows to milk—" she began. Then fell silent because, of course, they had no extra cows now, nor would they probably ever, and even the cows they milked at present belonged to Wade Collins.

"Daughter," Papa said encouragingly, "You got as many idees as old Ben Franklin. And you see what a name he made for hisself!"

But Papa was the one that needed encouraging. It showed in his eyes, more deep set than normal, and with the lines indelibly imprinted around them. It seemed an indisputable fact that money would solve every problem they had, including the dilemma over David, but try as she would, she could think of no feasible way to bring in another dollar.

"If we had extry jars we could at least can some poke greens for ourself," Mama said. "I canned a few, but we could can some more if we had jars."

"Them's the breaks," Papa said, looking and sounding far away somehow. It was an expression that Abby had learned to dread because it meant he was experiencing worries inside himself that he felt were too severe or too extensive to share with the rest of them.

There was a heavy silence for a minute, with only the sound of spoons against plates, scraping up peas, and Lucy's slurping her milk up through an onion blade straw.

"Abby-girl," Mama said, sounding bright. Too bright, really. "I been a-goin' through those things Aunt Myrtle sent and there's a real purty navy blue gabardine dress in there. We could make you a skirt out of it. Bein's she's heavy-set, it might even make Lucy Belle one, too. There's some blouses I might can cut down."

"Me and Abby could both fit in one of Aunt Myrtle's blouses," Lucy said brightly, "And still have room enough to turn around in it."

"They'd be good for church—or for whatever you needed 'em for," Mama added. It seemed as though they all avoided mentioning the word school lately, even though it was only three weeks away, and now Mama's face flushed just a bit because she had almost spoken of the forbidden. "Better light the lamp," she murmured, and fluttered from the table to the jar of matches by the cookstove and back again, touching a lighted match to the wick.

"I can help with the sewin'," Abby said dutifully, watching Mama adjust the flame meticulously. But right now things to wear were not really a concern. You could go to school on last year's clothes—unless you were like David and outgrew them, or wore them all out. Times past she would have wished for a bright dress instead of a drab navy. And not heavy gabardine, but crisp, shiny taffeta or dotted swiss. But that was back when she took food and money and things for granted and it seemed a long time ago.

In the silence that followed, the knock on the door sounded so loud and was so unexpected that Abby jumped a little. She hopped up quickly, grateful for a reprieve from the strained quiet around the table. "I'll see who it is."

Mrs. Wade Collins was standing there, a box in her arms. She was an oppressive figure, tall and big-boned, dressed immaculately in soft grey and pink with fingertips painted the same pink. Abby couldn't keep from wondering suddenly what she had thought the evening Connie came in looking, as David put it, like a dirt dobber's nest. Such filth was likely unheard of in the Collins' household.

"May I come in, dear?" Mrs. Collins asked.

Abby stepped back quickly and said, "Yes, ma'm."

Papa stood up and nodded courteously to Mrs. Collins, who acknowledged it graciously and assured him he could take his chair again, which he did, scraping it back up to the table and self-consciously pushing at his plate while waiting for her to speak.

"I just this minute came from Ladies Aid," she said toward Mama, smiling brilliantly. It was the type of smile used by actors in plays where everything must be exaggerated so the audience can see. It made Abby fidget, and she went back to her place at the table and scooted noiselessly into her chair.

"Will you come in and set with us?" Mama asked politely. She patted uncertainly at her hair, the two little rolls of it that were swept off her forehead and held in place with a bobby pin, and straightened her faded, feedsack housedress as though she felt dowdy and plain in the presence of one dressed so regally.

"I have only a moment," Mrs. Collins answered smoothly. "In Ladies Aid we've been doing quite an extensive charity work." She shifted the box she held as though it was significant. "I told the ladies—as president, you know—that we have a field worthy of our endeavors right here in our backyards. I was speaking of our poor tenants, of course. We've heard rumors that some of them are going to keep their children out of school for lack of proper garments. Considering the importance of schooling, I was heartbroken when I heard. I told the ladies last month, quite a number of our tenants are in dire straits and could use any item of clothing we could get together. And, bless their hearts . . ."

All eyes were fixed on Mrs. Collins as she leaned over with an air of purpose and set the pasteboard box down on the blackened floor they had all been too tired to sweep. It was strewn with sand that had tracked in on their feet and that blew in ceaselessly beneath the doors and around all the windows, and Mrs. Collins' sharp gaze took it all in.

"So!" she exclaimed, straightening her tiny grey hat with the fluffy pink feather. "I have no idea how you feel about charity, but sometimes we just don't have much choice in the matter. Especially in today's economy. Even the best of us are having to learn to tighten our belts."

Abby thought of the new automobiles that seemed to abound at the Collins' neatly painted white house with an upstairs, the elegant clothing worn by them all and wondered exactly which belt Mrs. Collins was learning to tighten.

"There are some very durable items of clothing here, all for youngsters," Mrs. Collins continued, smiling on the three children. "They might need buttons or snaps replaced, or a snag repaired, but they are clean. And I'm sure there are years of good wear in most of them." She paused, still smiling a bit, and looking around at each of them expectantly. Then she added magnificently, "I hope you won't consider this so much a work of charity as a little extension of ourselves!"

Lucy whispered curiously to Abby, "Are we pore?" and Abby shushed her quickly and quietly, and clasped her hands in her lap to wait out this small ordeal of Mrs. Collins' patronage with polite patience.

"We're beholden to you," Mama said, without meeting the eagle-eye gaze. She was pushing at her hair again, and straightening the collar of her dress.

Mrs. Collins nodded, and declared with shining eyes, "I feel a charitable attitude is the business of everyone who is fortunate enough to have plenty. As for myself, I never throw anything away. Waste not, want not, you know! I told the ladies this evening, it gives such pleasure to be able to bestow goods where goods are needed and appreciated, and all of them agreed."

Mama smiled uncertainly, nodding, and said again with a beseeching glance toward Papa, "We're beholden to you. And tell the ladies—"

Papa cleared his throat and stood again and took up where Mama had paused, "—that we're beholden to them, too. Mighty beholden. But the Easons, you see, aim to make their own way. Charity is a good thing—for them that needs it. Tell 'em our thank-yous. But we—" his voice faltered the barest bit, "—we're expectin' some money to come in. We're gonna buy our young'uns some new clothes outa Montgomery Ward's catalog."

Abby looked doubtfully at Papa, her mind sluggish and confused all at once with wondering exactly what Papa was getting at. New clothes? Money?

Everything Papa had said, he'd said politely and respectfully, but Mrs. Collins was looking as startled as Abby felt, and her smile was weak. "Well," she said faintly. "The ladies don't mind sharing in the least."

"I know they don't," Papa said mildly, as though trying to smooth it all over so that Mrs. Collins' feelings would be spared. "And we sure are obliged. But some other folks prob'ly needs these-here things worst than us. I'll help carry 'em back to the car, and we sure do appreciate it."

No one said anything, even Lucy, just looked at each other in wonder and curiosity, then down at their plates or off across the room at shadows thrown by the flickering lamp. When Papa got back, he was silent as he sat back down and began buttering the cooling cornbread. Finally he said, sounding not quite convinced, "They mean good. I know they mean good."

"There might've been some good things for the kids, Travis," Mama began meekly.

"My young'uns is gonna have new clothes this year," Papa said bluntly, as though it was an established fact already. When all the time everyone understood it wasn't. "My young'uns ain't gonna wear hand-me-downs no more. Now, mind, I don't exac'ly have nothin' against hand-me-downs theirself. But it's the way they are handed down that can sometimes jist gald a man's gizzard."

Abby picked at her cornbread while the others ate. It was worrisome the way Papa had given Mrs. Collins' charity box back. Though he never cared for charity and certainly never sought after it, he had never acted exactly that way before. Aunt Myrtle gave them things every once in awhile and he had not taken offense at it even once.

After a minute Mama, in a wavering voice, asked what they were all wondering, "Travis, how're we gonna git all them new clothes?"

Papa's face was grim and there was that brief look of something like defiance that had worried and puzzled Abby since the first time she had noticed it because it simply was not Papa's true nature to defy or resist. "Jist don't fret about nothin', Maudie," he said, and though the words seemed dogged, they were also strangely gentle. "Jist don't fret yourself, hear? It's a man's job to figger out a way. And if he cain't then he ain't much of a man."

In silence—the kind of silence that always prevails in a funeral parlor—they finished eating. There was an indefinable feeling in the room even worse than the night in California that a man had come and tried to pick a fight with Papa just because he was an Okie and a fruit tramp. It was the feeling Abby recalled that Tots Caulifield, with his haunted expression, had inadvertently left behind the one time they had seen him. A feeling she had experienced catching that last glimpse of Clarence and Ludy Jones and their three little children as they drove off.

And suddenly she understood that to a man the worst kind of fear is not that of robbers and tornadoes and wars and the like, but that of his family being in want. And even worse, for that want to be perceived by others, freely discussed, having opinions passed upon it, causing the on-lookers to pick through their abundance and fill boxes to hand out with not so much compassion and camaraderie as with a smug sense of self-satisfaction. That is when the fear is surpassed only by the shame and helplessness, and that was what made some charity boxes totally unacceptable while others were gratefully received.

But even in the understanding of this fact Abby was not freed from the enormity of their situation, but was rather propelled even further into it. The atmosphere churning around them in the lamp-lit, silent kitchen seemed comparable to the whirlpool that the Ferguson's dog back at Tecumseh had gotten into. It started gently on the edge, just a ripple underneath the water, and then it got stronger and stronger until right in the center the force was so great it could suck even a grown man under. They had watched Brownie disappear and everyone had been helpless to do anything at all.

Somehow Abby felt as though they were all on the edge, with the undercurrent pulling insidiously. It was a giant whirlpool of uneasiness, a fear of hunger, a fear of the future, of the unknown. If somebody didn't do something they were all going under. Even Papa, for some reason. And that was undeniably what scared Abby the most.

If they could somehow get everything back as it was, when laughing together came easy, when playing thinking games and such was just a natural part of living. Back before the drought and the grasshoppers and David's predicament. If they could just manage that . . .

With a little shiver of desperation, Abby said softly, "Papa, why don't we play the wishin' game?"

Chapter Twenty-two

EVERYBODY JUST LOOKED at her for a minute with such bleak and emotionless faces, made almost ominous by moving lamp-shadows, that she wished she hadn't even mentioned playing the game.

Except for Lucy, who said with quick interest, "Let's do."

Abby stole a glance at Papa and he nodded, but didn't say anything for a moment. He breathed heavily, wearily, then gazed across the half-lighted, shadowy darkness in the room, out through the window to the sky that had closed itself up to them, holding back moisture when moisture could have helped save them.

"Well, daughter . . ."

He stared some more, a long time, until Mama seemed to get nervous. "Better git this butter and milk wrapped and put by the window," she murmured, and busied herself getting the tea towels and re-wetting them and winding one tightly around the milk jar and another around the covered butter dish. Then she sat back down again.

Papa hadn't said anything all that time. Then he drew another deep breath. His blue eyes glowed dully in the lamp light, and he said very softly, his voice vibrating with some hidden feeling that was trying to come out even while being carefully repressed, "I'd buy us all a train ticket."

Just that, and nothing more.

After a minute Abby asked, unexplainedly breathless, "Where would we be goin', Papa?"

Papa didn't answer for a bit. All their eyes were looking toward him, waiting. Lucy's naively anticipating good things, David's guardedly intent, Mama's wary and uncertain, Abby's suddenly apprehensive. Papa looked tired, with the wrinkles and lines all around his eyes and mouth that weren't noticeable when he was smiling or talking. Papa was thirty-nine, but now he looked as old as Grandpa looked in his last picture. Grandpa, who had died of old age at forty-nine.

Finally he said slowly, "We'd be goin' to a better place. To a new life where . . ." He fell silent again for a moment, as though he was feeling his way along in order not to say more than he intended. "Where a hard working man could coax a livin' outa the land and provide for his fam'ly halfway decent."

And Abby saw that his hand was shaking a little as he picked up his plate automatically and handed it to Mama to be scraped. She felt something stir within her that she'd felt many times before, but never so strongly as now. It was a longing so intense that she literally ached inside with it.

When it came her turn to wish, she looked at no one, but at the base of the flickering lamp and said what she had always wanted to say.

"I'd buy some land," she said. It was almost a whisper, and the kitchen grew quiet, so quiet that the little gurgle of the pot of beans that cooked on the stove sounded loud. Tomorrow's dinner, because they would be in the fields and meals had to be cooked the night before.

"I'd buy some land," she began again, and her voice was a little stronger this time. "At least one hundred and sixty acres. It'd be ours, and nobody else's. We'd tend it right, so Johnson grass wouldn't spread, nor stickers, nor careless weeds. We'd have a tractor and a planter and a go-devil, maybe, and some cotton trailers. When we pulled the bolls we'd take it all to the gin and git all the money for it, not jist part." She was bolder now and there was a burning energy inside her chest that was helping push out the words. "Then we'd go down to Puckett's Grocery and pay off ever' last cent we owe, and to Turner's to pay the feed bill. Then we'd go buy David and Papa some Levi's, three pair apiece, and me and Mama and Lucy some taffeta dresses or dotted swiss ones for church, and some print ones for school. And we'd go over to the First National Bank—or the Farmers—and put some money in there. It would be for David's college and for mine and Lucy's if we decided we wanted to go later on. And all the people'd look at us and say, there goes them Easons. They used to be sharecroppers, but now they **own the land.**"

The beans still bubbled and gurgled loudly on the stove, and the dishwater in the pan on the back burner began sighing and hissing as it reached the point of boiling. In the wake of such unusual fervidness displayed by one of the family, no one seemed inclined to speak. Abby looked at Papa for no reason at all and she saw a strange, naked, hungry look on his face. It caused her heart to begin pounding painfully, even harder than it already was. Because she knew then without being told that that was Papa's wish, too, and always had been.

She knew the unity he felt with the land because she felt it, too. There were unexplainable, invisible ties there that had kept him toiling on all these years when it would seem hopeless and even ridiculous to those who had never felt the call and pull that the land could exert. Abby had experienced it for as long as she could remember, so she understood. Papa loved the land possibly more than she did. To breathe in the lovely, earthy aroma of warm, newly-turned ground ready to receive the seed, to work the land and try to coax the best from it, to walk over it and to observe the growing things. And he had never owned any of it for himself, not even a handful.

David laughed a little then, not a real laugh, but humorless and embarrassed. Breaking the intense silence with the odd high, then low pitch that sometimes occurred because for more than a year now his voice had been trying to become settled into a natural deepness like Papa's, but veered off course at unexpected times.

"Jist chasin' dreams," he scoffed bitterly. And Abby knew, and probably the rest of them, besides Lucy, what he was really thinking about. "Like chasin' the wind, only harder. At least sometimes the wind stops. Dreams never do. They're always two steps outa reach."

The weariness lines around Mama's eyes were very pronounced, too, and she said quietly, "Don't make fun of nobody, David."

Lucy said in a small voice, "Myself, I don't wanta go to college. I jist barely wanta go to school."

No one else seemed to have much to say after that. David never did take his turn at wishing. Mama started putting away the peas and wrapping the leftover cornbread in another damp tea-towel because miller bugs had started coming in soon after she lit the lamp. They were fluttering haphazardly, hitting the globe and falling here and there, even into the food when it was not covered or put out of sight.

Abby began washing dishes in the pans they set on the table and Lucy dried them, standing on top of two thick, out-dated Montgomery Ward catalogs so she could reach things better. It was David's job to check the water in the horse tank and fill the water buckets for the house, so he disappeared outside to get that done.

Papa stood at the kitchen door looking out into the darkness for a long time. One work-worn hand gripped the facing with its peeling crusts of paint, making his muscles bulge out under the browned skin with its curly mat of sun-bleached hair.

When Abby finished the dishes she went to stand beside him. "Is it gonna rain, Papa?"

She could see in her mind the cotton, like rows of dusty, wilting soldiers, the grasshoppers popping up here and there, eating away viciously and the ground parched for want of moisture.

Papa looked mildly startled, as though he had come back from a long way off, then he peered out at the sky. "Well, daughter, there's a bank out there, see?"

He gripped her shoulder, but gently, and she moved closer to him in order to see out. The scant, dark ridge of clouds in the southwest looked too far away to promise any moisture. That set the nagging inside of her in motion again.

But what bothered her more than that was the fact that Papa's hand on her shoulder was still trembling as much as it had when he handed the plate to Mama at the supper table. The uneasiness deep inside her that never quite went away anymore stirred even more. She looked up at him and saw he was not looking at the sky now, but into her face. Then away, out into the darkness again. When he spoke his voice sounded strained and sad, "It'll rain one of these days, Abby girl. It always does."

"It ain't too late for rain, is it?" she asked.

"Don't worry about the crops none," he said, still sounding odd and almost foreign. "The crops is gonna take care of theirself. Them and the good Lord."

"We didn't need those things Mrs. Collins brought anyways," Abby offered, thinking maybe that was partly what was bothering Papa.

Papa nodded and gripped her shoulder harder.

"We'll make do. A Eason ain't no Eason if he don't figger out a way."

Then he drew a deep, uneven breath, and his voice came low and gentle, maybe because he wasn't feeling much spunk right then, and he said, "Don't pay no mind to David. His spirit's jist under the weather right now. He knows as well as anybody that sometimes—most all the time—dreams git caught up with. But jist if you keep on a-chasin' after 'em. And jist if they're worth the catchin'."

They couldn't even look at each other, her and Papa, their eyes filled to the brim with tears. But she nodded anyway, and said, "I know it, Papa." Sounding as though she were sure, even while uncertainty continued gnawing at her insides like a sore. She couldn't keep from thinking of Grandpa and how he had died so prematurely that he never got to realize his dream. And Papa, who very possibly would never catch his dream either.

"Papa?" She reached out a hand and fumbled with the latch hook, wondering if she should ask, then decided to go on. "What did Gran'pa pine away for? What was his—dream?"

Papa didn't answer for a minute. Then, when he did, he sounded mildly reluctant. "Same as mine and yours, Abby-*Madchen*. I reckon he jist wanted enough land of his own to make a livin' for his fam'ly. Only times was even harder back then. Maybe that's why some of his boys got notions they shouldn't of. Though that wasn't a good excuse."

When it appeared Papa wasn't going to say more, Abby asked curiously, "What kind of notions?"

Papa breathed deeply. "Notions to strike out and find some other way to live."

"You mean they left home?"

Papa nodded.

"What did Gran'pa do, then?"

"He tried to go on. Work the farm, but Gran'ma wasn't well back then and took a right smart of seein' to. And there jist wasn't enough hands to work the crops. And—I jist don't know . . ."

"So he give up?"

"He didn't intend it like that, daughter. But—I guess you'd say he lost his *Licht*. Lost his will."

Abby thought of self-consuming plants and wilting spirits, of David and Papa, but it all seemed too much to deal with suddenly, so she merely asked quietly, "Did his boys finally come back?"

Papa stared out into the night again, rubbing his jaw and looking as though he was pained at some memory. "They come back. For the funeral. And they stayed on and tried to make up for it all. But that ain't somethin' a body can make up, hardly."

"Which boys was it, Papa?"

Even as she asked it, Abby knew without a doubt who one of them had been because of the look on his face. And she tried to imagine in her mind her own Papa running away from a place where he was desperately needed and she could not.

"It was me and your Uncle Lewis and your Uncle Clyde," Papa said heavily. "And me bein' the oldest, I'd say it was mostly because of me."

Mama was listening, paused with one hand on her hip, the other on the table where she had been emptying up pints of heavy golden cream to churn into a half-gallon jar. "What's did is did, Travis. Ain't no use goin' back over it now. You was jist a boy, sixteen."

Papa nodded.

Mama added apologetically, as she resumed scraping the last of the cream. "Course it ain't no business of mine, a-tryin' to tell you what to think about and what not to think about."

"Was you tryin' to foller a dream when you left, Papa?" Abby asked anxiously.

"I reckon," Papa said, his low voice gruff.

"What was you after?"

Papa stared some more. "Mostly adventure, I guess, and—money. Things. Jist a lotta things. I was wrapped up in what I wanted and not what was best. A body has got to keep that kind of hankerin' separated from the reg'lar kind, the kind that's worth the goin' after."

Abby squeezed the door facing with one hand until her nails were as pink as Connie Collins, but edged in white. "David's—is the reg'lar kind, ain't it, Papa?"

Papa nodded, his gaze trained again on the narrow bank back in the southwest, and the stars that were closer by shone sharp and bright. "I'd say there ain't no question about it. But he needs to remember somethin', too. He needs to remember sometimes things has got to be put off out there in the future. Browning said, 'A man's reach should exceed his grasp, or what's a heaven for?' "

Abby nodded solemnly, recognizing the quote from "Andrea del Sarto" because Papa had said it many times before. But all those other times his voice had exuded confidence. Somehow he sounded different this time, as though the words were play-like ones designed to cover up the real, stark issues.

As if he had suddenly made some decision or other, he turned to Mama, who was still bustling around doing things the way she did when the situation wasn't quite right. "Maudie, I'm goin' to town on some business. I won't be long."

Mama nodded, as though Papa going off to town

at night was nothing unusual, even a bit scarey. "I'll wait up, Travis."

Papa tucked at his shirttail and squared his shoulders. "I'll try not to be too long," he repeated, and the door slammed softly behind him.

They all watched him go in curious silence, heard the car door open and close, the starter turn over, then catch and start the motor. David, just coming in the front door, looked too, but said nothing. Lucy was cutting paper dolls and couldn't be concerned for too long over anything else. Abby got her book and found where she'd left off last night. Mama stood at the door looking out even after the sound of the car faded away. Finally she turned toward them. "Time for bed, kids."

As usual, Lucy resisted. "Cain't we stay up till Papa gits back? Maybe he's buyin' us somethin' good."

"At nine o'clock?" David said sarcastically. And he continued gazing out into the darkness too, his blue eyes squinted and sullen, hiding from them the thoughts he would not share.

"Cain't we, Mama? Cain't we jist wait and see if he's gittin' us some candy, or somethin'?"

"No." Mama's voice sounded unusually sharp. Then she said very quietly, but in a voice faraway that indicated her mind was with Papa, who would be on Highway 30 by now, half-way to Erick. "Ya'll need your sleep. We're gonna try to finish the field tomorrow. It's gonna be a hard day."

Chapter Twenty-three

ABBY WAS NOT sure what awakened her. Even without any covers at all she felt steamy and clammy, and the patched sheet beneath was damp and warm.

Or it could have been the hot wind billowing the feed sack curtains out over her once in awhile and making her think a spider was crawling over her arm.

It was Mama's voice, low but distinct, and a little angry, that brought her abruptly out of sleep. "Travis," she was saying, "how could you even think of such a thing?"

Papa's voice was intense, a low rumble, "Ain't we all tried to think of some way? Ain't we waited for the rains and the rains never come?"

"I know it, but—"

"What else can I do, Maudie? You think I ain't fought it over and over in my mind for two months and tried to reason somethin' out? You think I ain't dyin' a little ever'day when I think what I'm puttin' my fam'ly through?"

"Travis, I know that—"

Mama's words were not touching Papa at all. "You think that don't eat on a man till his insides is achin' with wantin' somethin' dif'rent for 'em? And—David, Maudie. You think I'm gonna stand by and let that boy git turned against his own Papa for holdin' him back? You see how he has changed—not nothin' like he used to be."

"But that ain't no way to git somethin' for your fam'ly, Travis. You know that as good as anybody."

Papa's voice was shaking. "Then you figger it out if you can. I tell you I'm over a barrel, and I been a-gittin' over it for quite a while. There's got to be a change, one way or the other."

Abby held her breath, afraid they would hear her breathing, afraid she wouldn't find out what awful thing Papa was going to do or maybe already had done. Afraid she wouldn't, and afraid she would.

"Anson Dorrel said he'd set me up and be the go-between," Papa continued doggedly. "You've seen him at town. He always wears a suit and smokes a cigar and sets at that little office by the bank. You know, on Broadway, as you're goin' down to'ard the post office. Said we had enough shinnery hills around so nobody'd notice nothin'. That big patch down by the cowlot, Maudie."

Mama's voice was cold and angry. "Nobody not noticing ain't the question, Travis."

"He's been after me before," Papa went on as though Mama hadn't spoken, maybe thinking she'd give over if he could explain it enough. "He's got the equipment and stuff. Won't be nothin' to buy. It ain't a means to git rich, or nothin'. It's jist a means of stayin' outa the porehouse. It's for David and his school, and—"

"I ain't havin' no part of it."

Papa's voice lowered, filled with a pleading—a helplessness that Abby had never heard in him before. "I ain't askin' you to have no part of it. I ain't askin' you to turn a hand. I ain't askin' you to do nothin' except—jist stand by me, Maudie."

Mama started crying. Abby raised up in bed, listening hard, fighting to keep from sinking into that awful whirlpool of the unknown that hovered so closely again. "Travis, I cain't—I cain't stand by no bootlegger."

Bootlegger?

Abby had heard of bootleggers. David called them gutless and lawless. She could not for the life of her think why Mama would say she couldn't stand by a bootlegger, unless— Suddenly sickened, she leaned back on her pillow and told herself she had not heard correctly.

Silence stilled the next room. It was worse than words. What was Papa thinking right now? What was Mama thinking? Bootleggers, gutless scourges to society.

Then there was the squeaking of the bedsprings and Papa was up pulling on his pants, his feet making the little shrieking noise as they swiped down through each pantleg.

"Travis—"

Papa didn't answer. He was dragging his shoes out from under the edge of the bed. The springs creaked with each movement as he sat on the side to put them on.

"Travis, where you goin'?"

Still no answer. Mama was getting up now, urgently threatening, "Travis, you answer me."

Papa's voice came low, harsh and desperate, "Maudie, do you think I'd do somethin' like this if it wasn't a haf-to case? D'you think I'd do it if there was any other way. Don't make it harder for me to hold up my head."

Mama was crying softly. " Don't worry about holdin' up your head, Travis Eason. Try bowin' it. That's all the good Lord wants from a'body. But you've been too proud ever since I first knowed you."

"Now, git off of that prayin', Maudie. I ain't never been much of one for prayin' and I ain't a-gonna start now. My prayers would sound like I was a beggin'. You know I always respected Him, but I gotta git over this here hump jist like I did all them others—by myself. And all I'm askin'—" His voice dropped to a hoarse whisper, "All I'm askin' is my woman to stand by me."

There was a powerful silence, so dreadful that Abby was digging the nails of one hand into the palm of the other without realizing it.

Mama's voice came, quivering and breathless, "Promise me one thing, then. Promise me the kids don't hafta know. Is that too big a promise, Travis?"

"No, Maudie," Papa said, his voice heavy with relief. "That ain't too big a promise. They won't know. Lord knows I don't want 'em to."

"And—" Mama continued, "Promise me you'll never start to git up and leave durin' the night. Why, you jist started to walk out and not tell me nothin'. Not even speakin'."

"Maudie, don't cry no more." Papa's words were muffled now and he was probably hugging Mama with his face buried against her. "I ain't ever gonna leave. *Ich liebe dich.*" He sounded like a little boy when he said that, and Abby wondered if that was how he used to say it to Grandma. *"Ich liebe dich.* I love you."

The words weren't distinguishable after that. Just sounds of them crawling back into bed and Papa reassuring and soothing Mama. The promise was sealed and everything was back as it should be except for that word. Bootlegger. What had Mama meant? At last Abby slept, not sure of the implications. If there were anything at all of which she was certain, it was that Papa would not be associated with a bootlegger for any amount of money.

"Abby, Lucy. Time to git up."

It had rained a little in the night—a good sprinkle that would not allay the heat nor bolster the crops, but that had perhaps brought the dust down out of the skies and settled it back underfoot where it belonged, at least until the wind got up again.

Throwing off the clammy sheet, Abby looked out, smelling the damp earth that would soon be giving off shimmery waves of steamy heat. It was not even daylight, and the shinnery trees and car were shadowy outlines in the unusual stillness.

At the breakfast table, Mama acted as though nothing at all had happened in the night to make her cry. The only indication that she might be disturbed was that she talked continuously and never looked directly at Papa.

"We smelled the rain a-comin' in the night," she said, passing out hot biscuits from the pan. "Here we are, needin' a toad-strangler and all we git's enough to warsh the dust off their back! I guess somebody ain't payin' the preacher."

With her head almost in the oven replacing the biscuit pan, she continued, "Our last day in the patch till snappin' time. How can time pass so, like a wink, when all the time you're out there it's goin' like cold molasses out of a syrup pitcher?"

She poured Papa some more coffee and passed the milk jar to David. "We can easy git through today. Then all's the choppin' we'll hafta do'll be Wade Collins' garden and his corn patch."

Abby crumbled her biscuits up and spooned gravy over them, listening as Mama went on and on.

"Good thing it's nearly over, too, what with school jist three weeks from tomorrow. Abby-girl, we're gonna make a order outa the catalog before the week's out. You be decidin' what you want. A dress with a circle skirt, maybe, and a wool skirt outa black watch plaid, they call it, and a white blouse? Long white anklets, if you want 'em. Or colored? I seen some red ones once't, all fancy with some kinda knittin' stitch."

Abby nodded, her eyes wide with the thought of actually ordering rather than just looking. "I'll look tonight."

"And Lucy, there's a purty dress I saw one day. Red and green and white stripe with a red collar. It'll set off your cheeks and all. And—" She turned to David and used Papa's little-boy name for him, "Davey-*Knabe*, I'm gonna buy you three shirts. Three shirts, Davey. You already got one good'n. And that-there yeller one ain't bad."

David glanced up. He had been taking in Mama's chatter intently, Abby had noticed. "I gotta have some pants, Mama—pants." he said. "Everything's too short and wore out."

"We'll git some pants, too," Mama promised. "Two or three pairs." She glanced at Papa, staring silently into his plate, cutting up his biscuits and gravy with a knife and fork.

"Jist as soon as—the money comes," Mama added. She jumped up and started wrapping the butter dish and jar of milk in wet tea towels, as though she realized she had said too much. "Ever'body shake a leg. We wanta be sure and not lollygag or we might not finish like we aim to. Papa's going' to town on business . . . ."

It was a wonderful feeling knowing you were about to hang up the cotton hoe for the year, Abby thought, except for garden work, which was nothing compared to cotton chopping. Even as the morning wore on and the heat rose out of the dampened ground, causing their shirts to cling limply and the atmosphere to seem thick and oppressive, there was an air of expectancy and relief in their movements and demeanor.

Papa brought them a sackful of red delicious apples from town, and they each got a whole one. He got back in time to sharpen the hoes one last time and helped finish the last two rounds. But his mind was somewhere else, as though he wasn't a part of them anymore. When Lucy started telling Little Moron jokes he hardly seemed to hear, but just kept his eyes on the rows ahead of them as though he were trying to study out things that were too hard to study out. Always before he would be making some jokes of his own.

David, though, was gradually coming out of his shell apparently because of the talk about new shirts and pants and the thought of money. While he and Abby tackled a patch of Johnson grass on their rows, he speculated thoughtfully that Papa must have changed his mind about the offer of money from Aunt Myrtle and Uncle Lewis to help with school.

In one of his rare, insightful moods he added quietly, "I guess it'll hurt his pride some. We can act like we don't know anything. That might help."

Abby wondered then if she should tell David what she had heard in the night, just lay it out and see if he could explain it. She decided she wouldn't since he seemed satisfied with his own deduction about affairs.

On the way home, David answered most of Lucy's jokes and riddles, adding extra bits of wit the way Papa usually did. He did it in the former dry, sarcastic way he inherited from Mama, with a touch of Papa's arrogance, as though it was all a bother and much too juvenile to really be of interest to him. But Abby could tell he was putting forth a special effort to be more like he used to be, perhaps to help Papa. She was thinking uneasily about the circumstances that were allowing them to regain David, while at the same time allowing Papa to distance himself from them.

David was saying thoughtfully, "When they was givin' out noses, Lucy Belle thought they said roses and she said, Gimme a big red'n!"

"You're fulla baloney, too."

"When they said brains, Lucy thought they said trains, and she went down to the depot."

"I don't even know where the depot is in Erick," Lucy came back scornfully.

David's face was still strained, though, as it had gradually become over the last few months, and even a bit thin, making him look somewhat older than almost seventeen. But he was smiling again—a little, and the smile transformed him into the boy he used to be. "And when they said ears, she thought they said beers, and she said, 'I'll take two big'uns!'"

"David," Papa said abruptly. "That's enough pickin' on Lucy. Ain't no use runnin' foolishness into the ground."

The mood changed. Papa had always reprimanded before, but not exactly in that tone of voice, and especially not when David was doing one of his routines. Now he sounded impatient and touchy, even angry. Abby and David's eyes met, then David merely shrugged and stared out the window, quiet again.

Mama chattered, "I think we could find enough roastin' ears to have for supper tonight, children. Don't that sound good—big ears of corn drippin' with cow butter? Abby, we'll probably need to empty up the cream so's we can churn. Lucy can help. Davey-*Knabe*, you can pick us about a dozen ears."

It was only the middle of the afternoon and they were at the house. Mama said David could put away the hoes and file and water jug, then pick the corn, and he and Abby could shuck it while Lucy started churning. Then they could all do anything they wanted. David asked if he could go to Richard Elliot's and Mama said yes.

"Let's look at the catalogs," Lucy suggested to Abby after the butter was taken up, washed, and pressed into the butter dish. They pulled out the catalogs and got a pencil stub and an old envelope and started making a list of the clothes they liked. It would have been a little like Christmas if it hadn't been for that lump of bewilderment that lay heavily in the pit of Abby's stomach.

Mama was ironing their only good dresses, which meant they would be going to church Sunday. She didn't have a real ironing board so she used a one-by-twelve covered with a ragged quilt that stretched across from the iron bedstead to the back of a chair. Occasionally, they would show her a dress or skirt they liked. She would say, "Ain't it the cat's pajamas?" the way Papa would have. Or, "Now, that's cute as a bug's ear, I reckon." They were pleasant words, yet they seemed artificial as was her smile. It all had to do with last night, somehow.

"Girls," Mama said, "I'm gonna see if Papa won't git ya'll a set of them World Books later on. Wouldn't that be a sight?"

Abby felt a surge of excitement. Was something about to happen that would taint their entire lives?

"Abby-girl, take yours and Lucy's dresses and put 'em on hangers in the closet. And remind me when I git through here that Lucy's has got a button off. I'll hunt one up and you can sew it on."

The only closet in the house was in Mama's and Papa's bedroom. Abby took the dresses Mama handed to her and searched for empty coat hangers amidst the few clothes hanging on the rod. Then she saw it. Bag after bag of something was stacked at the back of the closet. Imperial Sugar were the words printed on the sacks. Twenty-five pounds, each one of them.

Abby's heart leaped. Mama must have planned on

making a lot of jelly or cakes and pies and things. Maybe some peanut brittle, like she usually only made at Christmas or on birthdays. She hastily hung the dresses and hurried back into the front room.

"Mama, what are we goin' to do with all that sugar in the closet?"

Mama's face registered panic at first, then she bent over David's good shirt as she ironed and said, "Papa put it there to—well, you know how he likes watermelon preserves? I'm goin' to make him some. A lot of them. And plum jam. You kids—Abby, you and Lucy, you oughta go out and pick me some pasture plums if you can find any left that ain't wormy."

"Oh, cain't we do it tomorrow?" Lucy wheedled, still deep in the catalog.

"Well," Mama said, "I guess, but tonight after we eat the watermelon that's coolin' in the tank—we'll cut the rind all up. You girls can help me. We'll cut it into little squares and let it set all night covered with sugar so's the juice'll git drawed out, then I can cook it down till it's all thick and syrupy until the rinds is candied, jist the way Papa likes it. And—we might even take some to the preacher on Sunday."

Abby asked, "Can we make some peanut brittle?"

"I bet we can! If you girls'll shell some of them peanuts a-hangin' in the gunny sack down there at the well house, I bet we can make the biggest batch of peanut brittle you ever saw."

Back to the catalogs—to the bright plaid skirts and vests and snowy white blouses, the shiny oxford shoes, lovely anklets of all colors, some of them fuzzy and soft looking as a sweater, and so long they would reach the knees. Abby added to her list, but it was hard to concentrate, even on a fascinating task such as choosing new clothes for school. Glory be, she thought. Store-bought clothes, not things cut from Aunt Myrtle's castoffs. And sugar stacked in the closet to make peanut brittle, and watermelon preserves and plum jam. The Eason family fortunes were sure taking a sudden change for the better, Abby thought to herself.

Chapter Twenty-four

WHEN YOU HAD new clothes, going to a strange school for the first day wasn't so bad, Abby decided. She had chosen her black and red plaid skirt and crispy, white blouse with a red ribbon to tie under the collar. She had black oxfords that smelled of new leather and shoe dye—that squeaked pleasantly when she walked, and white anklets that reached her knees.

David, acting as though shaving was part of his routine, was working up a lather in Papa's shaving mug when Abby came into the kitchen for breakfast.

Papa whistled, more like himself she thought, and said in mock sternness, "Now mind, Abby-girl, I don't want no fellers callin' here till you're sixteen."

"I'll be sixteen next month, Papa."

Papa looked dumbfounded. "I'd of swore she was goin' on fourteen," he said to Mama. "We'd better change that to eighteen. No fellers till you're eighteen. And Lucy—well, don't she look purty in that dress! Lucy don't want no feller, no how. She said she was perfectly content to stay home with her Papa and Mama in their old age."

He winked at Lucy, but she was nodding her head vigorously, "I cain't stand boys, anyways, Papa."

And after David's shave, Papa exclaimed, "My! If he'd of left a mustache I'd of mistook him for Clark Gable, there for a tad. Wouldn't you, Mama?"

Tall, lean and lanky, David grinned a little, one-sidedly the way he used to, his blue eyes sparkling, his formerly strained face more relaxed. Abby knew the reason for the big change was because he was going to get to go to school after all since the fortunes of the Eason family had taken a turn for the better. "Well, Clark

Gable better move over if I can't make the grade in school," he said with exaggerated vanity, "cause I'll be headed for Hollywood and the pitchers." Then he turned to Abby and winked. "Frankly, my dear, I don't give a hoot!" Being gathered around the breakfast table, they all had a good laugh, bringing back some of the good times of the past.

Later, the school bus deposited them in front of the handsome red brick schoolhouse. Someone in the office told Abby and David which hall led to their rooms. Lucy, palefaced and tongue-tied, had gotten off at the grade school across town all by herself.

David seemed even taller and more broad shouldered than usual. He was dressed in his new Levi's and a dark plaid shirt. Abby thought smugly to herself, just wait till Connie Collins sees him in his new clothes; if she liked to look at him before, she'll just love looking now—if she isn't still mad.

She said to David in a loud whisper as they walked down the hall, "Maybe if Connie Collins is here, you might git a chance to say you're sorry about her gettin' muddy."

David looked at her incredulously. "I didn't ask her to get on Cherry and I didn't cause her to fall, and I didn't slap nobody. It might of did her some good to get down in a mudhole once't. So give me two good reasons why I should say I'm sorry about anything."

Abby couldn't even give him one reason especially when he had that indignant look on his face, so she just shrugged and watched him as he strode toward his room in that cocky swagger he had acquired in the last year or so.

She clutched her new black patent leather purse, shivering inside, and watched David disappear through a door. She looked around hesitantly. Even in her anxiety she could enjoy the smell of the first day of school—the pencil shavings and rubber erasers and newly painted concrete floors. Even new books gave off a lovely, scholarly scent.

A bell rang loudly and insistently right above her head, and she quaked. She simply had to make herself go into her room. Only two or three stragglers were hurrying down the halls and she made herself begin walking with them.

Outside the eleventh grade room she stood for a minute trying to summon nerve to go in when a smiling, young woman with a shiny brown braid knotted atop her head, stepped out to pull the door closed.

"Dear, do you belong in the eleventh grade?"

Abby nodded with a smile, acutely aware of the long braid which probably made her appear younger. Maybe she would cut if off or comb it out and let it fall over her shoulders the way Connie Collins did. Or even wear it wound and perched on top of her head as this perky teacher did.

The woman stepped back, gesturing toward the roomful of students inside. "Do come in. I'll introduce you if you'll give me your card."

Abby handed her the card and the woman perused it, pursing her full red mouth thoughtfully. Then, "Abigail. What a lovely name, and such a beautiful skirt and blouse you have on, Abigail. Do come in, dear."

They stepped inside and Abby, fighting her timidity, was literally unable to lift her head and look straight into the sea of strange faces.

"Class, we have a new student this year. Her name is Abigail Eason. Each of you stand and give your names."

Abby twisted the handle of her purse while names were rattled off in rapid succession. The names made no impact on her at all because she didn't see which voice went with each face. Besides, she could scarcely think for wondering if anyone could hear her heart thudding.

There were only two empty desks. One girl raised her hand and said, "Mrs. Tate, may she sit behind me?" So Abby made her way to the back, tripping slightly over the foot of one boy hastily thrust out while Mrs. Tate wasn't looking. She sat down and laid her notebook paper on the desk top and her purse on top of that, then folded her hands in order to control their trembling.

From the front of the room Mrs. Tate smiled, announcing, "Abigail, I had just told the class to prepare to write a theme to be handed in at the end of the hour. I have to go to the office for a few minutes to straighen out some errors concerning our new English workbooks. The theme is to be at least one hundred words and will be titled, "My Happiest Summer Memory." Errors in spelling and punctuation will count five points each. Any questions?"

Abby opened her mouth to say, "No, ma'm," but all that came out was an embarrassing whisper that made a boy near her snicker, and she shook her head, feeling her cheeks burn. She pulled a sheet of paper out of the package on her desk and took a pencil from her purse.

As soon as the teacher left, the room began buzzing. The girl in front of her turned and whispered, "My name is Darlene. We went to Yellowstone this summer. I'm going to write about that."

Abby nodded and smiled, wondering what the girl would think if she knew Abby had spent almost the entire summer in the cotton field.

"What did you do?" Darlene asked curiously.

Abby shrugged, "Not very much," she whispered.

"Hey, Neal," the boy across the aisle said in a stage

whisper to the boy behind him. "The new bootlegger's girl is not bad. Not bad at all."

Bootlegger! Abby kept her face trained downward, made herself write, "My Happiest Summer Memory."

"I bet she spent the whole summer helping her old man make white lightning!" Neal chortled. "Her happiest summer memory! I bet she learned to like it, don't you, Randall?"

The girl ahead of her whispered, "You shut your mouth, Neal, or I'm tellin'."

"I'm worried sick," Neal smirked.

Randall said insinuatingly, "There's only one thing worse than being a sharecropper. And that's being a..."

Before he could say it, Abby thrust her face toward him and burst out in a harsh whisper, her anger causing her to forget momentarily all resolutions at righting her grammar, "Listen here, mister, there ain't nothin' wrong with bein' a sharecropper. At least it's honest work. I ain't ashamed of bein' a cropper, for now, anyway. But someday..."

Randall snickered toward his friend. "She's got lots of fire in her."

Darlene said soothingly, "Don't pay them any mind, Abigail. They're goons."

Abby sank back slowly, wanting to sink right into the floor. Someday—what? Bootlegger. Sharecropper. She would a thousand times over rather be a sharecropper than a bootlegger or moonshiner. But she didn't have that choice. Papa did, though.

She forced herself to shut everything else out and, with trembling hands, began writing. She had learned long ago it was much easier to tell in writing exactly how she felt than it was in the spoken word, and she could do it slowly enough to use proper grammar, which she found almost impossible to do when speaking.

> "Papa is a sharecropper so that makes his family sharecroppers, too. It is hard work, but it is honest work, and that counts for more than money, Papa always said.
>
> "My happiest memory this summer was the same as it has been all my life; working and being together with my family. Sometimes we play thinking games while we work. Games that make us use our minds and help us to learn things, and it's fun at the same time.
>
> "Papa says the good Lord can use an ignorant man, but He can't use his ignorance. So while we work he tries to make sure his kids don't have any ignorance for the good Lord to have to put up with.
>
> "Sharecropping is hard, but at least our whole family is together and making a living. Hard work—"

"Hey, bootlegger's kid!" Neal whispered for all to hear.

Darlene hissed, "Don't even look at him, Abigail."

"Does your old man give out samples?"

Abby held her pencil tightly, her eyes downcast, and tried not to hear, or even to think about what was being said.

"Abigail," Darlene said softly, "Come over to my house sometime. We have a radio, and we could listen to Henry Aldrich or Captain Midnight, or something. And we could walk down to Hood's Drug Store and get a cherry fizz, or even go to the show. The newspaper said *"The Yearling"* will be showing at the Rogue next week."

Abby nodded, and though Randall and Neal were still spouting off, she and Darlene looked at each other and smiled. She was still trembling, but she bent over her paper and began writing again.

> "—is no disgrace. A disgrace would be if your family was lazy or stole things, or tried to make a living in other dishonest ways . . ."

When David got on the bus to go home Abby saw

immediately he had had a bad day, maybe even worse than hers. His face had a sober, almost pinched look, and his blue eyes were dull, hiding some indiscernible emotion. Disappointment and frustration caused her to grip the rod across the back of the seat and feel a little helpless for a moment.

Connie Collins slipped into the seat beside her as though it was the usual thing. "Abby, could I sit with you?"

Bringing herself determinedly up out of the defeat she had felt because of David, Abby answered a bit hazily, "I guess so." Though Connie had smiled at her from afar several times, they had not actually spoken since the horse-throwing incident.

Connie looked perplexed. "I've been meaning to tell you I was sorry for—just walking away that time I came to ride the horse. I heard you call, but—" She shrugged, not quite certain how to continue.

"It's okay," Abby assured her. She had never been a grudge-holder, anyway, but it was David that deserved the apology more than anyone.

Connie stared out the window for a moment as the bus pulled away from the school. "Abby, some kids were saying things behind David's back today, and one or two to his face. I thought you should know."

Abby's mouth suddenly went dry. Then the bootlegging stories had made it to David, just as she had guessed. For a moment she felt anger at the heartlessness of people, but it quickly passed, giving way to acceptance as usual. "Like what?" she asked.

"Just all sort of things. Lies."

"Kids always do that to sharecroppers," Abby explained, which was certainly true, but she only wished it was that simple this time.

"I know," Connie said. She studied deeply for a

minute. "I'm afraid David got into trouble over it. He had to go to the office."

Abby stared at her. "David's never got into trouble at school in his life."

"They made me so mad," Connie said through her teeth. "Picking on sharecroppers as though they were dirt or something. It's stupid and disgusting."

"It's just one of those things," Abby soothed, wondering in the back of her mind what kind of trouble David had gotten into. Even now he was sitting with his head turned to the window, staring out unseeingly at the town, and probably wouldn't have given an answer even if she had been close enough to ask.

At the showhouse, the Cisco Kid was playing and Puckett's was having a special on sugar, 99c for ten pounds. On down at the Dixie, crisp, new school clothes filled the window and a big sign said, "Men's Levis, $3.98 while they last." Abby took note of it all as they passed through town, and of the people meandering by. There was that pretty Mrs. Holmberg from out east of town with her tiny daughter and two sons. And to think that morning David had seemed recovered from all the uncertainties and difficulties of the summer. Now he was right back where he started from.

"Abby," Connie said softly and decisively, "I'll be your friend forever, if you want me to be."

Connie really meant it, Abby could tell. Somehow all the misunderstandings with David had brought a change. Abby had been noticing the difference in her at church. Even the expression on her face had modified and she seldom, if ever, whispered behind her glove or sized up newcomers with haughty stares. And David, in all his stubbornness, was so blind he either couldn't see it, or just didn't want to admit it. "I think that'd be nice," she said.

"Will you start sitting with us at church?" Connie asked.

Abby pictured in her mind all those flowers—and the one weed. Even though she had a few nice clothes now, she still wouldn't fit on the back row. So she shook her head reluctantly and said, "I might sometime. But not yet."

At Connie's questioning look, she added lamely, "I'm used to sittin' with the family."

Connie sighed softly, nodding, "I'd sit with you all but David would think it was for his benefit."

Abby agreed. At this stage in his life, David seemed to take exception to even the most innocent gesture.

"Abby, he's still mad at me. I think he's madder at me than everybody else put together."

Because she couldn't begin to lay out the intricacies of David's plight in a way that would be understood by an outsider, Abby merely pointed out, "It's not everyday he gets slapped by a girl."

"I know. I don't know what got into me. I'm so sorry that ever happened."

"Well, maybe you should tell David."

Connie slumped against the seat. "I can't. He just expects me to crawl to him or something. I tried to be nice to him before when I first met him, and then I tried to apologize about some things that I thought might be bothering him. But, it just didn't work."

"I don't blame you," Abby said, secretly, but benignly, thinking Connie probably didn't know how to crawl anyway, figuratively speaking.

They were letting one of the Davidson boys off and Abby glanced toward the house to see if Ches Davidson, Jr., was at his station by the broken front steps. He was almost a fixed part of the litter, head tilted, staring transfixed, at the bus. When Mr. Williams, the bus driver, waved, Junior waved back automatically and a tiny, reticent smile turned up the edges of his mouth. And he trudged back inside, his long, tedious day having been made by the casual gesture of one who was out there actually sitting in the busses or the road graders, making them go.

"Besides, he can apologize to me," Connie said, suddenly on the defensive. "I think he meant for me to fall off that horse, if you really want to know. You heard what he said. And he acted as though I didn't know anything, and he knew it all."

Abby just shook her head. About the time she thought Connie was through with high horses, she would hop right back on one and take another ride.

At supper, after finding out all about Lucy's and Abby's day, Mama tried to draw David out, talking in a bright, interested voice. "Are you gonna like your teachers, Davey?"

"They're okay."

"Did you git to take some of that fancy 'rithmetic?"

"Yes'm."

"Any purty girls in your room?"

"A few."

"Well, then," Mama said gaily, "Why ain't there a smile on your face?"

David wiped his mouth, studying his milk glass for a minute. "Cause I guess sometimes a body don't feel like fakin' it."

He glanced with hostility at Papa, who didn't see it, since he was looking down at his plate.

Lucy announced suddenly, as though she just remembered. "David, you got a whippin' at school today, didn't you?"

Everyone looked at David, but he just glanced coldly at Lucy and said nothing.

"Well, Davey-*Knabe*?" Papa said, sounding as though he didn't believe it anyway, that he thought Lucy was surely mistaken, and that he was giving David plenty of room to straighten it all out.

"It was worth it," David said, tight-lipped.

"It was three licks," Lucy added. "Ronny Bentworth heard it and told Tim Bentworth at noon. Tim Bentworth's in my room. Ronny Bentworth was gittin' books for the teacher or somethin'. Tim Bentworth said Ronny Bentworth said it sounded like a bull whip a-poppin', even with the door closed. He said—"

"That'll do, Lucy Belle," Papa interrupted, still looking at David. "What've you got to say, boy?"

"Nothin'," David said. Abby could hardly believe her ears, David giving Papa that kind of answer.

"Well, you surely got somethin' to tell us," Papa prodded. "You ain't never had a whuppin' at school that I knowed anything about."

Abby stole a look at David. He looked desperate. That confirmed the fact that the licking was due to Papa's bootlegging somehow, and David didn't want to come out and say it in front of all of them.

"I beat up a kid," David said very unemotionally.

Papa winced, but he asked casually, the way he did when he was wanting them to think a thing through, "And did it help matters?"

David stared at his glass some more. "Yes, it did."

"How did it help?"

"It shut him up."

"And what did he need to be shut up for?"

"Talkin' out of place."

Papa pushed back his plate a little, even though he

wasn't yet through eating. "Must of been somethin' purty bad."

David moistened his lips but didn't answer.

"Jist how bad was it, son?"

Without looking up, David advised, "I don't think it'd do no good to talk about it."

Papa nodded thoughtfully and drew his plate back toward him and began scraping up the last of his beans.

"You was doin' better, Davey," Mama said softly, anxiously. "More like your old self."

Lucy put in pompously, "I don't know why anybody'd git a single lick on the first day of school, let alone three."

David looked at her unsmilingly. "I shoulda put you in that cane press that time when I had the chance, and hooked up the horses to turn the stile till all the juice was squeezed right outa you."

Lucy's eyes grew wide and scared at the thought. "You better not never try that!"

"Don't be sayin' such things, David, even if you don't mean it," Mama said. "I don't understand, we got you all them new clothes and pencils and a notebook."

"Ain't no cane presses around here, nohow," Lucy comforted herself, licking a drop of bean juice off her finger.

Mama continued, "You even got spendin' money now, in case you ever want a girlfriend to buy somethin' for."

"And where's all the money comin' from?" David asked grimly.

Mama looked instantly troubled, even more so than she had when Lucy told about the three licks. She tried to smile, ignoring David's question. "Seems to me like Connie Collins and some of them other girls has got their eye on you."

Papa looked up quickly, his blue eyes shrewd and thoughtful. "We'll talk about it somewheres else, David," he announced. "If'n you got a crow to pick, you can pick it with me—in private."

David scooted his chair back and stood, straight and tall and seemingly calm. But from Abby's position she could see that the hand clenched at his side was trembling uncontrollably. "I don't feel like talking about it anyplace. I'm goin' outside."

Abby's insides seemed to wither and die for a minute. The only other time David had deliberately set himself against Papa was the night he told him he was staying with Winburn Tolsey, no matter what. But it had been different then. David had sounded scared and unsure of himself. Now there was an awful, defiant look burning out of his eyes and he sounded a little reckless, as though he didn't care who he stood up to anymore.

The door slammed softly. Papa got up, too, almost casually. "I'll be back, Maudie."

"You goin' to town?" Mama asked.

"No, jist outside for a while. Me and David's got to talk."

Nervously, Mama got up and started putting away the food, then brought out a gallon jar filled with dried pinto beans. "Abby, while you girls is doin' the dishes and I'm lookin' the beans you can tell me some more about Darlene. Maybe you could have her stay over sometimes. We could make some lemonade and maybe pop some of that popcorn we got shelled the other night."

But Abby's mind was outside, out there in the dark somewhere with Papa and David, maybe down at the windmill. For somehow she had a foreboding that even now words were being exchanged that shouldn't even be said, feelings were being trampled upon, maybe even destroyed.

Getting the dishpans of hot water off the stove and adding a handful of lye soap shavings, she listened, taut and uneasy, to the silence outside and to Mama's ramblings on the inside. She was through with the dishes, had just poured the water out the back door, when David came back in, followed by Papa. Both their faces were fixed into dark scowls. That the two of them had clashed was very apparent. Abby's mind was in a turmoil, trying to picture what must have been said, even while she wiped the dishpan with the dishrag and went over to the cabinet to hang them both on a nail.

Because it was his nightly task, David was checking the water buckets, but in that terrible, seething silence. Then, very abruptly, he turned back toward Papa as though he could hold in his feelings no longer. In a tone of voice he had never before used with Papa— or anyone else—he gritted out, "You're a common crook is what you are! You taught us one thing, and now you're sayin' maybe it's okay to be something else..."

Chapter Twenty-five

THE NEXT MORNING Abby awoke reluctantly. She felt burdened the moment she opened her eyes. Slowly the events of the night before came to her— David's outburst, Papa's giving him the belt in a ruthless manner as she and Mama and Lucy had stood helplessly by.

The cold-faced boy sitting at the table and eating in silence was a stranger. Across from him was Papa, just as silent, just as hostile.

Mama's chattering kept the silence from overpowering them. Abby preoccupied as she was with concern over the bewildering state of affairs, was unable to converse at all.

Never would she have dreamed of David's becoming a rebel. Antagonism had never been a part of his personality. He was always happy-go-lucky, had an even temper and was a softy. Always before a new calf or any baby animal had been enough to reduce him to a bowl of mush.

Each bite Abby took wanted to stick in her throat. She tried to pay attention to Mama's chatter even though no one else was. Lucy was always too sleepy in the mornings to be of much help conversationally. To add to the family complications, looming in the foreground was the prospect of facing Neal and Randall in the classroom again today.

After helping with the dishes, Abby neatly dressed with apprehension. She chose a green and black skirt and bolero to match, and even pinched her cheeks just a little when she glanced in the mirror and saw she looked pale. She considered leaving her hair down, but ended up braiding it. Then she wound it around on the top of her head and turned this way and that looking in the mirror while nobody was noticing. It looked rather fetching but much too pretentious, as if she were trying to be something she wasn't. She dutifully undid the pins at the last minute and let the braid hang down her back as usual.

At the door of the eleventh grade room she took a deep breath and made herself go in. Mrs. Tate smiled and she managed to smile back. No one else paid her any mind as they were coming in, getting seated and pulling books out of desks or looking for last minute assignments.

Darlene caught her eye and smiled, beckoning her to come over. "I saved your seat," she whispered.

"Thanks," Abby said gratefully, sliding into the desk. She wondered if Darlene had heard her say she was a sharecropper's kid? She would just have to tell her today in case she hadn't understood and wanted to renege on her friendship. It was the only honest way.

"Hey, Miss Moonshine's back!" Neal whispered loudly from across the aisle.

Abby ignored him. Mrs. Tate rapped on her desk, then began calling the roll.

Neal whispered to Randall, "Maybe we oughta get to know her better. It might come in handy if we get thirsty ."

"Abigail," Darlene whispered, "Let's sit together in the lunch room."

Abby nodded, grateful for Darlene's willingness to help her ignore the boys across the aisle.

In the lunchroom Abby and Darlene were surrounded by chattering, giggling girls and Abby didn't get a chance to tell her. Even though she worried about David sitting stone-faced and alone across the lunchroom, she was beginning to feel almost as though she belonged.

Briefly she considered keeping her status to herself, but her conscience was too touchy for that. Besides, Darlene, as well as everyone else, would know eventually. Randall and Neal knew, and Mrs. Tate knew because of the essay she had written the day before.

So while they were sitting alone on the back steps of the school before the bell rang, she blurted suddenly, "We're sharecroppers!"

"What?" Darlene asked, not comprehending.

"We're Wade Collins' sharecroppers."

"You're a cropper?" Darlene asked, staring.

Abby nodded anxiously, waiting.

"I remember Neal sayin' it," Darlene said slowly. "I guess I thought he was just teasin' you. You don't look like a cropper."

"Well, we—" Abby flushed a little with shame. "Papa got some—extry money."

"Bein' a sharecropper's no sin," Darlene shrugged.

Abby shivered with relief.

Darlene continued curiously, "Why does Neal keep callin' you a bootlegger?"

Abby shrugged, and choosing her words carefully so they would be truthful, said, "I don't even know of any bootlegger here. Do you?"

"Not really. That Neal's crazy anyway. Nobody but Randall pays him any mind. If I was you, I'd just act like he's not there. Just look right straight through him."

Abby wished she was half as good at it as Darlene.

"There's the bell," Darlene said, pulling at her arm. She paused, grinning. "Anyway, we was sharecroppers, once't, before Mama got her Uncle's land."

Abby stood there with an incredulous look on her face, then rushed to catch up, and both of them started laughing.

Darlene's acceptance of her was offset later in the week by Stacey Dunsmore. Abby had learned long ago that every school has a Stacey. She is a self-proclaimed leader who draws the line between the have's and the have not's, and sets herself up as overseer of all social matters.

Stacey had been feeling Abby out since the first day, talking to her a bit, apparently not having made up her mind whether Abby should be 'in' or 'out'.

"I heard something about you," she said one day before English began.

"Oh?" Abby asked.

"Yes, I heard you're a sharecropper," She announced with a slight smile, her eyes snapping, her lips pursed, waiting.

Abby's heart started pumping painfully hard. All the other times people knew because of the way she dressed. In her heart, she had hoped it would make no difference to anyone. Now she knew it always would.

"Where do you get off trying to act like one of us?" Stacey asked accusingly.

"I don't know what you're talkin' about."

"Trying to pass yourself off when you are just a cropper."

Abby didn't know how to answer. She thought she was just being herself. How would Darlene answer, she wondered? "Well, pardon me," she suddenly blurted out, haughtily raising her nose slightly for Stacey's benefit.

Maybe she made a mistake, she thought as Stacey's eyes narrowed as she spoke, "No one who is anyone likes someone unless I say."

Abby replied, "If no one who is anyone don't like someone who's not anyone, then I guess that's their problem." Abby continued recklessly, hot-headedly and foolishly, "And if anyone don't think they can be someone unless Stacey tells 'em they can, then they are stupid."

Stacey looked challenged—surprised and confused, obviously unaccustomed to such treatment. She just stood, glaring.

The bell rang as Stacey blurted, "I'd advise you to get in your place."

"And where's that?" Abby countered boldly. "Under your throne?" She could hardly believe what she was saying. Standing up to the upperclass took backbone.

"I'd advise you not to make me mad," Stacey warned. "I can have every girl in high school turned against you in nothing flat."

Abby almost asked her if she could control Connie Collins and Darlene, too, but she didn't want to drag in names. Wanting to stop the conversation, she said almost pleadingly, "All I want to do is go to school and be a friend to whoever'll let me." She added under her breath just as Mrs. Tate rapped her desk, "And if that makes you mad, then that's your tub of peas, not mine." She secretly hoped Stacey hadn't heard.

The aroma of fresh cookies greeted Abby even before she opened the kitchen door.

"Oatmeal!" Lucy screamed as she exploded through the door ahead of Abby.

David, with hurt still on his face, walked around the corner to his sleeping room.

"David, Mama's makin' cookies," Abby said, before going inside.

"I'm not hungry," he growled.

"We got to go pick up shinnery roots after awhile. You'll need some energy."

"I reckon I've got enough."

"I'll bring you some out in a minute if you want me to."

David stopped, crammed one hand into his pocket, his back to her, and muttered, "If you want to."

Lucy was sitting at the table with a stack of cookies in front of her already. "David got another lickin'," she said with her mouth full. "Tim Bentworth keeps up with it cause his daddy's the principal and Ronny Bentworth's his brother."

"David best git hisself settled down," Mama exclaimed in very evident annoyance, tilting a pan of cookies off onto a tea towel. "Two lickin's in two weeks is disgraceful, specially if you ain't never had one at school in your life."

"Tim Bentworth's daddy says it's most always the sharecropper's kids and he wouldn't give you a plugged nickel for a dozen of 'em."

Tim Bentworth's daddy apparently didn't know Stacey Dunsmore too well, Abby thought. She said indignantly, "Tim Bentworth's daddy talks too much to be a principal. His word ain't the gospel. If he'd of knew David before . . ."

Sanftmuig, Grandma always said of Grandpa and Papa. Gentle and mild, with a touch of spice. That used to be David. Now it didn't apply to either Papa or David.

"David's a-gittin' mean, ain't he?" Lucy said matter-of-factly, touching her tongue to a crumb in the palm of her hand.

"No, he ain't gittin' mean!" Abby exploded. "Lucy Belle, you need to stop and think before you say those things."

Lucy countered, wide-eyed, "You're shootin' off your mouth two times more'n me—"

"That'll do, girls," Mama warned sternly. "David's jist at a bad age, is all."

If sixteen was a bad age then seventeen must be impossible, Abby thought hopelessly, because David had been seventeen for awhile now and things were getting worse. It wasn't only the age, she knew, but all the frustrating things that piled in on him. Dickens had once said of a certain period that it was the best of times and the worst of times. For the first time in her life, she could think of very little good. Too many people like Stacey Dunsmore and Neal and Randall at school. David and Papa at home. All the uncertainty and worry and fear made the worst of times, period. She wondered how it would all end.

"How come Papa and David cain't stand each other anymore?" Lucy asked innocently.

Mama laughed uncertainly. "Lucy Belle, you git the outlandin'est idees."

"They don't never talk or nothin' anymore," Lucy said. "Let alone laugh."

Abby laid down her cookie, all her appetite gone. It was true. The two of them never even looked at each other anymore, and didn't say anything unless it had to be said.

If they would just sit down and talk and try to understand each other. David could list all his objections and Papa could explain why he was doing what he was. They might still not agree, but at least the air could be cleared and they might possibly work out some sort of treaty or something.

But they were too much alike. As Grandma said, *Gleich Vater, Gleich Sohn*, like father, like son. Both of them grim and hard-headed and angry. Never able, or willing, to express feelings and say what they felt deep down, but just letting it seethe and grow inside until

Abby poured a pint jar of milk and stacked five cookies in her hand. To Mama's questioning look, she explained, "I'm taking these to David."

"Ain't he got enough gumption to come in and git 'em hisself?" Mama asked impatiently, but behind the impatience, Abby could see the worry in her eyes. Mama was as puzzled as she was over what was becoming of them all. In a tender voice she added, "Tell him to change clothes and git ready to pick up roots. And tell him we're gonna have one of our young fryers for supper. David's always been partial to fried chicken."

Abby had gotten to the door when Mama said, almost as if she was thinking aloud, "Girls, don't mention David's whuppin' to Papa. I'll tell him when the time is right—when it needs to be said."

Chapter Twenty-six

"DAVID, ARE THERE any bootleggers around Erick?"

He and Abby were picking dried corn off the dying stalks in Wade Collins' field due north of the Eason's house. They would halve it with the Collinses, storing their part so they would have delicious parched corn whenever they wanted it during the winter.

Somehow she felt the gnawing worry inside her would be eased if she only understood how bootlegging related to her family. She often wondered if David really knew. She hoped maybe he only thought the worst, without knowing all the facts.

He looked up at her quickly, studying her, his thinnish face grim, a sneer curling his lip.

Her heart constricted even though she thought she had steeled herself for the worst.

"Why?" he wanted to know, poking another ear of corn into the gunny sack.

"I jist wondered."

"What'd you wonder for?"

Abby spoke slowly so he wouldn't suspect she knew anything and so she could carefully construct her words. "Somebody at school was callin' somebody else a bootlegger's kid. And I jist wondered—"

"Who was it?"

"His name was Neal somethin'."

"I mean, who was he callin' that?"

She gave an impatient toss of her head so David wouldn't get suspicious. "Never mind. I'll ask somebody else."

She started on down the row but David's hand shot

out quickly and clamped painfully over her arm. He asked again, "I said, who was he callin' that?"

"No matter," she whimpered, a little frightened, sorry she had asked David, yet knowing it was too late.

"Was it me or you or Lucy?" he asked slowly.

"Maybe—but no, why would it be?" she cried softly. "Where would a bootlegger be around here, anyways?"

David stood silently, his fingers biting into her arm. She jerked away defiantly and stepped back. Surprised at his roughness, she hoped he wouldn't answer her question.

But he was. David began telling her anyway in a deliberate, measured voice rife with bitterness and wrath, "There's a bootlegger around here, all right. He's makin' rot-gut whiskey while all the time he tries to act like everything's like it oughta be. He says he's got a right to break the law."

David's words were cutting, and Abby tried to shut them out, but David continued to recite what must have been on his mind over and over, "He sets hisself up over ever'body as being something he's not, specially to his own kids. That bootlegger is the one you call Papa. That's who it is if you want to know."

She whispered through stiffened, almost non-working lips, "Papa makes whiskey? David, you're a liar."

"Everybody knows. They all knew it right along but me, and thought it was so smooth it was goin' on right under my nose all the time." He laughed softly, bitterly. "And all along I thought it would hurt his pride to take money from Uncle Lewis. I didn't know he didn't have no pride."

"M-maybe they're wrong, David," she quavered.

"Ask Mama. Ask her! See if she'll take up for him." He thrust his chin bitterly and defiantly into Abby's face, "And if you're brave enough, ask him and see if he doesn't bust you wide open with a belt."

Abby was sick. She knew it was true. "But he's our Papa, David! You call him Papa, too. You know you do."

"Not no more, I don't."

Her world crumbled. She lashed out, "I'm not going to believe it unless I see it with my own eyes. Papa wouldn't do it."

David turned away from her, shrugging, yanking another ear off the stalk.

"You're jist makin' it up, David," she said accusingly. When she saw he wasn't going to answer, she sobbed and began pounding his back with her fists. "Ain't you lyin'? Ain't you!"

He stopped and slowly put the ear of corn in each of his hands into the sack and turned to face her, his eyes filled with pain. Then in a constricted, subdued voice, he said softly, "I'm sorry. I shouldn't have mentioned it. This ain't nothin' fit for a girl to know about her daddy."

She shrank back, silent now. The two stood there looking at one another. "Is that why he busted you?" she asked over the lump that was aching in her throat.

David ducked his chin and seemed unable to speak for a moment. Then, "I reckon so," he answered.

"How come? It was him breakin' the law."

David breathed deeply, and in a tired, low voice, said, "I guess you was there and saw it, didn't you? He was mad, and I was mad and that's about the size of it."

Recalling that terrible scene in her mind once again, Abby blurted out in distress, "You shouldn't talk back to him, David. You never did that before."

"I haven't had no call to before."

For a moment she was silent, then she asked, "Will you and him ever get back like it used to be?"

David turned, quickly rubbing at one eye with his shoulder, yanked off another ear and thrust it into the sack. "I think it's too late."

This couldn't be happening in their family, Abby thought. A year ago David would have leaned over backward trying to please Papa. And Papa felt the same way about David. Papa always taught them that only the weak-minded or the weak-willed drank, and he wouldn't give you two cents for all the whiskey in Milwaukee. He was dead set against breaking the law, and while he said the Good Book taught not to spare the rod, he also didn't believe in spanking his kids while he was upset at them. He said they needed the rod of correction, not the rod of destruction. It seemed as if he had gone against all those things he had taught them all their lives. There had to be some explanation.

At the house Mama and Lucy were shelling corn Abby and David had brought in earlier. "Through picking a'ready?" Mama asked, her deft fingers forcing row by row the dried kernels off the cob and into a bread pan. Lucy was picking them off a kernel at a time, occasionally glancing around wretchedly as though hunting a way of escape.

"No, I need a drink."

"Not much in either bucket. Why don't you run and git another when you're done drinkin'?"

Abby nodded and lifted the dipper. Her heart raced and hammered. She gulped a mouthful and it went down so fast it made a dull ache in her throat.

"Mama . . ." Out of the corner of her eye she could see Mama nimbly shelling the corn. She decided she wouldn't ask, especially not with Lucy around.

"What?" Mama asked, without looking up.

"Uh—can we—parch some corn tonight?"

"Might as well," Mama said. "There's plenty."

"Is Papa gonna be here?"

"I reckon."

That was the mystery. Papa was almost always home. If he was making whiskey he would have to be gone or something. She would tell that to David and see what he said.

"Do you think he might be up to playin' checkers or something? Maybe a contest, winners take winners?"

"Your Papa's got a lot on his mind. But we'll see."

She laid the dipper down on the washstand and picked up one of the buckets. "Is he worried about money?"

Mama threw the stripped cob into an apple crate to be used in the Franklin come winter, and picked up another full ear. "You're dawdlin' now. David's gonna be a-hollerin' up a storm. You git that water, then go out there so's ya'll can git through by suppertime."

Abby had a feeling Mama wouldn't let on, even if she was asked. The one to approach was Papa. She would do it soon.

"Jist git your skillet hot, but not smokin'," Mama said from over at the table where she was kneading lightbread on a bed of flour in the dishpan.

Breathing in the yeasty aroma that filled the kitchen, Abby dipped two spoonfuls of meat grease out of the lard bucket and watched it spread as it hit the warm iron skillet.

"Now take a good handful of corn and stir it so's it don't burn," Mama continued. "Shake a little salt on it."

They had finished supper and had done the dishes. Papa had gone outside right after he ate and hadn't come back yet. It was too dark to be doing anything out there. Abby couldn't keep from wondering if that was significant.

"Mama," Lucy announced, only half-way in the house and holding open the screen door, "David's still in the car listenin' to the radio."

Floating faintly on the night air came Tennessee Ernie Ford's deep, smooth voice as he sang his new song:

> "Now, some people say a man's made out of mud,
> But a poor man's made out of muscle and blood,
> Muscle and blood, skin and bone,
> A mind that's weak and a back that's strong."

"Tell David to turn it off," Mama commanded. "I told him five minutes and not a minute more. We don't need no run-down battery."

"Papa told him a long time ago jist five minutes at a time," Lucy said. "But he's listened to about a million songs already."

The screen door slammed and Lucy disappeared into the darkness. All around them came Tennessee Ernie's song,

> "I was born one morning when the sun didn't shine,
> I picked up my shovel and walked to the mine
> I loaded sixteen tons of number nine coal
> And the straw boss hollered, 'Well, bless my soul!'..."

"Where's Papa?" Abby asked casually, stirring the corn methodically.

"Outside somewheres," Mama said vaguely.

"He already milked, him and David," Abby said. Mama did not answer.

> "You load sixteen tons, and what do you get?
> Another day older, and deeper in debt."

"Is he feedin' Wade Collins' other cows? Or his mare?"

Mama busied herself over the table, still kneading bread, seeming not to hear.

"Or what?" Abby prodded.

"Abby," Mama said strangely impatient, "I never asked your Papa what he was doing. I'm sure it ain't none of our business."

> "If you see me coming, you better step aside;
> A lot of men didn't, and a lot of men died.
> One fist of iron and the other of steel,
> If the right one don't get you, then the left one will."

Abby continued stirring the sizzling, swelling kernels of corn. Always before, everything one of the family did was everybody's business. Not because they were nosey, but because that's the way it was. "I think the corn's ready, Mama."

"Put it in a bread pan, then. And tell Lucy and David, because it's better when it's hot."

Lucy popped in. "He won't. Said he don't want no parched corn."

"You tell him to git hisself in this-here house before I tan his hide," Mama exclaimed crossly, working tirelessly at the bulbous mound of bread dough.

Slam!

Abby set the pan on the table. "I guess we could have some buttermilk, too," she said.

"That'd be right pert," Mama agreed. "Jist pour us all a glass."

"Papa, too?"

"No, wait'll he comes in."

"He's gonna miss it while it's hot."

"We can fix some more. If he gits in afore bedtime."

> "Saint Peter don't you call me, 'cause I can't go,
> I owe my soul to the company store!"

Listening to the last strains of the song, Abby bent over, pouring buttermilk out of the gallon jar into glasses. "You mean he might be outside quite awhile?"

"I don't know. He never said."

Abby took a bite of the salty, browned corn and it crunched deliciously, still hot enough that it burned her tongue a little. She took a drink of buttermilk. Lucy was coming in again, bearing scandalous news.

"He won't! Says it won't run down the battery, anyways."

"Well, I'll jist say . . ." Mama muttered. With her shoulders set and her dough-scabbed hands held askew, she marched outside. Lucy followed her until Abby stopped her.

"Just set down and eat your corn," she said firmly. "I think Mama can handle it." She was beginning to wonder, though.

Lucy sat down, making her reluctance very obvious, nibbling a handful of corn. "David's getting to be mean, ain't he?" she said.

"It's just he—we all got a lot on our mind," Abby said, sighing heavily. The old times were seeming more and more out of reach.

David was slowly coming in the door, sullen-faced with Mama right behind. "If you don't beat all," she scolded, gesturing with one doughy hand for emphasis. "Your Papa's goin' to hear about this."

"What's the harm of listenin' to the radio five minutes?" David wanted to know.

"The harm is, you didn't stop at five minutes. The harm is, your Papa tellin' you five minutes and me tellin' you five minutes, and you straight-out not payin' no mind," Mama raved. "That battery ain't built for runnin' half the night."

"There isn't anything to do around this place," David replied. "If he's makin' money now, he oughta get us a radio in the house, or let us go to the show or something."

Mama pushed at her hair with the back of her hand and left a faint flour track. "Here," she offered, "Here's some corn. And Abby poured us all some—"

"Now that he's bootlegging, that is," David added loudly and bitterly.

The color faded from Mama's face. "You watch your tongue young man. There's young'uns in this house."

"Don't nobody around here care any more?" David said harshly.

There was something in his eyes that frightened Abby. She involuntarily cowered down in her chair, clutching her buttermilk glass. "David," she said in a voice that sounded too loud in the stark quiet, "Let's all set down and eat some corn—please!"

Papa stepped inside. They had all been looking at David. Now all eyes shifted to Papa. He stood blinking at them in the lamp light, then turned to hang his battered straw hat on a nail near the door. "Something the matter?" he asked, glancing around at each of them again.

His question was met with silence, then Mama began rubbing her hands together over the galvanized bucket that was the trash can, slaking off the bits of dough in little rolls, and didn't seem to hear. Abby quavered, "Papa, we was jist eating some parched corn. You want some?"

"In a minute, daughter. Sounds good." At the table he paused to adjust the flame of the lamp, for it was burning unevenly and blackening the globe.

David hunched his shoulders, cramming his hands into his pockets, and looked at the floor. "I'm goin' to bed."

"At eight-thirty?" Papa asked. He was half-smiling

and his voice sounded almost lighthearted in contrast to the stinging words that had been uttered in the room previously. He was wanting to make up to David, Abby knew, trying to be friends again the way they used to be. His first such attempt since the cold war began, at least that she knew about.

Without glancing up, David muttered, "Nothin' to do."

They all watched him as he strode in a swagger to the door, Mama from over at the stove where she was pouring meat grease into bread pans, and Papa from the table as he pulled out a chair to sit down. In the quiet they heard the door to his sleeping room open and close. Abby relaxed a little. She'd had the feeling David was going to walk out and keep right on walking.

"Perseverance," Papa was saying, in what would have been a jovial tone except for an unmistakable undercurrent of uneasiness. "If a man can persevere, he can live—that's what I been a-thinkin'. It brings to mind how that-there committee up in Washington D. C., or somewheres, voted to abandon them oil leases over around Elk City. It'd been seismographed and a test hole drilled to 13,000 feet and they said it was a dry hole. But the president of Shell Oil, he said, let's try her again boys. That's when they hit the jackpot—a giant field. A "giant field," ya see, is what they call it when there's more than a million barrels down there. Ain't many giant fields in the world. Perseverance—and Shell Oil's stockholders is a bunch of rich people right today."

Papa rubbed his hands together, giving an appearance of contentment, but a remoteness in his eyes gave out a contradictory signal. "Well, don't this-here parched corn look fit for a king. And, daughter, I'll have some of that-there buttermilk, too."

Chapter Twenty-seven

PAPA WENT OUT again during the night. Abby had not been able to sleep and she heard him when he got up and pulled on his pants. If it had been spring or early summer she would have supposed he was watching the clouds for tornadoes, as he often did. She would have derived comfort from the fact and would have rolled over and fallen asleep. But this fall night tornadoes were not a threat.

She listened to the sounds of his dressing with little chills creeping down her back and along her arms. When the door closed softly behind him, she lay stiffly for a few minutes, then got up and slipped on her old shoes noiselessly.

Outside she caught the smell of wood smoke. It wasn't cool enough in September for fires to be lit yet. Sand peppered her face, arms and legs, and a tumbleweed gave her a start as it rolled swiftly by and slammed effortlessly into the side of the house.

Trees swayed back and forth and the windmill wheel creaked and groaned, trying to pump. Papa had apparently shut it down tight. Everything seemed unreal and spooky. Out of her mind full of unanswered questions and undefined fears, sprang these lines of poetry,

> "The wind was a torrent of darkness among the gusty trees,
> The moon was a ghostly galleon tossed upon cloudy seas."

She shivered. Papa had mentioned the shinnery hill by the lot that night she had heard him and Mama talking, so she went there, hitching up her gown a little. Shinnery grew so thick and was so intertwined with wild grapevines that she found herself struggling until she found the trail.

Pushing her way through, she reached the heart of the tangled growth to a cleared area where there was a fire and some steel barrels and wooden ones, some sacks of sugar and several contraptions she didn't recognize. And there was Papa.

The look on his face told her how startled he was. He said nothing—just continued to stir a barrel of swollen corn with a long pole.

"Papa," she whispered.

His voice sounded strained and unfamiliar. "Daughter, why? What're you doin' out here?"

Abby could scarcely speak. "I was a-huntin' you, Papa."

"You shouldn't be out in the dark this way."

There was steam coming from one of the barrels and Abby could smell a sickening sweet-sour aroma. She forced the words out that had to be said. "Are you bootleggin', Papa?"

His shoulders became rigid. Frowning down at the sour mash, he didn't answer. She repeated, "Are—are you makin' whiskey?"

He tried to sound angry. "Daughter, I want you to go straight in the house. Ain't no call for you bein' out this away. Git to the house now and git in bed where you b'long."

Abby's throat ached with the tears she was holding back. The wind whined softly, whipping through the dark trees. She shivered again. "Papa," she whispered, pleading, "I'm scared—for you, for us!"

"Abby-girl." Papa looked at her, his gruffness sounded more gentle. He said tenderly, "Nothin' to be a-scared of. I'll take you back to the house if you want me to."

That wasn't what she meant. She clasped her arms around herself and drew a shivery breath. "I'm scared about—about—"

Everything she wanted to say about the bootlegging, about their family seeming to come apart, about David becoming a stranger driven by pent-up bitterness and wrath—all the uncertainty that she didn't understand and couldn't accept and that had been building up into a tight ball inside her for weeks, suddenly exploded. It began in her chest, rising and pushing up out of her throat in deep, shuddering sobs.

She turned and started running, gasping and sobbing, trying to get her breath, almost unmindful of the shinnery branches slapping her face and scratching her arms, and pulling at her gown—the grapevines grabbing at her so that she had to jerk violently to free herself. She ran to the chicken house on the other side of the lot where she stumbled and fell against it, trying to stop the dry, breathless, gulping sobs that relentlessly wracked her body.

After a minute Papa reached her, put a firm hand on her convulsing shoulder. "Daughter—it's alright. Ain't nothin' to cry and take on about."

Inside the hens stirred on the roost annoyed over the disturbance just outside. Abby pushed herself flat against the rough boards that were still warmish from the day's heat, and clenched her fist against her mouth, but she couldn't stop the sobs.

Papa picked her up as though she was a little doll and sat down with her on the side of the horsetank, rocking her back and forth and soothing her the way she could remember a long time ago when she had nightmares. She huddled against him like she did when she was little and the whole family, including David, laughed and talked and worked and no one hardly thought of anger, fear or hunger.

Papa held her tightly, stroking her hair and murmuring things the way he used to. Finally, the sobs gave way to just trembling and an occasional whimper. She felt exhausted, used up, and she couldn't fight the burden of the problem anymore, even though it still weighed heavily upon her.

"Daughter," Papa said after a time, in a quiet, sad voice, "when you git all growed up and git married and have younguns of your own, then you'll be able to understand. You'll know then. A man does what he has to do to put vittles on the table for his bunch. They need clothes on their back. Sometimes he has to do things—even things he may not want to do. You'll understand someday. I just know you will. You've just got to understand."

Abby pressed her face into the roughness of his shirt and said in anguish, "I don't care about any new clothes, Papa. Let's send them all back."

"There's winter to think about," he continued gently. "Winter's a-comin' on. We didn't git nothin' canned. Your Mama put up a few peas and corn, and that's all exceptin' maybe some poke. We got a gunny sack of dried corn in the wellhouse and a few taters down in the dug-out. The sweet taters ain't gonna make, dry as it's been. We got maybe a dozen punkins. A few peanuts. You could nearly fit our popcorn in a Bull Durham sack."

"We could buy a hundred pounds of beans," Abby whispered, pleading. "Like we did last winter. Beans is cheap. And a big sack of taters down at Puckett's on credit if need be. That's all we'll need, Papa. We can make do."

Papa sighed and a gentle hand squeezed her shoulder. "It's come time for somethin' better. My bunch don't need to scrimp and scrape and barely git by year after year no more. And David, he has to have schoolin'. What was I gonna do? Cotton ain't worth nothin'—25c maybe. Ain't no extry jobs to be had. Don't you see, Abby-girl. My back is flat against the wall!"

The wind engulfed them. The sucker rod on the well clanged against the pipe as the wheel groaned and protested once again. Papa's arms were big and strong and for the first time in a long time, Abby felt safe.

"What's the matter with David, Papa?"

Papa shook his head. "I cain't git through to him. He cain't see that—that—" Words trailed to nothing in his desperation. Then he said angrily, "He cain't see that I'm doin' it for him—for all of my younguns. He just cain't see that. I've tried to explain it more'n once't. He's got his mind set. Headstrong, he is. I don't know— I jist don't understand . . ."

Abby clenched her hands because they were still trembling. "I wisht it was like it used to be."

Papa sighed heavily and clenched her shoulder again with his big hand. "Ain't no way to go back, daughter. I done thought of that. Lordy, how I've thought about it. Tried to think how it could all be changed and forgot and the slate wiped off. Ain't no way it can be done. Life ain't a slate. There's some things a body cain't undo."

Then he stopped, carried her to the house with her head pillowed wearily on his shoulder, both of them caught up in deep silence. In the house, he took off her shoes just like she was a little girl again, and put her back to bed, smoothing her hair back from her eyes and kissing her tenderly yet firmly on her tear dampened cheek.

Maybe the not knowing was better than the knowing after all, Abby decided. Papa was a bootlegger and bootleggers have set themselves against the law.

It was not a pleasant situation in which to be, yet a life of hardship kept Abby from succumbing to mortification. At school, she held up her head because an Eason wasn't an Eason if he didn't. At home, she did the same because there was Mama and Lucy to think of.

David, in his twelfth grade class, had gained a victory of sorts. At least he had those of his own sex subdued by muscle, and those of the opposite with his charm—aloof and untouchable though he was. Even the guys, who at first picked fights, were now mostly quietly sympathetic or at least passive or indifferent, and with his natural charisma, they would have followed him if he hadn't chosen solitude except for one or two cohorts such as Richard Elliott.

In the eleventh grade, Stacey Dunsmore alternately ignored Abby, or subtly picked at her, or boldly taunted, as the mood or situation dictated.

"Now I know why you're trying to make everyone think you're a sharecropper," she said one day, oddly elated for a change.

Abby, waiting for the bus to come over from grade school, shifted her books to another arm. She turned a little, pretending she hadn't heard, hoping Stacey and her friend would give it up and go about their rat-killing somewhere else. They didn't belong with the bus crowd anyway, living in town as they did.

"I kept hearing it, but now I know it for a fact," Stacey continued triumphantly, throwing a knowing look over her shoulder at Sherry. "Your father is a bootlegger!"

Heads turned as everyone looked at Abby, whose face flamed brightly by now. She said quietly, firmly suppressing the anger and humiliation she felt, "Papa's a sharecropper. We all are."

"Well, then why all the stories?" Sherry asked cattily.

"I don't know," Abby answered as helpless tears threatened, crowding the corners of her eyes. She turned away, looking for the bus.

"I think it's a perfect shame," Stacey said. "He should go straight to jail."

There was nothing to say. All the times of being ridiculed for being a cropper could not compare to this. The other times Papa was guilty only of loving the land and his family, and working hard to provide for them. But this other was much too complicated to lay out because the Staceys in the world could never understand —the desperation that would drive a man to step outside the law. The Staceys never had to go without for years and years, struggling for survival, living from hand to mouth, sometimes wondering if there would be one more sack of potatoes. The Staceys took food for granted, and pretty clothes—and nice houses surrounded by green lawns.

"Oh, there you are, Abby," Connie said, coming down the sidewalk toward her. "I had to find my history book and I lost you in the hall."

Abby looked relieved and managed to smile. Stacey and Sherry were standing there in disbelief that Connie, a senior in good standing, would even dream of befriending an Abby, and speak kindly to her.

"Did you have much homework today?" Connie asked, pretending to be unaware of an audience.

"Jist English," Abby replied. "A composition for a contest in the *Beckham County Democrat*."

David had drifted up to the group waiting for bus three and Connie glanced at him, then quickly away. She and David—as far as Abby knew—had not exchanged one single word since the horse-throwing incident, and from all appearances both had resigned themselves to a future of reciprocal silence.

"What's your composition about?" Connie asked.

Before Abby could answer, Stacey stepped nearer. "I guess you know her father is a bootlegger, don't you, Connie?"

Connie glanced up with raised eyebrows and commented, "I'm sure it's none of my business what he does."

Stacey tossed her head. "She *says* he's a sharecropper."

"Well, if he's president of the bank," Connie shot back, "Why should I care?"

"I think she's a big put-on, that's all."

The buses were finally pulling in one by one, noisy yet welcome. Abby had been unable to counteract all of Stacey's bluster, being appallingly short on spunk at the moment, but Connie said it for her in one parting shot. "One thing I can say, Stacey, is that I'm sure you know all about put-ons!"

Abby kept her head up as they entered the bus and found a seat, even when she glanced out the bus window as Stacey, child-like, made a face at her. Turning back to Connie, trembling, she asked, "Are the twelfth-graders gonna enter the newspaper contest, too?"

Connie didn't seem to hear. "Abby, I'm seeing more and more how—blind I was."

"How come?" Abby asked, though she knew already.

"I think of all the things that had to happen, just little things mostly, to cause me to see what I was before, and..." Her voice trailed as she chose her words, "And I wouldn't change any of it. Except for one thing."

And they smiled at each other then, somewhat sadly, and both of them knew she was speaking of the tall, sober-faced boy at the back of the bus who, even now, was staring out the window immersed in his own world.

Chapter Twenty-eight

THE FARMERS GATHERED at Cal's Cafe to contemplate the weather and the crops, transferring their interests from the hopeless state of the cotton to the dubious outlook for wheat.

September had come and it was the fifteenth of the month. Everyone knew sandy-land wheat didn't supply any pasture if it wasn't in before the fifteenth. Tight-land farmers south and east of town were only a little better off, their deadline being some time before the last of the month.

The pros and cons of dusting in the wheat seed were discussed, with most agreeing it was risky. A shower might sprout the seed but wouldn't supply enough moisture to bring it up. Deryll Sheppard had lost his seed the past two years that way. It had been the last straw, accelerating his downfall.

So again they were waiting on the rains, afraid to plow to get rid of weeds for fear of causing it all to blow away. Hands were in the meager cotton fields scouring over it for the first picking. Landlords were hauling it to the gin and watching it sucked from the trailer, hoping against hope for a decent grade and a sudden rise in prices. They would drop by Cal's again for a quick cup and the latest in homespun wisdom, national quandries, a regional anecdote—or even gossip (only they preferred to think of it as news).

Shell Oil activity over by Elk City was always good for several minutes (this was usually followed by remembrances of Spindletop, over in Texas, the "first great oil well in the world." How that back in 1901 it had gushed 100,000 barrels a day a hundred and seventy-five feet into the air, and attracted 10,000 sightseers the first two days. And someone always mentioned the fellow up by Ardmore who, when trying to sell his place, had explained apologetically about his water well, "Now, it's got tar in it, but it's real healthy drinkin' water." Oil!).

One day the big joke was that President Truman had heard of western Oklahoma's plight and immediately sent out the Red Cross to lend a helping hand. At the door of the first shack the volunteers knocked and said with great authority, "We're from the Red Cross." The cropper inside shook his head sadly and responded, "Man, it's been a right tough summer and I don't see how I can give you anything a'tall this year!"

On the more somber side was the problem of car accidents west on Highway 66. The exodus headed for California since the war ended (almost Thirties style) had increased traffic, and 66 had been built without a proper shoulder for some reason. Everyone said Lacy Albert was getting two or three calls a week for the emergency ambulance. Representative Carmichael from Sayre had brought the problem to Governor Turner's attention and a shoulder would soon be forthcoming—and yesterday wouldn't have been soon enough!

Then there was Bill and Lurleen Daggett's divorce. Everyone knew it was a direct result of the strain of the times. All of them recalled how the divorce rate had doubled during the two world wars. Upstanding citizens they were, too. He was a Rotarian and she was big in the Home Demonstration Club. Tight situations either brought people together or drove them apart and Bill and Lurleen had allowed the latter to happen after twenty-four years. There was no third party involved. It was agreed by all that stress was clearly the factor.

Weather conditions—namely the lack of rain—always exerts a direct effect on morale in farm communities so that all aspects of life are touched, not just the most obvious. At church Iva Findsterwald began fretting about her boy, Donnie, buried over there in a national cemetery in Hawaii, and about her youngest boy, Dickie, the one who quit school at sixteen and lied about his age and went off to the war in a burst of patriotic fervor due no doubt to his brother's death, she always added.

Of course, that was in '44. But the fact that Donnie was on foreign soil and Dickie might as well have been (having never settled down since that time) and the fact that she was inwardly fretting over what would become of the family financially (as was most everyone else) stirred it all up in her. Due to Ben Findsterwald's bad heart she couldn't worry aloud at home about the stunted crops, but she could talk to others and she did often to Mama at church.

"Restless, our Dickie is," she might say. "Always a-pacin' when he's at home. He tried schoolin' on the GI Bill, but he doesn't take to schoolin'. To confinin'. 'I'm a farmer, Ma,' he said. Well, lands sake, if he's a farmer, he could farm with us. Course, maybe it's best he's not, this year . . ."

And at another time, "The war did that to him, and losin' his brother. He didn't lose his life over there like our Donnie did. I'm thankful of that. But he lost his—his—" She shook her head, searching for the correct word, "—his direction or somethin'."

Abby noticed Mama sympathized with even more heart than she might have under different circumstances. She understood it was because Mama was learning more all the time about the trials of an offspring who had seemingly lost his direction, and perhaps even his spirit.

David's attitude was trying on all of them, Abby

thought, with his quietness, his blue eyes shadowed, and his lethargy. Whereas his mind and hands used to be forever busy with plans and schemes, they now both seemed disinclined, his spare time often spent in some fruitless activity such as slicing an elm twig to worthless slivers. Always before the end result of his whittling would have been some useful object—a butter paddle or mixing spoon or the little horse's head that he gave Mama for Christmas one year and which she still kept on the corner what-not shelf.

Mama whispered to Papa that maybe David was sick. Maybe he had had polio like one of the Edwards kids back at Tecumseh a year or so ago. Papa shook his head and said polio didn't last that long without getting either better or worse. "It's jist somethin' that'll have to straighten itself out," he said, without a lot of confidence. "It's his age, and everything."

Another time late at night Abby heard Mama say hesitantly, "Travis, maybe we shoulda thought about Winburn Tolsey harder. Maybe we shoulda let David—" And that was as far as she got before Papa interrupted, his voice hard and trembling with instant anger, "Don't never—not never again—mention Winburn Tolsey's name in this house."

"I jist thought—"

"Well, don't think no more."

The tone was so abrupt and unlike Papa that Abby lay for a long time considering it, unable to sleep. And for all that time there was not another sound in the next room. The next day went by with Mama and Papa not speaking a single word to each other that didn't have to be said, and the entire day would remain forever a terrible blot down deep inside Abby. Things like that hadn't happened in her family before.

That night she heard them talking at last, making

up, Mama crying and Papa soothing. She was so vastly relieved she pressed her face into her pillow and cried a little herself, realizing in the back of her mind she had imagined Mama and Papa divorcing the way Mr. and Mrs. Daggett had.

She slipped out of bed quietly so as not to wake Lucy, and knelt mutely beside the bed. Words failed her and she knelt in anguish and in awe of the magnitude of the problem tearing at the family.

Her only glimmer of hope was that God understands the need and eventually soothes the hurting heart.

Chapter Twenty-nine

CLOUDS WERE FLITTING like fluffy lambs in the pale blue sky, and grasshoppers propelled themselves through the air landing briefly only to spring up again.

Meandering through the pasture, slapping at the grasshoppers, searching for the cows and occasionally plucking a shinnery leaf, Abby wished the clouds would come together and give out some rain.

"Abby?"

Abby jumped and looked up to see Connie sitting there on a corner post!

"I didn't mean to scare you," she said apologetically, climbing down. "I was waiting for you 'cause I knew you came this way every evening for the cows."

"What do you want?" Abby asked, though she knew. Even though Connie had assured her that if David was the last boy on earth, she didn't want anything to do with him, Abby was inclined to take that with a grain of salt. Connie still had her days, even considering the drastic change in her attitude lately. She had also said she would never speak to David again unless he spoke first—and it had to be an apology at that.

Also, David had warned Abby if she mentioned Connie one more time he was going to slap her cross-eyed half-way into 1948. Whereupon, she had decided that if David ever did need her help in approaching Connie she would not turn one little finger toward doing it. It was disgusting the way the two of them were so outspoken in their mutual dislike even while throwing secret looks at each other at every opportunity.

"It's David," Connie said. "Abby, does he—hate me, or what?"

"About as much as you hate him I would imagine," Abby said.

Connie sighed deeply. "It's all my fault. All of it, isn't it?"

Abby didn't know what to say. Connie had never admitted any blame before. "Well, he's—David's got a lot on his mind, so maybe it's his fault, too," she answered. "It's jist a lotta things that—maybe you don't know about." To this day she didn't know if Connie knew for sure about Papa's bootlegging. The way gossip was passed around at school, most of the kids were conditioned only to believe what they actually saw.

"Maybe," Connie said softly. "But I know what happened that first Sunday. Even though I try to forget it."

"What happened?" Abby asked curiously. Maybe this would prove to be the other half of the story David so scathingly told her she didn't know about. She had missed church that Sunday because of a sickly stomach and it must have been then.

Connie stooped and picked up an acorn, absently tearing the little cap off the end and then pitching it all aside. "I thought he was so cute—nice looking," she said hesitantly. "But he wouldn't even notice me."

"Well, he's always been cautious about stuff till he gits it figgered out and decided in his mind," Abby defended.

"It sounds as though I'm conceited—but I knew he wanted to look at me as much as I wanted him to. You can feel things like that. But he never would. I offered to show him to his class, and find him a Sunday School book, and everything, but he just said no thanks." She blushed. "Boys pay attention to me, Abby, and when he didn't I said some things—to show I didn't care, I suppose . . ."

"What things?" Abby asked.

"About sharecroppers," she said. "I'm sorry, Abby. I was acting as bad as Stacey Dunsmore."

"Oh," Abby said.

"I guess I acted like I owned him, like he was my sharecropper and not Daddy's. Oh, Abby, it was awful," Connie cried.

"Well, the milk's done already spilt," Abby soothed.

"I don't blame him for hating me. He should."

"Nobody has a right to hate," Abby contradicted.

"Do you have any idea if he—likes me a little?"

Abby dug her bare toe into the dirt and absently flicked off a harvester ant while wondering what David would want her to say. "I'd say he likes you," she answered slowly.

Connie looked more hopeful but her eyes were still troubled. "Then why won't he talk to me?"

Abby thought for a minute. " David's at a disadvantage," she said finally. "Because you're rich and he's pore. Because your Daddy's a landlord—and he's a cropper. And because he's worred about—a lotta things." For good measure, she added dryly, "And because he's stubborn as a mule in a harness."

Connie smiled, barely. "I'm so confused. Abby, I don't know what to do. Do you—think you could talk to him for me?"

Abby leaned over and plucked a shinnery leaf, thinking. Not wanting to tell about David's foolhardy threat, she merely said, "I think it'd do more good if you did the talkin'."

"But he won't listen."

David was extra good at shutting people out having become quite proficient at it just the last few months considering he had had no previous experience. However, all the times she had known of Connie trying to talk to him, she had been a little huffy. She had seemed to learn something about humility since the mudhole incident though, and Abby had a feeling if David knew how she had changed he would be more apt to show some understanding. But she couldn't tell Connie all that, so she just said, "David's over on the twenty fixin' fence. It's just a quarter-mile."

"You mean I should go there?"

"If you're a mind."

Connie looked undecided at first. Then she asked hesitantly, "Would you go, too?"

"Well, I guess I could."

The twenty was deep-plowed but they had to walk through it, or go all the way around. It was sand with a little tightness mixed in, and so soft and springy their feet sank three or four inches with each step. If it ever rained, Wade Collins had said he was going to try a patch of wheat. But for now the field was bare except for Russian thistles that could spring up in a desert if they were a mind to, which meant there would be an abundance of tumble weeds later on as they cured out.

Had it been in the middle of the day Abby, barefoot as was her custom in the summer, could never have made it due to the heat in the soil put there by hours of glaring sun. More than once in the past she had blistered her feet under such conditions. But the sand had cooled enough that she could make fair progress by pausing occasionally with her feet in the shade of a thistle, and Connie paused with her each time, chattering nervously about some pearl earscrews that Mrs. Sailors wore one day that all the senior girls had a fit over. And about Stacey Dunsmore telling someone she felt naked without a pair of earscrews on. And weren't those new kind of earbobs beautiful, colored plastics that sold for a mere seventy-nine cents at the Ben Franklin?

Being in the open as they were David must have seen them coming but he just kept stretching barbed wire with his wirestretchers, winding the little pulley until the wire was tight as a fiddle string and hammering in staples. His shirt was unbuttoned, occasionally billowing gently with the breeze, and there was a huge three-cornered tear where he had apparently gotten too close to a barb on the wire. His solid arms and stomach were dust-streaked and sweaty and he looked weary after working eight hours in scorching sun and wind.

When Connie said hi, only his eyes glanced up, his head nodding slightly. Abby knew he hated having the two girls around when he was so dirty and tired, but David needed to learn some humility, too.

"We came to watch you," Connie said. She meant it to sound casual, but it didn't come out that way because she was obviously ill at ease.

"Watch out or you'll git dirty, too," David said without smiling. Abby thought, here we go again.

Connie flared a little. "Please don't put me down, David".

Neither of them spoke for a minute while David worked over the wire stretchers, undid them and pitched them aside. With his back to her, he remarked, "You shouldn't talk about puttin' people down."

Now was Connie's chance to apologize, Abby thought, but humility is fickle sometimes. Connie looked away, haughty but sad. "Don't you ever think anything good about me?" she asked.

David shrugged in a way that could have meant any one of a dozen things. The wind gusted at his shirt tail. He pulled it together, buttoning it and tucking it in.

"This war we're in. I don't understand why it's

grown into such a major battle."

David was getting more staples out of the sack and didn't answer for a minute. Then he laid both the staples and the hammer down and turned around, full-faced, with his thumbs hooked arrogantly in his belt loops. "Maybe that Sunday started it. Or maybe me being a cropper, I'm supposed to overlook everything?"

"I don't know what you mean," Connie lied in a small voice.

David recited, sarcastically, "I recall something about people that work the land for a living. About how it gits under their fingernails and how the flies buzz around their heads and hayseeds fall outa their hair. About how they contaminate churches and schools and—"

"Wait, David. I didn't mean all that, and you know it."

"And before that you was movin' in to halter-break me."

"I was only trying to—"

"And besides, how do you know you won't git somethin' standing this close to me?"

"Don't David," she said in exasperation, "You know better than that."

"I do?" he said, looking first across the field, and then at her face briefly, before lowering his eyes to the ground. "I heard every word you said. I knew it was all for my benefit, so I soaked it all up. I can tell you the rest of it, if you want me to."

"No," Connie said quickly, "That was before I really knew you."

"You don't know me," David stated curtly.

Connie drew herself back up. "Because you won't let me."

For a minute the situation looked almost as incurable as it had the other times Connie had tried to talk to David. The difference was this time they were talking, unsmiling and accusing though it was. It was as though he thought accusations might bring out some answers that simple discussion wouldn't. It seemed to Abby if he would tread softer he might get more satisfaction.

"I don't think you should run people down that way," he went on grimly. "Sharecroppers and such. You treat us bad behind our backs, then talk another way in front of us."

Connie whispered, "I know. I did do that at first. But, only after you ignored me. And—"

Abby couldn't keep quiet. " Well, you run down croppers, yourself, David. You know you do when you're in a bad mood."

David seared her with a look. "Why don't you go take a walk?"

Taken aback, she said quickly, "Okay." She moved a step or two back so David wouldn't notice her anymore and she stopped.

"I was wrong," Connie whispered. "I guess like you said once, I thought tenant farmers didn't have feelings and everything because they didn't seem to care. But—" Her voice was shivery now, with tears. "I guess I was wrong."

Abby hoped David would ease up some now that Connie was.

He was miserable and mixed up. He asked, almost inaudibly, "How can I have a girl that don't have no respect for my kind?"

Connie responded with difficulty, "I think I know how you feel, now."

The silence was heavy, the kind you can almost reach out and touch. Abby curled her toes into the sand, afraid to move lest David notice she was still present and go off on a tangent. But he seemed oblivious to her and everything else except the struggle of feelings he was experiencing.

He mumbled through a very slight smile, "Where you keepin' your high horse these days?"

Connie's voice trembled as she said, "Far away."

"Where's your mother keepin' hers?"

Connie looked down. "That's still a problem, David. But I hope—we can be friends, at least. Or more, if you want."

"Yeah," he breathed heavily, apparently formulating the outcome of this situation in his mind, not knowing whether to be discouraged or heartened, "The tramp and the lady."

"You're being too hard on yourself," Connie protested softly.

David picked up the hammer and barely tapped at a staple, then laid it down again. He ran his long fingers through his fawn-colored hair and crammed the other hand into his pocket, relaxing his shoulders. His expression softened some more as though new possibilities were presenting themselves. "Your mother and daddy'd throw a ragin' fit."

"Maybe," Connie said. "I guess we can cross that bridge later."

David stared off across the field, not certain just how to proceed.

Connie said in a low voice, "Another thing—I'm sorry I got so mad about the mud and everything. I should have apologized long ago. I'm especially sorry I slapped you."

David smiled at her faintly. "I was kinda sorry, too."

"It was awful of me," she acknowledged.

David's blue eyes squinted into that speculative half-smile and instinctively rubbed his left cheek briefly, obviously remembering back. "It sure was," he agreed. "I never been walloped so hard in my life."

Connie smiled self-consciously, blushing, her eyes to the ground. "I had wanted to impress you and show you I could do things like a real country girl. . ."

David's face turned to the sand and thistles on the twenty and the shinnery pasture beyond that, then to the blue-white of the sky and back down to his feet. "I don't believe it. You wanted to impress me?"

"Yes," Connie admitted softly.

"You was willin' to ride that killer horse to impress me?" He was gently teasing now and Connie blushed.

"I know. Daddy told me after I got home that Cherry wouldn't hurt a fly."

They both smiled, still not exactly looking at one another. "She was a buckin' dude, wasn't she?" David laughed.

There was a flutter of beating wings nearby and they turned to see. "Quail," David murmured, and they watched as the covey scurried for cover. "I been watchin' 'em all day. See how they're marked up, the color of the ground and dead leaves and all?" Connie nodded in silence.

"That's so they blend in with their surroundin's. It's a protection."

"Is it?" She asked, feeling the warming of David's attitude toward her.

He chipped off a piece of bark from the corner post near which he was standing, studied it absently, then threw it aside. Abby observed he was sounding for all the world exactly like Papa, "Sometimes they get scattered out of the covey and they sound a gatherin' call so they can get back together. It's instinct. The good Lord made them that way."

Connie's eyes were unmistakably filled with admiration. "David, you know so much about so many things. I listen to you giving answers at school, and—well, you're so intelligent."

He shrugged off the remark, self-conscious for a moment. Then, "You really wanted to impress me?"

"Ever since the first time I saw you."

"Really?"

"Really."

David seemed overwhelmed and shook his head again in bewilderment. It reminded Abby of the time he came bringing in a tiny rabbit he had found, how he so tenderly murmured things to it when he thought no one was listening, how he held its fuzzy little body to his cheek or cuddled it protectively in the hollow of his shoulder, or stroked it with one gentle finger.

He had that same sort of expression on his face now. Abby knew for sure he was a goner; he was Connie's forever if she wanted him. And apparently she did, for she was looking at him the same way.

He breathed, "You sure did set a purty horse that day. I never did see such a sight."

"Thank you," she answered with just the right amount of shyness.

"And when I put my hands around you to help you up . . ." He shook his head in wonder. "That was something. The closest I ever was to you."

Their eyes met. They smiled directly at one another. "I bought those clothes especially for you," she said. "Then they were ruined. Mother was furious."

Contritely, David admitted, "It was my fault. I was goin' too fast, actin' ignorant."

"Oh, that isn't what I meant," Connie said hastily. "I should not have been trying to show off . . ."

"I shouldn't of got so close to that mud puddle," David insisted.

"But if I had been holding on . . ."

"I caused Cherry to sidestep, without meaning to . . ."

Abby stood amazed. These were two people who had probably never apologized over a half-dozen times in their lives!

"I thought at first you were hurt," David said, looking pained all over again at that long-past possibility.

"Really?" Connie asked softly. "Would you have even cared?"

"Well, sure." He took a step forward, brushing her arm ever so gently, just the way he might have a baby rabbit. Then he stuck his hand back into his pocket. "To be honest," he said, "I was scared half to death for a minute. I kept thinking how easy you could have been hurt. Cherry might have stepped on you, the way she turned so sharp."

Connie's eyes were shiny with feeling. "Then—you didn't hate me, or anything?"

He looked down at her tenderly, struggling without success for some words that would benefit such an awesome feeling. Connie looked into his eyes, knowing the answer to her question. Abby felt like an intruder.

"Hate you, Connie?" David said, obviously controlling his emotions. "I couldn't even if I tried."

Abby turned and walked away, picking oxeye daisies along the fence row. She glanced around once, not wanting to miss it if he did kiss her. They were just standing there, still not touching, smiling a little and talking some, feeling extremely shy with each other, but feeling as though they had a lot to say.

Abby could not help laughing aloud, scaring up a cottontail with her glee. She threw her handful of daisies into the air in sudden exhilaration. They floated for a second, then landed, scattered prettily over the dusty, shinnery-choked earth. Then becoming her practical self again, she meticulously gathered them up, thinking how nice they would look in a pint jar of water sitting on the supper table.

Chapter Thirty

"I'LL CARRY THE big ones and you carry the little ones," Abby told Lucy, looking out over the field which was showing the effects of a succession of snappy cool nights.

There were cornstalks with papery, dried blades flowing up and out and rustling in the slight breeze. Blackeyed pea vines, shades of dull green, red and brown, some of them still gamely sporting the white blooms that were shaped like tiny, delicate butterflies. Wasps and bees and all kinds of other insects floated lazily from vine to vine, sipping from various blossoms. The orange of the pumpkins dotted the field brightly in the afternoon sun adding a touch of gaiety to the otherwise somber scene of the waning of summer.

Abby always thought of James Whitcomb Riley's poem when she saw a field of corn and pumpkins. He had probably been inspired by such a scene when he wrote,

> "The husky, rusty russel of the tossels of the corn,
> And the raspin' of the tangled leaves, as golden as the morn;
> The stubble in the flurries—kinda lonesome-like, but still
> A-preachin' sermuns to us of the barns they growed to fill;
> But the air's so appetizin'; and the landscape through the haze
> Of a crisp and sunny morning of the early autumn days
> Is a pictur' that no painter has the colorin' to mock—
> When the frost is on the punkin and the fodder's in the shock."

It was the frost they were trying to avoid. There were, like Papa had said, about a dozen or so of their part of the pumpkins had grown to maturity. They had to be taken to the cellar before a hard frost would render them useless, causing them to turn to mush and rot. Wade Collins' part would be piled at the end of the field for him to haul away in his new 1947 Ford pickup truck.

Lucy complained, "There's more little 'uns than big 'uns, Abby."

"We'll both work till it's done," Abby answered briskly.

"Why ain't David a-helpin'."

"Because he's got a lot harder job than we do, shocking sudan bundles for Wade Collins."

"I heard him say he was going to Richard's."

"That's after he gits through. It'll take the better part of the evening shockin'. Now, come on. We gotta git this done today because we start boll-pullin' after the weekend."

When they were coming out of the cellar from taking the third load, a sleek black car was setting in front of the house. It looked as out of place there amidst the weeds and sand as one of those curious new contraptions called tee-vee would have in the Eason's front room. (Tee-vee was like a movie-picture David said, only the picture was hazy so that you must squint a lot to make anything out, like looking at a photo through a piece of gauze, and all the rich folks were crazy over them regardless of what they could or couldn't see.)

Abby and Lucy stood staring silently at the car and Abby wondered if it was anything like Winburn Tolsey's new Cadillac. Even wondered briefly if it was Winburn Tolsey, himself, coming to whisk David away from them.

Two men in dark suits and ties were stepping onto the broken front step. Abby went closer. "Papa ain't home. Mama, neither."

One of the men smiled at her in a practised, professional way. "Might you be able to tell me where Mr. Eason could be located?"

"They're in town on business, a-gittin' groceries and chicken feed."

The man pulled out his wallet and showed Abby a card which meant nothing to her. She couldn't even focus her eyes on it, the uncomfortable awareness of the men was so great. "We have authorization to look around the place a bit." He tipped his narrow-brimmed derby politely, then seemed to have a second thought. "I observed your coming from the cellar. Anything down there?"

"Pumpkins," Abby said.

The men looked at each other and one of them nodded slightly. Lucy was hanging back behind Abby, apparently afraid, but Abby watched the men disappear into the blackness of the unlighted dirt cellar feeling only curiousity and a bit of uneasiness. Maybe they were going to buy Wade Collins' farm, the old house and all, and wanted to look it all over first. The Easons might have to move on again after cotton harvest—or at least before next spring planting.

From the cellar the men went to the well-house, then to the hay shed and the chicken house. Then they came back around to the horsetank and poked around in the mossy water with long sticks and even peered into the trash barrel.

All at once Abby had an acutely disturbing thought. If bootlegging was against the law then these men could be the kind of law that you read about that didn't wear uniforms or badges. They could be trying to find Papa's bootlegging place or some of his whiskey. They might even take him off to jail, as Stacey Dunsmore had suggested they eventually would.

"Lucy," she said so sharply that Lucy jumped and

whirled to face her. "We gotta git a move on. Git them punkins carried, like Papa said."

Lucy was looking concerned and whispered, "What if them men steals somethin'?"

"There ain't nothin' to steal," Abby scoffed. She would have to do something—she wasn't sure what—if they headed for the shinnery hill. To Papa's advantage, the shinnery and grape vines grew so thick they made it looks as though nothing ever had, or ever could, get through them.

"They might git Wade Collins' mare and his colt. Or the cow and calf."

"They ain't got a trailer," Abby said matter-of-factly. "Besides, I'd admire to see 'em corner Cloudy, wouldn't you?"

They were carrying the last of the pumpkins when Papa and Mama drove up. Lucy rushed to them and whispered loudly, "Some men's here noseyin' around."

Papa got out the big box of groceries and looked unconcerned. "I noticed the car. Who do you reckon they are?"

"We don't know," Abby said, taking the smaller box Mama handed her. Then she looked at Papa direct and straight, wanting to somehow warn him without causing Lucy to know anything she didn't have to know. "They might be with the federal government or something."

Just then the men came around to the front of the house. Abby couldn't keep from wondering what they were thinking about the sagging corners, the whipped out unkempt yard. Probably at their houses they had smooth green grass and flower beds.

Papa shifted his box to one hip and he and the men shook hands and talked for a minute while Abby and Lucy and Mama went inside to start putting things away. Mama kept looking outside every little bit. She was ill-at-ease when the men stepped inside just ahead of Papa.

"Go right ahead on," Papa was saying cordially. "Jist look the place up and down. That's your job."

Abby wondered if any of that sugar was still in the closet. But Papa wasn't worried and in a few minutes the men came back into the kitchen and said they were much obliged. Papa offered them some coffee but they had to get on they said, and Abby was glad when the door closed behind them.

"Who was they, Papa?" she asked, acting disinterested.

"Git out some bowls and spoons and set the table," Mama said to Lucy. "Abby-girl, skim the milk."

Abby got out the milk jar and the ladle to scoop off the cream, still watching Papa, who was standing at the window looking out, and waiting for an answer. "Where's David?" he said.

"He was gonna go over to Richard's after he finished shockin' bundles."

Mama stopped stirring the soup. "He knows to ask first."

"He said there wasn't nobody around to ask," Abby explained.

"Well, he better learn not to jist pick up and go without there's somebody around to ask first," Mama exclaimed. "He better git hisself back here by supper if he knows what's good for him."

Abby got the milk skimmed and poured, and set all the glasses over on the table, even David's, although she had an awful feeling David might not come home tonight. She had had that feeling several times lately and nothing ever came of it, though. It was just that he and Mama had had another run-in over his playing the car radio the other night and David had muttered to Abby that someday he was going to take off and just keep going and not look back.

She looked at Papa, still staring out the window with a faraway look on his face. "Who was those men, Papa?" she said again, softly.

Papa didn't move. "Jist some federal men, like you thought. Revenooers. Ain't no worry of yours—or nobody's."

They ate and David didn't come. Finally it was bedtime. "He'll show up directly," Papa said. "Probably not noticing the time, it bein' Saturday night. You gals go on to bed, now."

The car starting up awakened Abby. She wondered if it was Papa going out to find David, but the car seemed to screech away in a burst of speed in a way Papa had never driven it before.

Papa came barging out of the bedroom dressed only in his underdrawers and looked out the window. "Somebody's got the car!" he said under his breath.

Mama was right behind him with his clothes. He pulled them on, leaving his shirt unbuttoned, and slid into his shoes without tying them. "I'll have to git down to Wade Collins and use his telephone to call the law," he said over his shoulder.

Abby shuddered, sitting up in bed and huddling into the worn sheet as though it was a cold night. "Did David come home?"

Mama nodded. "He brought Richard home to stay the night."

"Who do'ya reckon got the car, Mama?"

"No tellin'. It's a sight the way people's agittin'. Instead of gittin' a decent job, they're dependin' on robbin' for a livin', jist a-breakin' the law right and left." She seemed suddenly perplexed, probably remembering that Papa was breaking the law, too. "The mystery is, Papa always has the key in his pocket. He don't never leave it in the car."

"Some people can wire 'em up and start 'em," Abby said, nervously chewing her lip. "David can. He showed me once. He didn't really do it—jist showed me he knew how."

Mama's face looked pinched and weary. "Go onto sleep. Papa'll see everything turns out right."

Chapter Thirty-one

PAPA WASN'T HOME yet at breakfast. Had to go to town, Mama said. She looked even worse than last night, her eyes circled with grey shadows, her face lined with fatigue, but closed up the way David's usually was.

"What did he have to go for?" Abby asked, sliding into the slatbacked chair.

Mama pushed at her hair and acted as though she didn't hear. "You girls hurry and eat. We're gonna pick up rotten-ended watermelons to feed Wade Collins' cows. Lucy, you ask the blessin'."

"How come?" Lucy asked, sighing.

" 'Cause the good Lord wants it, that's why."

"I know why the blessin'," Lucy explained, frowning. "I cain't figger out how come we hafta pick up rotten watermelons."

"The blessin' first," Mama said, with unusual patience.

"God is great, God is good, and we thank Him for this food," Lucy intoned. And with hardly a pause she asked, "How come?"

" 'Cause they ain't no good for people—most of 'em sour, and all. But cows'll eat 'em, right enough. Saves feed."

"How come they got to have rotten ends?"

"Dry weather. But there's a right smart of good 'uns. Little, but good." Mama spooned mush into each bowl and Abby added a small lump of butter to hers. "Wade Collins'll give us some of the good 'uns for pickin' 'em up," Mama added.

"How come on Sunday?"

"We start snappin' cotton tomorrow."

Abby had never seen Mama with so much patience. It was a bit worrisome. She wanted to ask about the car but she didn't want Lucy to have to know in case they hadn't gotten it back. Or in case it was David that got it, and he was far away by now.

"I'm gittin' tired of workin'," Lucy began. "Why don't old Wade Collins—"

Abby interrupted sharply, feeling as though Lucy's complaining was the last straw. "Cain't you just do like you're told for once and not always be tryin' to wiggle your way out of stuff?"

"I ain't half as bad as David!" Lucy defended herself. That reminded her of something. "Is David goin' to hafta help?"

Mama nodded, buttering skillet-toasted pieces of lightbread, and Abby breathed easier. "Ain't no call for him not to, is there?"

"How come he's not eatin'?"

"He'll eat," Mama said with such confidence that Abby wondered briefly if last night had been only a bad dream.

Mama set the mush back on the stove to keep it warm and brought over a plate and set it down. "I nearly forgot the salt pork! Won't it taste good with toast and mush?" She started to sit down, then jumped up nervously. "There they are now."

David came in first, sullen, swollen-faced, one eye half-closed and ringed with grey and purple, the other blood-shot. There was even dried blood on one cheek. Behind him came Papa, his face drawn and weary and defeated, but cold and angry, too.

"Warsh up," he said curtly to David.

"We was jist startin' to eat," Mama said. She dished up two additional bowls of mush.

"What's wrong with David?" Lucy asked, her eyes bright, curious buttons.

"He got hit," Papa said, "Eat your breakfast."

"Who hit him?"

Papa snapped, "I said eat your breakfast."

Abby's stomach flopped. Everyone concentrated on eating and David sank heavily into his chair. "I ain't hungry."

"Eat anyways," Papa said in a flat, hard voice.

They all quietly finished eating. Even Mama was silenced by Papa's tone and mood.

It was that way for the remainder of the day. Papa drove the tractor, getting off once in a while to help them carry the putrid-smelling melons that were swarming with wasps and sweat bees to the trailer. When they got the trailer full they all rode the half mile or so to Wade Collins' pasture and threw the melons across the fence. The herd of cattle crowded around, chomping noisily into the melons and enjoying their feast.

After they got the souring ones out of the field they had to start over, getting only the very small ones that wouldn't have time to ripen before a hard frost, and the ones that were black on one end, but not yet ruining. These they would store in Wade Collins' barn for him to feed later. David spoke only when spoken to the entire day, a terrible scowl on his bruised face. More than once when they happened to be apart from the others, Abby started to ask him what happened. But the rebellious look in his bleary eyes stopped her each time. One part of her was angry with him for causing the whole family so much misery. Another bigger part of her ached and cried silently for him. What was going on in his mind? Did he think none of them cared for him, or what?

After supper he silently drifted outside. Abby

rushed through the dishes, sick with worry. Was he going to run away? Maybe he would be better off if he did, since he and Papa had seemed to become such bitter enemies. But even entertaining that radical idea scared her worse than ever.

Papa had to go to town on business again. Mama went into the bedroom and stretched out across the bed with a cold rag on her forehead, and Lucy, hardly seeming to be touched by the gravity of their situation, was cutting paperdolls out of the catalog. Abby slipped out of the house quietly.

David wasn't in his room. She found him around in the back sitting on a bale of Johnson grass hay. He was staring unseeingly at Wade Collins' cow walking the fence wondering where her calf was. Wade Collins had taken it to the butcher the evening before.

David didn't even stir when Abby sat down on the sand a few steps away, drawing her knees up under her chin, clasping her arms around her legs. Gould's verse, "Now the day is over, night is drawing nigh, Shadows of the evening steal across the sky," was happening now. It was almost night, a peaceful time—at least it should be.

After awhile she said softly, "What're you thinkin', David?"

She didn't expect an answer, but in a minute he said, "That I shouldn't of been born."

She chided quietly, a bit impatiently, "That ain't no way to think."

Silence for a minute, then he added, "And that I wish there wasn't no such thing as croppin'."

"It's the only chance some folks has got to make a livin'," she reminded him, wondering how far she could go before he would shut her out as he had been doing all of them lately. "Folks that cain't buy their own land

and tractors and things don't have no other way to farm, if it wasn't for croppin'."

"Some livin'."

"You don't have to be one when you grow up."

"I'm already growed up," he said, then added glumly, "Once't a cropper, always a cropper."

"Oh, that's just a sayin' and you know it."

He took a deep breath. "We're fourth generation croppers."

"So? Papa or none of them got any schoolin' much. You're getting schoolin'. And you're smart like Papa. A bunch of teachers has told you that, not just Mr. Tolsey. What'd that one teacher—your science teacher —what'd he say that time?"

"I dunno."

He did, of course. Papa used to mention it every once in awhile. "He said you was a genyus with your hands and your head, too."

"What good's a genyus out in a cotton patch?"

"Well, don't stay in any cotton patch," Abby jabbed back, still impatient. David was just having pity parties. She had thought maybe Connie Collins would pull him out of that, but it seemed as though he had two lives now, the one at school and on the bus with Connie in which they sat or walked together and talked deeply and even held hands, and life at home where he mostly spoke when spoken to, and never laughed.

She continued, "After you graduate you can go to college, now that—" As though a cup of ice water had splashed in her face, she stopped abruptly, recalling the circumstances that would allow David to attend college now.

"Ain't no share cropper ever went to college. And I sure ain't goin' on bootleggin' money."

Abby declared indignantly, "Even Booker T.

Washington found a way to go to college. Went to Hampton Institute. And he was borned a slave. Tells all about it in *Up From Slavery.* He even advised presidents part time."

"What's Booker T. Washington got to do with it?"

"Oh, you're just bein' bullheaded. Ain't you never heard of workin' your way through? That's what I'm thinkin' about doin' myself. If I decided to be a teacher instead of a farmer."

"A girl farmer?"

"Sure. A girl *Pachter.* What's wrong with that? Course, I'll probably be married. Maybe. Just work and save money and then go to college. It won't hurt if it takes a few years longer."

David scoffed, "Still chasin' dreams, ain't you? He's makin' whiskey, and you're chasin' dreams all day."

She looked straight at him until he finally gave her a reluctant sidelong glance. Then she said quietly, "You'd be better off if you chased a few yourself."

He shrugged, as though it was a bird-brained suggestion, and they both fell silent. The windmill creaked and groaned as a puff of wind gusted through the wheel and caused it to turn for a minute. Water trickled from the pipe into the tank. In the lot Wade Collins' cow called again for her calf. It was a sorrowful, questioning, high-pitched sound that caused Abby to want to go comfort her. She had observed that animals are kind of like people are about their children. They want them close, and to know everything is well.

"Papa just wants what's best for us," she said, staring up at the first stars that had popped out, tiny splashes of gold on a deep blue velvet.

David said nothing.

"You think he couldn't jist up and leave us settin' and go off to the city and stay? It wouldn't take much for jist him to get by if that was all he was worried about."

Still nothing from David.

"You think he'd break the law jist on account of himself? You know he wouldn't."

"You glad he's bootlegging, or what?" David asked in a hard voice.

"No, I ain't glad," she puffed up. "But I can see why he's doin' it. I cain't agree. But at least I can see why."

"I figgered you'd take up for him eventually," David said flatly. "You always do. Just like Mama."

"I might take up for him," Abby countered, "But that doesn't mean I'm takin' up for what he's doin'."

"What's the difference?"

"A lotta difference."

"He always said do like old Abe Lincoln and stand with anybody that stands right, and part with him when he goes wrong. That's what I aim to do."

That was true, and Abby could think of nothing to come back with. Finally she said hesitantly, "I don't think Abe Lincoln meant to go against your own family, though. It was him that said a house divided against itself can't stand up. So if it was Abe Lincoln, maybe he'd say go to Papa and try to explain how you feel—without goin' stark, raving mad—"

But she knew that was useless to suggest to David so she didn't bother to finish. It seemed as though he was getting more and more proficient at being stark raving mad.

It was full dark now, and all around them was noisy with night sounds. The night birds, a ceaseless throbbing of crickets and locusts (jar-flys Abby called them, because Papa did) and the shriek of the windmill wheel, shifting with the changing wind. Even some frogs had managed to find the dampness under the horsetank, and made that their home. Wade Collins' cow was getting more insistent, probably because when it was good and dark it made the lonesomeness worse. She was pacing the lot, where she was locked in so she wouldn't charge through a weak place in the fence in her desperation, and she occasionally bellowed in distress.

"Old Daisy wants her calf," Abby said, pityingly.

David got up and wandered over and picked up a dried cornstalk from the pile by the lot fence, forever a sucker for animals. Especially sorrowing ones. He held the stalk through the fence and Daisy came to him, sniffing and blowing, and reached her tongue out for a bite. Abby came up and stood beside him. They watched Daisy chew hungrily, her sorrow forgotten for a moment.

"How come your eye is black and everything?" Abby asked experimentally.

"Fight."

"Who with?"

"Some kid."

"You didn't never use to fight."

"I didn't ever use to have a reason."

"What was your reason?"

"My business."

"Papa's bootleggin'?"

No answer.

"How come you didn't come home till so late last night?"

"Didn't feel like it."

"Didn't you know you'd get in trouble?"

A silent shrug.

"Was it you that drove the car off?"

"Yes."

"Where'd you go?"

A faint smile played about his lips. "Connie's, for one place."

"To her house?"

Again David said nothing.

"You went to her house? What did her mother say?"

He moved his shoulders vaguely. "Her mother didn't know. I been visitin' at her window twice now, since that day in the pasture. So I just dropped by there last night to see if she wanted to go to town."

"To town? Did she?"

"Naw. Said it wasn't right to slip out."

"What good's visitin' at a window?"

Again he smiled slightly and shrugged carelessly. "She knows she's been kissed now."

"You kissed her?" Abby asked in disbelief, thinking of David's unusual hesitancy toward Connie that day in the pasture.

He looked serenely out across the lot, his uninjured eye glimmering.

"Where?"

"On her lips. Where do you think!"

"No! I mean where were you? At her window?"

He nodded again, hiding his slight grin by pretending to be interested in something to the opposite direction from Abby. "You didn't think her mother'd let her come outside, did you?"

"Did her daddy know?"

"Nope. I reckon he would of charged me through a wall, if he had."

"What'd Connie do when you kissed her?"

Grinning self-consciously, he said, "Everything she was supposed to."

"You mean—did she put her arms around you? Through the window and all? And kiss you back, or something?"

"Sure. That ain't no big deal, is it?"

But David's slightly foolish expression told her it was a big deal. He leaned with his muscular arms against the fence, his back straight and proud, preening for a moment in the knowledge that Abby was properly impressed with his prowess. "I'll tell you something else," he said, becoming slightly braggadocious, "I kissed her two times last week, and five times last night."

"Five times!"

Abby shook her head, trying to fathom that sort of boldness. "What's it like? Kissin', I mean."

He shrugged, blushing, "I dunno. It ain't something you can describe exactly unless you're Elizabeth Barrett Browning. Just picture yourself floatin' off on a cloud or wakin' up in heaven or something like that."

Abby tried to picture those conditions but they didn't really seem related to kissing.

She reached out a hand and scratched Daisy's ear through the fence, contemplating all the things David had said. She could picture him kissing a girl one time, maybe, or even two. But five times? That seemed as though it might be bordering on intemperance.

"Where'd you go after that?" she asked thoughtfully.

"Town."

"What's at town that you had to steal the car for?"

"I didn't steal the car."

She was quiet for a minute, giving David time to get over her accusation. It was a wonder he hadn't pierced her through with his verbal sword by now, or merely refused further comment. "Did you stay in town all night, or something?"

At first she thought he wasn't going to answer this time. Then, "Yep. In jail."

"Jail!" She looked closely at him in order to assure herself he was only making a joke.

He got another corn stalk for Daisy and watched her chomp into it. "Reckless drivin'," he said calmly. "Disturbin' the peace. Out after curfew. Besides," and he looked at her straight, his swollen black eye menacing, his other one blue and exactly like Papa's, piercing into her, "We was drunk, me and Bobby Jack Davidson."

She looked at him, mortified to silence.

"We was drunk on his whiskey," he added defiantly.

"Why?" Abby whispered.

"Seemed like a good idea."

"Well, it wasn't," she said angrily. "Now everybody in town'll think the Easons ain't no better than some of the other sharecroppers, or thieves or just any old bit of trash. And Bobby Jack Davidson isn't anybody fit for you to run around with."

David snorted. "You sound like somebody else I know. And I told him, just like I'm tellin' you, the Easons aren't any better, anyways. Not now, they aren't. We got a bootlegger for an old man. How do you like them apples?"

"You told that to Papa?"

"Why not?"

"What'd he do, then?"

"Said he was goin' to bust me."

"Well, you needed it. Did he?"

"Nope. I said he'd never see me again if he did."

"You should be ashamed," Abby said, near tears.

"What for? As long as he isn't ashamed of what he's doin', I'm not ashamed of what I'm doin'." And David sauntered away, hands in his pockets and swinging his shoulders in that cocky swagger of his.

"That doesn't even make sense!" Abby half-shouted

to his back. "Papa is ashamed." But David kept going.

Daisy was walking the fence again, bellowing, then listening and looking searchingly into the darkness. Abby saw her through a blur of tears, and tried to swallow the ache in her throat.

Papa had always said, with Thomas Moore, "Earth has no sorrow that Heaven cannot heal," and she had always clung to that belief. Now, for the first time ever she was beginning to wonder if it was really true. So many things had happened that she never would have dreamed of. Values and feelings trampled, almost surely irreparably. But the deep pain and longing inside her caused her to whisper helplessly into her hands, as she had many times of late, "Oh, Lord, help us get back like we used to be."

When Daisy called mournfully for her baby again, Abby slipped through the fence and put her arms around the cow's warm, flabby neck, soothing her, talking to her, and crying just a little for both of them.

Chapter Thirty-two

DAVID AND CONNIE'S romance enjoyed considerable preeminence. Even down at Cal's Cafe it was alluded to once or twice between comments concerning the unusual rat problem at the Rogue Theater or the scattered rains that had allowed most of them to get their wheat in at last. Some of them were of the opinion Wade Collins would send his croppers packing as soon as cotton was out, thereby putting a quick end to the impossible attraction.

At school the teachers discussed the affair between classes, speculating about the improbable couple, handsome and so sweet to be sure. Just to think—the sharecropper's son and the landlord's daughter. That didn't happen often if at all, even in rural Oklahoma. A Romeo and Juliet situation; very indescribably romantic—with little chance of survival.

And like Romeo and Juliet's parents, Connie's were understandably hostile, especially Mrs. Collins, so the talk went anyway. Her jurisdiction, however, didn't extend into the schools (even if her husband was on the school board) and forbidding contact would not have been logical considering the couple had most classes together and both rode the school bus daily. So for the most part, diplomacy was displayed in public while in the privacy of her home, it was reported that Sue Collins was having a hissy fit, insisting the Easons should quietly transport themselves across-state.

Actually, speculations were that David would be leaving anyway, what with the trouble with his Dad (which wasn't surprising since sharecroppers and their equivalent always are somewhat unstable anyway). Then the Collins' problem would be solved without further complications unless . . . . David decided to take Connie with him.

Twice David was called into the principal's office and reprimanded sharply for displaying too much intimacy in the hallway. For those unusual displays of verve and boldness, his prestige shot to an all-time high. A few girls even tried, behind Connie's back of course, to overthrow her position. Stacey Dunsmore was one of them, and after striking out she took the failure out on Abby—as well as anyone else who crossed her path.

At home, the cold war raged on while cotton was gathered and wheat fields plowed and planted and bundles hauled in. Abby had read of such things in books—members of families disagreeing and becoming strangers. Now she was experiencing it. Living with strangers in the house drastically changed the atmosphere. Abby had the feeling that David wouldn't be with them much longer.

It was one of the few situations she had struggled with which literally defied any solution. Even if Papa quit bootlegging, the damage was done, and as he had said that one night, there was no way to go back. Some things you couldn't undo; they merely had to be forgiven—and David showed no tendency toward that. Besides, they still had to have money to exist one way or the other, and cotton prices weren't going to sky-rocket just because people needed them to.

So life went on, with occasional laughter and ordinary occurrences, even some unusual ones (such as Lucy's being invited to a birthday party by a classmate whose father was on the city council). The fact that the entire class received the invitation instead of the usual select few, did nothing to dampen her enthusiasm. She was so jittery and excited on the day of the party that she lost her breakfast before getting on the bus that morning.

Oddly enough, Abby found she was able to function by setting her mind to it. She occasionally experienced a bleakness that caused her to stare into space for a moment, wondering how it had all come about and where it would all end.

Probably the greatest burden of all was not being sure about anything, namely David's plans for the future, which caused Abby to bring the subject up one day while the two of them were stacking sudan bundles for Wade Collins in his stack lot.

David was throwing them off the flat-bed wagon and Abby was rolling them into place; two parallel rows with heads inside so birds couldn't steal the grain, topped by a single row lengthwise in the middle, then more parallel rows until the entire stack was shaped like a small house with a sloping roof, designed to keep out moisture. Abby didn't mind the work, but she was wary of centipedes and other critters that often made their home in the caked dirt on the bottoms of the bundles.

David stopped once to try to remove a grass burr from his hand with his pocket knife, and Abby leaned on the wagon nearby, watching and working up her courage to ask the question that hounded her.

"David," she finally said, softly and hesitantly, "You thinkin' about going away sometime?"

He didn't move or anything except for the knife he was prodding gingerly into the heel of his hand as he attempted to ferret out the sticker. Finally, "What makes you think that?"

"They're sayin' it at school."

More silence. The sticker was out at last and David was poking the knife blade into the weathered boards of the wagon bed.

"Are you?" she asked, breathless for some reason.

With finality he said in a low voice, "I reckon."

Her heart skipped painfully, though she had anticipated the answer. "When?"

"I dunno yet."

"What about Connie?"

"I dunno that yet."

"You goin' to Winburn Tolsey's?"

"No. I won't drag them into this. He's probably got other cats to skin by now, anyway. Besides, I gotta make it on my own. I've gotta show everybody I can make it without anybody but me."

"Everybody needs somebody."

"Someday, but not right now."

She sighed, picking at a splinter of wood. "Do you think Wade Collins 'll send us packin'?"

"Not if I leave first."

"Is that why you're goin'?" she asked, almost wishing it was, but knowing it wasn't.

David shook his head, not so much in a negative reply as in an unwillingness to even make a comment. Then he said in gruff reassurance, "Old Wade Collins is not goin' to do something that stupid. Mrs. Collins might try, but not him. He'll put the hindrance to her if she doesn't watch out."

"David, couldn't you and Papa . . . .?" It was useless, she realized, but she pushed on. "Couldn't you figure out something without leavin'?"

He looked at her, his blue eyes squinting for an answer. "Seems to me you got more questions than I got answers."

She wanted to plead, but for once she didn't. She had come to the conclusion that his going was inevitable, and maybe even for the best.

"Have you thought about Mama—how she'll fret?"

David shrugged, emphasizing his youth and uncertainty. He pushed the pocketknife into his pocket, stood up and began working again, silent and somber, and Abby did the same.

The air was autumn crisp, the sumac a lovely purple and red, the chinaberries a brilliant yellow, but for now the beauty was wasted on both of them as they set about finishing the stacking of bundles for Wade Collins.

At breakfast Abby broke open her biscuit and poured on sorghum molasses, watching it ooze off the sides and drip stickily onto her plate. She was taking her first bite when Lucy slammed the door and announced, "David ain't in his sleepin' room!"

Her heart skipped, but she continued calmly cutting up her biscuits. Mama turned from the stove. "He may be in the outhouse, or helping Papa finish chores. Go see, Lucy, or he's goin' to miss the bus."

David had done it. Abby had been half expecting it since he had mentioned it last week. It had happened, she was certain. Another prodigal like the Bible mentions, only David didn't have any substance to take with him. Not that she knew about anyway, except for one dollar and forty-three cents. He had not accepted one penny of bootlegging money, even though Papa had offered it.

She couldn't finish her biscuit. Her stomach began twisting and rolling. She felt tears welling in her eyes and spilling down her cheeks. "Mama," she said faintly, "I think I'm gonna throw up—"

"Here," Mama said hurriedly, "Let me fetch the slop bucket."

Holding her middle, Abby made her way to the bed in the front room and lay across it.

"Do you need this?" Mama asked, setting the galvanized bucket beside the bed.

"I hope not," Abby whispered.

"I'll git a cool rag for your head," Mama said, and under her breath as she hurried away, "Lands, if it ain't one thing, it's two more."

Lucy was in again, stuttering in her excitement. "Papa ain't seen David neither. He looked in the outhouse and jist everywhere. He's lookin' in his room now jist to make sure."

Papa came in. "David's gone. His bed ain't been slept in."

He sounded matter-of-fact and unconcerned, but Papa was good at disguising his feelings. "I'm gonna run over to Richard Elliot's and see if he knows where he is."

Abby sat on the side of the bed as Papa left, wondering if she should tell them David mentioned leaving. She leaned against the rail for a minute. Her heart was thudding. "Lucy, we better hurry and get ready," she said weakly.

Mama had been looking out the window at Papa leaving in the car. She turned back to Abby. "Child, your face is white. Maybe you better stay home today. Must be a stomach complaint going around. I'll mix you a raw egg and milk. Wish I had some Black Draught for tea." And to Lucy, "Git a move on, Lucy Belle. The bus is gonna be here any minute now."

"Without David or Abby?" Lucy asked anxiously.

Mama was in the kitchen now putting away the breakfast almost no one had touched. "Git your teeth brushed," she said.

Lucy whimpered, whispering to Abby, "I don't wanta go without you, Abby. What if something is wrong with David?"

"David's alright," Abby reassured her. "Hurry now . . ."

"I'm too little to go by myself," Lucy persisted tearfully. "Tell Mama."

"Lucy," Abby said weakly but firmly. "You're almost ten. David went to school by hisself when he was six. I went to school a lotta times by myself when I was six or seven if David stayed home to work or was sick."

When Lucy was at last gone to the bus, Abby lay back and closed her eyes, totally unrelaxed. Where was David now? Out on Highway 66 walking? In somebody's car, miles away? Hurt maybe? Scared? "Oh God, take care of David," she sobbed under her breath.

Papa drove in a few minutes later and Abby sat up expectantly and Mama rushed to the door. He came in silently, brushing past Mama's inquisitive glance and sat at the table, his face gray and lined with weariness.

"Travis?" Mama wanted Papa to speak, steadying herself with one hand on the back of a chair.

"I went to Richard Elliott's," Papa said in a monologue. "Richard was down to his daddy's store. They all was. They was missin' some money. Richard wouldn't say nothin' at first, then he said David told him he was gonna break in and git some money so's he could take a bus somewheres. Run away. David's run away, and now Buzz Elliot's got the law after him."

Mama turned away, her hands pressed to each side of her face. She walked in a daze to the window in the front room, over to the dresser, and then to the wall. She leaned her forehead against the heavy brown wallpaper with the dull pink flowers and deep inside her there began a long, low wail that got louder and higher until it seemed to pierce everything within Abby—that same, strange piercing as when Daisy cried for her calf. Then Mama began sobbing uncontrollably.

Abby ran to her, but Papa had already reached her. Mama turned away, standing uncertainly and fearfully backed up against the iron bed rail like an animal, her eyes wild and frightened, breathing hard.

"Now, Maudie—"

"I want my boy," Mama said, weeping, pushing at Papa as though she didn't know what was going on. "I want my baby boy, Travis."

"Now, Maudie, it's gonna be alright," Papa said gruffly, rubbing her back with one hand and trying to gather her into his arms. "You gotta git aholt of yourself."

Mama squirmed and pushed away and leaned her forehead against the wall again, moaning and rocking back and forth, still crying. "It was the bootleggin', Travis. That's what the last straw was. The bootleggin'."

Papa's face contorted into a look of raw realization, then shock, then rage. In the next instant the anger was gone and he slumped defeatedly, melting against the dresser with one arm, rubbing his whiskery jaw with the other hand.

"I know it," he said brokenly, breathing heavily, his eyes closed. "Oh, *Gott*. Oh, *Gott*! I know it."

At school the next day, David's name was heard in every conversation. The stories about him grew out of proportion and Abby listened in a daze. He had a gun, some had said. He shot at one man, she heard. Said if his old man could bootleg, he could do worse than that. He had robbed Elliott's grocery store by breaking a window and cleaning out the cash register when the Elliots were just barely scraping by anyway. He had gone to Dallas. No, he was going to Oklahoma City. He ran away. No, they said he was picked up by this weird looking truckdriver and kidnapped. He was headed for Borger to work in the carbon plant. No, it was eastern Oklahoma to the sawmills. He had asked Connie Collins to go, and she had come within an inch of doing it, but her father said he'd kill them both.

Connie? Abby decided to talk to her, and found her during the noon hour sitting on the back steps of the school by herself. She looked up, her face tear-stained. "Everyone's talking bad, Abby," were her first words. "David wouldn't have a gun or rob a store."

Abby sat down beside her dejectedly. "Richard Elliot said he robbed it."

"I think Richard's making it up."

"Richard was his friend."

"I know, and David told me Richard loaned him that money, and I believe him."

"You talked to him before he left?"

She nodded, looking down at her hands, wondering if she was talking too much. "He came to tell me goodbye."

"Did he say where he was goin'?"

She hesitated, but she had to tell somebody. "He wasn't sure. Maybe to eastern Oklahoma, Sallisaw or Poteau, or somewhere. He wasn't going to write because—well, it would make problems. He wants to work and save some money to go to college."

A flame leaped hot inside Abby. David was still chasing dreams. Great! At least he hadn't given up.

"Abby—don't tell anybody. He wanted me to go at first. Said we would get married. And I wanted to so much, but I told him we had to wait. Wait till we're older and we both know for sure. Abby, I'm afraid he got mad at me," she sobbed. "But I didn't know what Daddy would say, much less Mother."

"He told you he's still gonna try to go to college someday?" Abby asked again, just to make sure she had heard that part correctly.

Connie nodded affirmatively, her damp eyes sparkling. "David's smart, Abby. You've no idea. All the teachers talk about it. Even Daddy thinks so. But Daddy doesn't—" Her eyes were downcast again. "Daddy doesn't know if it's a good idea to—like a sharecropper. Like him that much I mean. What I mean, he said we're used to different things . . ."

Abby smiled a little, thinking deeply. "Someday," she said softly, feeling the hope burn briefly inside her again. "Someday maybe he won't be a sharecropper. Maybe none of us will."

Chapter Thirty-three

THE CADILLAC THAT drove in late one evening was long and sleek and a very soft blue. Standing at the window, Abby could see through the barren branches of the elm tree as Mr. Tolsey got out and went around the car to open the door for his wife.

A tremor of dread went through her. Quite likely the Tolseys were coming to tell them something about David. That he was living with them now, and going to school, but that he would rather not see them just yet. Though they desperately wanted to learn of David's whereabouts and to find that he was well, she felt Papa was not up to hearing the other part of the news.

"I think I heard a car," Mama said from the stove where she was draining hot grease from the skillet of fried potatoes. At the same time Papa stepped inside the back door carrying two foaming buckets of milk.

"I'll strain the milk," Abby said hurriedly. She set out the empty milk jars and got the clean tea towel and began pouring the milk through, her anxiety mounting as she waited for the knock.

Papa was washing his hands when it came. Mama set down the steaming platter of potatoes and went to answer the door.

Framed by the doorway, the Tolseys looked the same: he very lean and fit and authoritative, she very dainty and self-assured. Mama stepped back, shocked, almost as though she had been slapped. Impulsively, she stuttered out an invitation for them to come inside. Then she turned reluctantly to Papa.

"Travis, we—got company."

Papa was drying his hands, and though the lines

around his eyes seemed to tighten a bit, his expression didn't change much. "Looks like we do at that," he said. He turned to hang the threadbare towel on the nail near the washstand and took his time about turning back to the couple who stood waiting expectantly just inside the door.

Papa's lack of cordiality, and especially the absence of a greeting, filled Abby with great uneasiness. Mama stood stiffly with a hand still on the doorknob, and Lucy stared, wide-eyed in the presence of such nobility.

"We were driving through," Mr. Tolsey began after clearing his throat. To Abby he seemed as ill at ease as they did, like back when they first began their ludicrous pursuit of David. "We are on our way to Kathleen's parents for Thanksgiving. We thought we'd just stop in and say hello to you people, and to David if he's here."

Papa pushed one hand part-way into his pocket and studied for a moment. "David ain't here."

His voice sounded accusing, and the Tolseys must have felt it. Mr. Tolsey forced a slight, questioning smile. "I guess we didn't pick an opportune evening then, did we?"

"I reckon not," Papa answered.

Abby glanced furtively at Mrs. Tolsey, and the baby blue eyes were the same, vaguely pleading, disappointed, yet confident. As she moved slightly her soft, flowered dress swished gently about her dark-hosed legs. A pearl necklace and earbobs shone richly, picking up the various pastels of her dress, and the high heeled pumps she wore were a lovely blue, as well as the handbag she held. "We're truly sorry to have missed him. I don't suppose he will be in any time soon.?"

"I reckon not," Papa said again, still unsmiling.

"Well, then—we'll be on our way," Mr. Tolsey said.

"I see you folks are about to have dinner." He touched his wife's arm lightly as though to steer her away, but he hesitated briefly. "You might just mention to David that we were in town and would have enjoyed visiting with him for a bit."

For a moment Papa said nothing. Then, in a hard voice he said, "I don't reckon we'll be a-seein' him for a while."

Abby had been rinsing the straining cloth and now she hung it on the curtain rod so it might dry in the night breeze. She didn't dare look, but from her side-vision she could see the way Papa's one hand was hanging limply at his side, yet was compulsively clenching and unclenching. For a moment she felt even more acutely the tension in the room.

The Tolseys turned back in silence and curiosity, waiting for an explanation. When Papa failed to elaborate, but continued to view their visitors with disgust and undisguised animosity, Mama felt compelled to explain, "David, he ain't—with us jist now. He—we . . ."

She turned helplessly to Papa and in the brief, electric silence that followed, Lucy's voice pierced the air, declaring proudly, "David, he up and run away."

"Lucy Belle," Papa reprimanded quietly. "Git on over at the table and set down."

"I don't understand," Mrs. Tolsey said softly, the large blue eyes troubled, starting to fill with tears.

Papa spoke quietly, deadly, his squinted blue eyes trained on Mrs. Tolsey, his words quite obviously for the benefit of her husband. "We don't rightly understand it, neither. All we know is that sometimes the folks with money steps in where they don't belong and they start in a-spouting off some cock-and-bull notions to boys that ain't full-growed enough to let it slide off and then them boys, they git so fulla idees that they ain't got room for reasonin', nor for no idees except what they think they need now and not what's best in the long-run." Papa's voice trembled, his anger and bitterness gushing out of his mouth. "We don't understand it neither, like I said, but we got a purty fair idee how it all started out."

Mr. Tolsey stepped forward instinctively to shield his wife. "Mr. Eason, what you're trying to say is that Kathleen and I are responsible?"

"All we know is, David was a boy anybody could git along with before he met you. He didn't never cause no ruckus. He worked hard with his hands. We was all together and doin' good—"

Mrs. Tolsey's delicate white hand fluttered to her throat and lightly grasped the string of pearls about her neck. "But we had no idea—"

Her husband interrupted, "I regret the impression you have formulated, Mr. Eason, but David is not and was never common laborer motivated. I've recognized you as an intelligent man with sound judgement, and I believe you understand the simple facts. Now—I'm not saying David was not a good worker. I'm saying that his intelligence simply has to be tapped. His type of intellectual endowment is seen so infrequently that it has to be classified as singular—very, very unique, very rare indeed. Now, I ask you—could we stand by—"

"It wasn't nobody's place to come in and turn him against his own people," Papa said harshly. Suddenly he seemed to remember his audience, his youngsters, one of whom was standing inertly near the table, the other sitting at the table and absorbing with curiosity and interest the strange exchange. His voice lowered, but the bitterness remained. "And that's what took place. That's exactly what took place."

"I'm sorry," Mr. Tolsey said. "I truly regret this. However, Kathleen and I felt we were on legitimate ground. I am in the education business, and it is my business to recognize and develop intelligence. Our sole purpose in expending time, energy and, yes, even money on David's behalf was for his personal gain. And even more importantly, perhaps for the gain of mankind. For I believe his capabilities—"

Papa said grimly, "Right now I cain't git too excited about mankind. It's what took place in my own house, and it's who caused it that's a-botherin' me."

For a moment Papa and Mr. Tolsey stood measuring each other, the hostility and bitterness between them literally scorching the air in the room. Abby clenched the edge of the table expecting the slightest movement to set off an explosion. Mama was motionless with her back pressed to the cabinet, and even Lucy dared not to speak a word.

"Very well, then," Mr. Tolsey said, the grueling silence broken. "Very well. I see we've made an enemy, Kathleen." The hard lines of his mouth broke slightly as he looked toward his wife, but the eyes remained narrowed, hard and anxious.

"Oh, Winburn," she began softly. Then the always-confident voice broke, and tears appeared on the long, dark lashes.

Watching her, Papa's voice became subdued, but the antagonism was still very much present. "A man can jist be pushed so far. A man can jist lose so much before he has to say it's enough. You can surely understand that?"

Mr. Tolsey patted his wife's delicate shoulder and fixed Papa with another accusing look. "Somehow I gathered from a letter I once received from David that there were perhaps problems of a domestic nature that

could hardly be ascribed to—shall we say—outsiders."
Once again Papa's free hand began clenching and unclenching. He seemed not to hear or chose to ignore the allegation. When he spoke his voice vibrated with the agitation and helplessness he was feeling. "I'm askin' now that the two of you leave and that you don't never set foot on a place of mine ever again. I'm askin' that. I ain't tellin', mind. I'm askin' because I'm trying to be nice and civilized."

Mr. Tolsey nodded, " As you will. Kathleen?"

But Mrs. Tolsey gently pulled from the grasp of her husband's firm hand and turned back. There were tears in her voice and on her face. She looked sympathetically to Mama, then said to Papa, "Mr. Eason, I do feel we owe you an apology." She looked quickly at her husband, hoping to get a glance of approval. He stood, stoney-faced and silent.

"Not for recognizing and attempting to promote David academically. But I fear we—" and here she brushed quickly at a tear— "we did get too personally involved. You see, we had wanted a son for many years, Winburn and I. And there was something about David—"

"Kathleen—"

"Please, Winburn." The baby blue eyes pleaded with him briefly. To Papa, she continued, "You see, there was a kind of bond building among the three of us—I can't explain how or why. It's just that we love—care about him very much. And I'm afraid we allowed that to enter into the relationship. It just happened. We didn't plan it, and perhaps we inadvertently allowed it to cause us to become—self-assertive, even pushy. I—"

"Kathleen, we will be on our way now."

Nodding, Mrs. Tolsey added quickly, "I beg you to forgive us. And I'm so very, very sorry about David's and your misunderstanding." She turned to Mama. There was a smile exchanged, and Mrs. Tolsey's delicate hand sought out Mama's, and she squeezed it hard but tenderly. Abby could see that an understanding, a sympathy for one another was exchanged at that moment.

Then they were gone, and Papa was standing unmoving with the one hand still thrust into his pocket, and a look of strain and trouble on his face.

In a very uncertain voice, Mama said timidly, "Travis, it's time to eat."

Neither the potatoes nor the pot of beans were steaming now, and the homemade lightbread was drying on a plate. Abby busied herself pouring the milk and Mama sliced up an onion, all of them uncomfortable, waiting for Papa to move or speak.

"I reckon I won't be eatin' right now," he said.

"But I made a big skillet of 'taters," Mama reminded him.

"I better go shut the windmill down. Looks like the wind's up."

"I can put aside some of the 'taters. There's plenty of beans."

Papa was moving wearily for the door. "No need. I'll eat somethin' tomorrow."

"Oh goody, Abby," Lucy said after the door had quietly closed. "We git all the 'taters we can eat."

Abby nodded, trying to smile as she placed the glasses of milk around.

"Miz Tolsey's the purtiest lady I ever seen," Lucy added. "Ain't she to you, Mama?"

"She's purty, all right," Mama admitted quietly.

"Wish I had a dress like hers. Someday, when I git big . . ."

While Lucy fantasized aloud, Mama and Abby sat in a strangely resigned silence wondering what would happen next and how all of it had come about in the first place.

Chapter Thirty-four

"CLASS," MRS. TATE said, rapping for attention. "As you know, sometime back I had each of you write a composition on a subject of your choosing for a contest sponsored by the *Beckham County Democrat*. I was pleased with the results. A number of you show exceptional ability to express yourself through your writing."

She straightened a stack of papers, smiling a bit. "I received word from Mr. Herring, the editor, that we have a first place winner in our class."

The class gasped softly. This was an honor usually won by a senior. The recipient would receive a certificate in front of the entire student body at the end of school and have his composition and picture on the front page of the newspaper.

Abby glanced at Darlene, who was exceptionally good at writing, and mouthed the words, "I bet you won."

Darlene smiled, shrugging. "I doubt it," she mouthed back.

Across the room Stacey and Sherry and a girl named Tracy were whispering. Stacey's face was pink with excitement and expectation and Abby knew she thought she was the winner. She pictured how Stacey would react when Darlene's name was called and felt a sort of haughty satisfaction. Then she reprimanded herself good. She would not fall into the trap of envying and despising as so often happened to sharecroppers and others who were the subject of ridicule by others.

Mrs. Tate was still smiling, pleased with the interest shown by her students. She continued, "I'm going to ask the author of the winner composition, Abigail Eason, to come forward and read what she has written."

Abby was mortified. The possibilty of winning had never, ever entered her mind. The blood rushed to her head and started pounding in her ears. Her knees became weak and her palms sweaty. For a moment she was glued to her chair. There was a buzz of voices around her and for some reason she looked over at Stacey Dunsmore.

Stacey looked as thunderstruck as Abby felt, and for a moment their gazes seemed riveted. Then Stacey tossed her head, looking the other way, and Darlene was whispering, half-laughing, "Are you gonna just sit there?"

All eyes watched her as she made her way, terrified, to the front. She felt them all around her because she could not lift her head nor train her eyes to any point other than the floor. She was certain she would be unable to speak once she reached the front with all of them staring, some harboring good will, others bad.

She trembled as she took the paper from Mrs. Tate, who smiled encouragingly. She opened her mouth to read and the words came squeaky and unstable at first.

> "Having been a sharecropper all my life, I have learned some things about work and even more things about human nature."

She cleared her throat and made an effort to stabilize her voice, to read with conviction, because she knew she was speaking the truth.

> "It seems to me that people are divided into two classes: Those who have and those who do not. Sharecroppers are in the second category because they do not have many of the world's goods, such as nice houses and clothes and cars. I believe it is a mistake to draw a line between two groups of people just because they dress differently or do not use good grammar or have extra money. I believe people should be judged by

what is in their hearts and minds and not by what their hands do for a living nor what kind of clothes they carry around on their backs, nor how much money is in their pockets.
It is character that counts.
There have been times when I was ashamed of being a sharecropper. But Papa always said the most noble position in the world is not where we stand, but how we stand—and in what direction we are headed. Sharecropping is honest work and that is what matters."

She glanced up again and Stacey Dunsmore was staring at her sullenly. Abby smiled unexpectedly—a smile utterly void of malice or envy. Suddenly there was only pity, but even that was quickly masked because she knew Stacey could probably stand any kind of attitude toward her except pity.

"I will try never to be ashamed of sharecropping again, though I will also work hard to try and step up the ladder another rung or two if the opportunity comes.
A man named John Ruskin, who believed in education and morality, once said, "The highest reward for a man's toil is not what he gets for it but what he becomes by it." By the help of God, and with the love of my family, and because of the work of my hands, I hope to become a better person. I hope to prove that, in God's sight, there is really only one class of people."

She looked up as she finished and some of the kids seemed lost in what she had just read and others looked as though they would snicker if the teacher wasn't present. Some nodded ever so slightly, some were embarrassed, as a certain segment of the population always is when the truth has been spoken.
Abby looked at Darlene, who nodded her approval, and she looked at Stacey once more, who looked right back at her, poker-faced and hostile. There will always be Staceys in the world, but there are also Darlenes. And, the next week when the composition and Abby's

picture—taken in front of the schoolhouse—came out in the newspaper, it was Darlene who meticulously clipped it out, taped it to a pink piece of construction paper, and presented it to her.

It was the Staceys you learned to put up with, Abby decided, thereby developing patience and character. But it was the Darlenes who make life more worthwhile.

It had snowed some more in the night, one of the earliest snows Abby could remember. Early December, and at least three inches of snow covering the ground and the shinnery trees like a picture from a Currier and Ives calendar. Still snuggled cozily amidst the quilts on the bed, Abby could see the whiteness sparkling in the first rays of morning sun.

"'Late lies the wintry sun a-bed'," she thought dreamily. " 'A frosty, fiery sleepy-head; Blinks but an hour or two and then, a blood-red orange, sets again'."

She wondered idly if R. L. Stevenson had lain in bed this way and watched the few sun rays peering out lazily, over-due because of the faraway drift of clouds in the east and skimpy ones overhead. Probably not. Probably R. L. Stevenson had hopped out of bed early so he could get in a good full day's writing.

She should be up, herself, but it was nippy cold, even though Papa already had the Franklin roaring with the fire built from shinnery roots and coal they had bought down at the railroad yard ("slack" coal, the kind that had been handled so much it was mostly dust, causing it to sell for much less than chunk coal). She blew out a breath and a puff of vapor appeared, hanging in the air briefly. That proved just how cold it was, so she would stay in bed until she was called. It was Saturday, anyway. No school.

Normally at this time of the year there would be no

school for them even on a school day. Sharecroppers' children spent several weeks in the fall and winter helping gather in the crops. Often the entire school let out for awhile, but whether school was closed or going on made little difference. As Papa used to say, the Easons were smart enough to catch up, so a few weeks' absence wasn't going to be too earthshaking.

This year, for the first time ever, the crops was so small that Mama and Papa were gathering during the day and she and Lucy only after school and on Saturdays. With the snow now, there would be no boll-pulling for anyone until it melted and the cotton dried out again.

In the kitchen Mama was making breakfast and talking to Papa. Almost like old times, but Abby could see Papa in her mind, probably sipping coffee, his face still almost as grey and somber as the day David left.

"I got to git that hen broke up," Mama was saying. "She's been a-tryin' to set all week, now. That's one more egg a day we could be gittin'. And when I go in there to try to gather the other eggs, she takes to me like a floggin' rooster. Lucy's scared clean to death of her. I never seen such fight in one hen."

"We'll git a gunny sack and tie her over the clothesline some time today," Papa said, sounding as though he was only half-way listening.

"Course, we don't use as many eggs now," Mama said.

Now. She meant now that David was gone. Now that they were sure he was gone maybe forever, and not merely hiding at a friend's house for awhile or pulling some other such shenanigans.

"Still," she added, "we don't want to hafta buy none. They're goin' up sky-high in the stores. Pucketts is a-gittin' thirty-nine cents. Somebody said Funderburg's Meat Market's was forty cents."

"Everything is high," Papa said.

There was silence. A spicy aroma was beginning to waft its way into the front room. Mama was apparently baking pumpkin for breakfast, delicious with cold cream poured over it. There were sounds of salt pork snapping and sizzling in the iron skillet and the little squeaks of the table as Mama kneaded and rolled out biscuits.

Then abruptly, but with that strange tonelessness that was always present, Papa said, "I'm gonna tell Anson Dorrel I'm through. For good."

There was absolute quiet except for the salt pork popping. Abby had heard of Anson Dorrel, but she couldn't remember where. It seemed as though that was the name Papa had mentioned the night he told Mama he was going to bootleg.

"Travis," Mama's voice trembled, then she couldn't go on.

"I don't know how we'll make do," Papa said heavily.

"You won't never be sorry," Mama said, and Abby could tell by her voice that she was trying hard to keep from crying. The table began squeaking again as she finished the biscuits.

"The harm's been did," Papa said in a low voice. "Already been did. Quittin' won't change that."

"We have to go on," Mama encouraged. "Got to forgit. The Lord will take care of us."

"It ain't somethin' a man forgits," Papa said. "Turnin' his own flesh and blood again him. Makin' him into a thief."

Abby held her breath. Except for that one instance during Winburn Tolsey's visit, this was the first time she knew of that Papa had mentioned David since the morning they found he was gone.

"Still, you cain't let it—you cain't let it keep a-eatin' on you so, Travis," Mama said softly. "It's been nigh on to two months."

Papa was quiet for a minute. Then, "I guess it ain't somethin' a man gits over. I guess he jist takes it to the grave with him."

Abby's throat constricted and she felt a familiar dread envelope her. Papa had seemed to die a little every day since David left. It had started to a certain degree when David had first rebelled against him. Maybe Papa was going to be like Grandpa, and pine himself away over circumstances that were long ago out of his hands.

Mama ventured uncertainly, "I been thinkin' we might—be able to find David if we really tried. I've been thinkin' where he might be."

"Wouldn't do no good," Papa said without hope.

"I been a-thinkin' he might be at Winburn Tolsey's by now." Then Mama added hurriedly, meekly, "I ain't aimin' to make you mad, bringin' up his name."

"It wouldn't do no good, finding David, bringin' him back," Papa said. He didn't explain himself, but Mama knew, as well as Abby, what he meant. They had lost David long before he left home and nothing, not even dragging him back and forcing him to stay would remedy that fact.

Papa added without malice, "And Mr. Tolsey—Mr. Winburn Tolsey—" He paused as though thinking out what he wanted to say, "Even Mr. Winburn Tolsey ain't my enemy no more. Never shoulda been. The enemy is what was inside of me, what was inside of David. The thing that grows and gits too big to handle and starts a-callin' the shots and makin' us do what we know better'n to do. That's the enemy. Winburn Tolsey didn't help out none, but he's jist a man like me."

"You done good, a-thinkin' that," Mama said

gratefully. "Awful good. 'Cause it takes a good man to think that-a-way."

A chair scraped back from the table and from the sound of his voice, Papa was standing now. "I'm gonna hunt up Anson Dorrel."

"You ain't gonna eat first?"

"I ain't very hungry," Papa said. "I'll eat some dinner."

"I can have the biscuits done in fifteen minutes."

"I gotta go," Papa said, and there was a touch of the familiar bitterness in his voice. "Now, before I remember that I'm might-near cuttin' off my own lifeblood, and that of my bunch."

"We can make do, Travis," Mama said. Her voice was still trembling, but she sounded determined. "Us, and the Lord. Now you git on and do what you know in your heart you gotta do."

Papa breathed heavily. "I imagine the good Lord done give up a long time ago on helpin' Travis Eason."

The letter came from Aunt Myrtle later that day. Standing by the roaring Franklin, Papa intended to read aloud as usual, but ended up reading for a minute in silence, then handed it to Mama and walked into the kitchen and poured some coffee. Mama read the letter to them a bit haltingly with Abby looking around her shoulder,

> "How's the weather? We're snowed in, but snug as polar bears. Lewis wanted me to write and see if David would be interested in some financial assistance ($$) toward college? Never mind if he has other plans. But we'd be glad to give him a boost, get him started working on those differential analyzers (only I think maybe they're beginning to call them calculators these days). Now, we know how you feel about charity, but this is not charity. Lewis will expect to be paid back (with interest, no doubt!) Lewis is looking for great things out of that child

and is just wanting some insurance that he'll be included in the gravy line someday when David gets rich and famous—and our 'holdings' turn loose, or backfire! You can let us know . . ."

Mama's voice faded out even though there was a bit left unread, and she refolded the letter laboriously with shaking hands. She laid it on the dresser where it remained undisturbed except to dust it off when the regular dusting was done.

Chapter Thirty-five

IF THERE WAS ever a time when anyone lost should return home, it would be Christmastime, Abby reasoned. David had never been away on Christmas. And she was just sure he would have been thinking of them for several days now because of the season, if for no other reason.

They had a tree, the *Tannenbaum*, but it was small and scraggly. Papa had been sick with a fever off and on for over a week, so Abby and Lucy had walked all the way down to the Northfork of the Red River, three miles away, and cut the tree. They had taken the little hatchet with which Papa or David used to fell a tree with two or three blows, but the girls applied more than a dozen ill-placed whacks before the tree finally collapsed at their feet. Then they took turns dragging it with cold-numbed hands three miles through the slushy snow and biting wind until the branches were a muddy, dripping mess. They had to set it out overnight to dry.

For an entire day Abby mulled over in her mind ways to fix up the tree. She had the feeling a pretty one would brighten everyone's outlook, especially Papa's, who was sinking more into sickness every day. Besides, if David did come they wouldn't want him to think they had slacked off on decorations.

They finally made paper chains from catalog pages like last year, and strung possum berries, but they were out of popcorn. The tree looked skimpy as Abby scrutinized it all day. If they just had construction paper they could have made little fans the way they did one year. Papa had thought those fans were the cat's pajamas, she recalled.

At last she thought of something else, and asked Mama hesitantly, "You know the peanuts down in the wellhouse?"

Mama was making divinity candy, stirring the boiling syrup and water carefully, and didn't look up—just nodded.

"Do you think me and Lucy could take some Crayolas and color some of them and put a thread through them with a needle and hang them on the tree?"

Mama glanced up, her face pink with the heat. "Why, that's a right fine idee, Abby-girl."

So she and Lucy set to work, spreading things out in the front room. "Let's make 'em bright colors, like yellow, and orange and red," Abby suggested.

"Maybe Papa would color the red 'uns," Lucy said generously, since red was her favorite color.

Papa was stretched out on the double bed, rolled in a quilt, his eyes closed. "He might not feel up to it," Abby said.

But Lucy asked anyway, and Papa struggled wearily out of the bed and came over and sat on Grandma's rocker near the stove, breathing shallowly, his eyes teary, his face flushed. He took the peanuts and the red crayon Lucy handed him.

"Is your fever broke?" Abby asked anxiously. Mama had been rubbing turpentine and meat grease on his chest for several days now, and heating flannel clothes to drive the medicine in. And he had ingested several doses of coal oil mixed with sugar.

Papa nodded and said weakly and unconvincingly, "Gittin' better all the time, Abby-*Madchen*."

Abby smiled at him quickly. Abby-*Madchen*. That was Grandma's name for her. "I wish Grandma could come," she said.

Papa nodded again, but said nothing because he took a coughing spell that lasted several minutes.

Of course, Abby knew it was best Grandma wasn't here now. "But vhere iss Dafid?" she would ask.

"He's gone," they would answer.

"Out back?" she might say. "*Im Freien?*" Or, "Doing *der* vork?"

"Jist—gone, Grandma," they would say again.

And perhaps her hands would grip the black purse nearer to her and her voice would tremble as she asked them again, in fear and confusion, at such a strange, unimaginable happening. How would they be able to explain to her that David had left them, make her understand the reason for it when they hardly understood it themselves?

The peanuts added a pretty touch to the tree, though the colors were a little duller than Abby had thought they might be. "Mama, do we have enough flour to make snow?" she asked, knowing she shouldn't think so extravagantly.

"Well," Mama said hesitantly. Then she brightened. "I know what you girls could do instead. We have that-there purty foil that was on Aunt Myrtle's Christmas present last year. Why don't you cut some stars out of an old shoe box and cover 'em with that foil?"

The stars were a great success. For several minutes Lucy and Abby stood back and admired them as they shined gently, swinging amidst the branches from their thread holders.

"Wouldn't they look purty with Grandma's *Kerzen?*" Abby asked.

Lucy looked at her blankly.

"The candles, remember?"

Lucy ran to Mama, wildly excited. "Can me and Abby make some candles?"

"We don't have no wax," Mama said.

Lucy deflated instantly. "Aw, we never do git to make candles, or nothin'."

"Wait 'll tonight," Mama said thoughtfully. "And I'll show you somethin' you'll like."

"Candy?" Lucy asked.

"Candy—but something else, too."

"Presents?" Lucy guessed again, getting more excited.

"I'll show you tonight, after it gits dark."

But Lucy kept on. "Santy Claus?"

Mama and Abby laughed a bit. "Nothin' like that," Mama said. "Jist something that'll make a purty sight."

For Christmas Eve supper they had chicken broth soup, rich with Mama's egg noodles, and sweet potatoes that Abby had scrubbed with a rough cloth and rubbed with bacon grease before baking them. Papa had been able to eat hardly anything for almost a week, but he ate a helping of each and even looked a little better afterward. All during supper Abby half-expected David to come blustering in, cold and tired, but happy to see them, and his mouth running in that wonderful, rapscallion way he had. He would have his arms full of presents for all of them, bought with his own paycheck. The presents she didn't care about that much, but it being Christmas he probably would want to surprise them, and she knew he would just have to bring Lucy one.

Then they would all go in to the Christmas tree and David would pluck a peanut off and eat it and remark disparagingly about the tree. "The next time why don't you try to git a *little* one." he would say, even though he would secretly think it looked nice, and was plenty big enough. He would eye the few presents beneath the tree, shaking or squeezing them, with his blue eyes glimmering mischievously (for they had included some for him, just in case). Then Papa would read from the gospel of Luke and they would all sing, "Silent Night."

David didn't come though. Once when the front door rattled, Abby's heart jumped into her throat. When she finally went to the door under the pretense of seeing if it was snowing or anything, there was nothing there, only the wind howling around the corners of the house and the shadowy, leafless elm tree moving ceaselessly.

Abby and Lucy did the dishes while Mama cleaned up the stove where the fudge boiled over. Then they all went back into the front room. Mama had set candy out in bowls. There was the fudge for David, the peanut brittle for Abby, and the divinity for Lucy. It had been that way for years. Of course, the candy was really for everybody, but each of them had their favorite.

"Time to open the presents," Mama said, managing to sound cheery. "Lucy, you be old Santy's elf and hand 'em out."

"What'll I do with David's?"

"Jist—leave 'em under the tree for him."

Abby automatically squeezed her two gifts, trying to guess what they were, while she watched everyone else open the things she had given them. For Lucy she had made a family out of acorns, carving tiny facial features and making little bonnets for the ladies out of cloth from the ragbag, and hats for the men out of scraps of ducking. Lucy was carried away in throes of delight, especially when she found Mama (with Abby's help) had made a tiny playhouse with divided rooms out of a shoebox, and furniture out of colored cardboard. Abby had even made curtains for the windows. For Mama, she had strung china berries saved from the fall for a long necklace and they really did look almost as pretty as jewels, translucent and golden. Mama put them on and declared she liked them better than plastic beads because they didn't look artificial. For Papa, Abby had used some pliable leather scraps and stitched together a pouch to hold pliers. A double slit at the top allowed him to slip it over his belt, and Papa remarked how handy it would be when he was out fixing fence.

Then Abby opened her own gifts. Lucy had used a match box with spool wheels to make her a box that looked like a wagon. "You can use it for a jewelry box," Lucy explained importantly, forgetting Abby owned not one piece of jewelry, not even a pair of plastic earbobs or an imitation pearl necklace. Then she seemed to have a cunning thought. "Unless you'd rather let me take my little acorn-people rides in it!"

Lucy had also drawn pictures for Abby and labeled them with everyone's names. David, a tall, skinny stick, and short, pig-tailed Abby were turning a rope while Lucy jumped it. In another picture they were all sitting around the supper table with an impossibly long-legged turkey on a platter in the center. Lucy was holding a drumstick which had apparently come from some mysterious second turkey, because the one on the table still had both of his. In another, all of them were chopping cotton except Lucy, who was sitting on the car fender eating an apple with a huge smile almost gashing her face in half.

Abby's present from Mama and Papa was a bottle of Gardenia perfume with a beautiful lid of red plastic that fanned out into the shape of a large flower. Lucy begged to use some of it and tipped it against her collar generously, accidentally letting some of it gurgle down the front of her blouse. After that, the whole house smelled faintly of gardenias and cedar and everyone agreed it was rather nice.

Mama went mysteriously into the back room and came back with the Dresden dolls. They were unbelievably charming sitting near the tree, the smooth porcelain gleaming dully in the lamp light. They were like a symbol of all the lovely things tucked far back into the recesses of Abby's memory. All the togetherness, all the other Christmases, all the shared love. They didn't have David now, but they had good memories to bring out anytime they wanted. Maybe they would have to be content with that. Could they? Could, especially, Papa?

After they had admired the dolls Papa told them rather weakly, but more like his old self, that Dresden china was made in Southeast Germany at Meissen, near Dresden, and likely that was where the dolls had come from. Then Mama disappeared into the back room again. This time she came out with a lovely, pure white candle. It was long and slender and perfect, and was set in a tiny crystal holder. They all marveled over its beauty, daring only to look and not touch, lest it be ruined.

"Where'd it come from, Mama?" Abby asked almost in a whisper.

Mama glanced knowingly, and a bit shyly at Papa. "It's our weddin' candle. Remember, Travis? Grandma made it for us. It's been up in my little cedar box all these years."

"Mama," Lucy said, becoming excited. "It's gettin' dark in here. Can we light it? The lamp don't put out much light."

Mama's work-worn hands held the candle lovingly, one finger smoothing the waxy whiteness. "If Papa wants to. It's jist been lit once't. While we was sayin' the vows."

They all looked at Papa, whose chest was rising and falling shallowly, making tiny wheezing noises, and he nodded. Mama got some matches and set the candle by the tree, next to the Dresden dolls. "Blow out the lamp, Abby."

Abby leaned over the lamp on the dresser and blew. Mama struck the match and held it to the candle. The flame caught, almost went out, then came to life. The silver stars dangling on the tree reflected the rays and they all watched in awed silence. Never in her life had Abby seen anything more beautiful.

She saw Mama and Papa smile at each other faintly and Papa, still breathing with difficulty, reached for Mama's hand. Maybe they were remembering the wedding more than nineteen years ago that Mama said had been held in Grandma Eason's front room, with no one present excepting the family and the minister (the *pastor* Grandma called ministers, with the emphasis on the last syllable.).

Looking at the candle now, and imagining what joy and anticipation of their new life together Mama and Papa must have felt back then, Abby felt a bit of hope shining again inside her. Even if David didn't come tonight, he would soon.

Very softly, and a bit hesitantly it seemed, Mama began singing in her clear, perfect soprano. When Abby joined in, then Lucy, the voices were more sure. Finally, almost at the last, even Papa sang, "Sleep in heavenly peace, Sle-ep in heavenly peace."

Sometimes at night in bed when the cold north winds were whistling and whining around the corners of the house, Abby would think of David, wondering exactly where he was in that "far country," and if he ever thought of them. Maybe he didn't have much time to consider his family, immersed as he was in his new life, probably finishing high school and making money and friends and buying clothes, and most of all, climbing eagerly ever upward toward his goal. "A youth, who bore, 'mid snow and ice, a banner with the strange device, excelsior!"

She and Mama still thought David would come to himself one day, as the prodigal son in the Bible had. Maybe he would never be back with them to stay, but both of them believed with intense zeal that he would take steps to mend the cords he had so thoughtlessly broken when he left back there in that outpouring of bitterness and rebellion.

Often on such sleepless nights, Abby's mind would wander from thoughts of David to other memories. She would try to remember what it had been like back when she was young and naive and relatively unconcerned—a babe, really—and she could not. Once, in a moment of wonder, she realized that somewhere along the way she had become an adult, all the while unaware that the metamorphosis was in motion.

It was not at all the way she had thought it would be, a sudden stepping over into a new world, a sudden desire to go to parties and wear earbobs and nail polish and high heels and sheer nylon stockings with seams in the backs. It was more a quiet acceptance of the unchangeable, and a determination to accept life no matter what it handed—or what it took away.

And, deeply contemplating in the darkness of that unusual night, she again pressed her face into her pillow and whispered, as she had so many times, but feeling an exceptional peacefulness now, *"Gott Segne Unser Heim."*

"One thing I can say about Wade Collins is, he don't

mind stickin' his neck out to help a body," Papa said, his breath rising in puffs over his head. He coughed harshly, the way he had been doing since his sick spell at Christmas.

Abby looked up from her place by the Franklin and held her finger between the pages of her book to mark the place. Papa had just come in from town where he had helped Wade Collins take the last load of cotton. He shrugged out of his worn mackinaw and hung it on a nail behind the door.

Mama was sitting by the fire, too, shaking cream in a half-gallon jar in order to make butter. "What'd he do?" she asked curiously.

"Wanted me to help him butcher hogs in a day or so. He'll give us one for helpin', besides all the renderin's, since his bunch don't take to hog lard." Papa got by the stove and rubbed his rough, reddened hands over the heat. "Meat to last till spring, or past."

Hope shone in Mama's eyes. "I always said Wade Collins was different, someway. Even when we heard Miz Collins got all up in the air last fall, Wade Collins jist took it in his stride."

Papa nodded, turned to warm his back and had another spell of coughing before he could say, "It's bitter cold out there, jist right for slaughterin' hogs."

"Here, Abby," Mama said, handing her the jar of cream. "I'll git Papa some hot tea."

"Papa, listen," Lucy said, bending lower to her open school book and reading in her slow-paced, stilted way, " 'Then let us reflect with pleasure, that labor is the source of treasure'. I have to tell what it means." Her pencil hovered over the tablet expectantly.

"You tell me," Papa said.

"I don't even know what the big words mean, let alone the whole thing," Lucy complained. "Reflect?

Labor? We ain't even got a dictionary to look 'em up."

"Reflect means 'think about'," Papa said. "Abby, you tell her what labor means."

"It's what we've been doin' in the cotton patch," Abby hinted, churning the jar vigorously against her lap.

"Pickin' cotton?" Lucy asked incredulously.

Abby laughed a bit, looking at Papa. But he hadn't seemed to hear, being lost in thought as he was so often. "Labor means 'work'," Abby explained. "Now read it over and use think instead of reflect, and work instead of labor."

Lucy lowered her head obediently and read silently, forming the words with her lips. "What does 'source' mean?" she asked then.

Abby thought for a minute. "I don't know how to explain it, exactly. Do you, Papa?"

"What?" Papa asked. So Lucy repeated the question.

"Where a thing comes from, might give you an idee." Papa said, after studying on it for a bit.

Abby had thought of an explanation, too. "Like Brother Whitten says, God is our source of hope," she said, turning the jar slowly to check the progress of the cream. "In other words, He is where our hope comes from."

Mama handed the steaming cup of tea to Papa, who was coughing again. "At least that proves you listen to the preacher once't in a while, Abby-girl. How's the butter comin'?"

"It's thickenin'," Abby said, showing her.

Lucy was deep in her book again. After a bit she looked up and exclaimed, "I don't no more believe that than a man in the moon!"

"Don't believe what?" Abby wondered.

385

"This here is tryin' to say work is pleasureful."

"Well, it is in a way," Abby said. "For instance, when you know you did a good job, don't that make you feel happy?"

"Not me, it don't!" Lucy said.

"Oklahoma's motto even talks about work," Abby persisted. "It says, 'Labor conquers all things'."

"I bet they jist made that up," Lucy said disparagingly.

"I think that quote from your book's purty apt," Abby egged her on. "Who wrote it?"

Lucy squinted at the book again. "A-non-y-mous. I never heard of him."

Abby looked, too. "That's anonymous. It means they don't know who wrote it."

"Well, I don't know why they're a-puttin' it in a book, then," Lucy said, slightly indignant. "There's plenty of things wrote by people everbody knows, like Henry Longworth Wads—Henry Wadsfellow Long—Henry—"

"Henry Wadsworth Longfellow," Abby said.

"Yeah, and all them other people," Lucy said, bending back down to her work.

And Abby thought, "In happy homes he saw the light of household fires gleam warm and bright," for the mention of Longfellow always prompted her to remember that line from "Excelsior." And for just a moment she felt again the longing ache inside that never quite went away. For times past. For David. For Papa.

"Sidemeat and tenderloin and sausage," Mama was saying. "And pork roasts, too. Do you think we might sugar-cure one of the shoulders, Travis?"

"I don't see why not," Papa said vaguely.

"We'll be eatin' fit for kings," Mama said thankfully. "Everyday like Sunday, with meat and all."

She continued to shake the jar, checking it occasionally. Finally yellow flecks of butter began to appear. She shook some more until the butter collected into one nice-sized lump and then set it on the floor beside her chair, thinking for a minute.

"With all the snows we been havin'," she said, "Crops'll be better'n ever this year, come spring. They say snow's got something in it that's as good as store-bought fertilizer for the ground. And it's been cold enough to kill a lotta the grasshopper eggs, I bet. That'll help a bunch. Things is looking up some, ain't they Travis?"

But Papa didn't hear. He was looking out the window, his blue eyes slightly dull and unsmiling, his face somber, lost in thought.

"Well," Mama said briskly. "I better git this-here butter took up and warshed or we won't have no buttered biscuits come mornin'."

Chapter Thirty-six

IN FOUR MONTHS they had almost gotten used to David's empty place at the table. Occasionally Abby still forgot and set him a place, then with an oddly painful embarrassment, she would hastily take it up again. They didn't mention David much—Papa didn't mention him at all—just went on about their business as though a part of them wasn't missing.

In fact, it seemed as though they didn't talk much at all anymore, except Lucy. On this particular night at the supper table it was rather startling when the kitchen door opened and a tall, ragged young man with a scraggly shadow of a beard stood in the dark. Just stood there looking in at them with piercing blue eyes, silently and hungrily. It was David.

No one said anything for the longest time, then Mama rushed over to the door, her breath coming in little gasps. "Davey?" she quavered.

He stepped inside, closing the door. "Mama," he said. Just that, then his voice broke and he could say nothing more. His whiskery face began to crumple and he helplessly bowed his head over, down to Mama's shoulder.

He leaned there against her as though he was a little boy again—a little boy in a man's body. Mama's arms gripped him tightly, almost desperately, and she sobbed and they swayed back and forth. David was hugging Mama, weeping, too, very quietly, ashamed because he hadn't cried in front of anybody for so many years.

Lucy ran to Papa, whispering loudly, as though she didn't know, "Is it David, Papa?"

Papa nodded, his sunken blue eyes staring at his plate.

Abby could hardly speak but she had to say something. She wanted to try and change the dull, unreadable look on Papa's face. "He—he growed a beard," she managed. "And his hair. He—needs it cut, don't he, Papa?"

"How come he's so dirty?" Lucy asked. "And how come he's so tall and his shoulder-bones a-stickin' out?"

Papa merely shook his head. He couldn't speak.

David did look even skinnier and he had grown an inch or two in height, Abby thought in wonder. And his shirt sleeves sticking out from under the cuffs of his faded, too-small Levi jacket, were in tatters, filthy. The bottoms of his pants were shredded. All that in four months.

"I—I'll git some bath water on to git hot," Abby said. She jumped up, jittery and uncertain, and emptied the entire two buckets of water into dish pans and set them on the stove to heat.

Mama became more composed and was saying in a trembly voice, "We jist got through supper. But there's beans and pork hock left. Some poke greens. We had fried taters, too, but they're all gone—"

"Beans sounds good," David said, his voice strained and heavy with emotions he was still trying to keep pushed down. He dragged his chair out and folded his hard, skinny body into it, stretching his long legs out beneath. Lucy sat down in her chair again, poker-stiff, trying hard to keep from looking into his face. He and Papa hadn't even looked at each other yet.

"How's Lucy Belle been?" David asked, his reddened eyes and craggy face smiling at her a little.

Lucy ducked her head down between her shoulders

and tittered uncertainly, then went back over to sit on Papa's lap.

"Lands sake," Mama said, "Here I set and didn't git a plate out."

"I'll git one," Abby said from the cabinet. And to cover all the overwhelming feelings inside her, she said briskly and impatiently, "My lands, David. Are you gonna eat without warshin' them hands?"

He grinned weakly, his blue eyes glittering through the film of tears. "Always the old mama hen, ain'tcha, Ab?"

She plopped the plate down, and a fork and knife. "Here, let me git some more butter out, and the cornbread."

She wished Papa would say something to David, or that David would do something to show Papa he was glad to see him. But they seemed to ignore one another. Papa was just sitting there, not looking around, with one arm loosely slung around Lucy.

Abby poured a big glass of milk and waited while David downed it and then she poured him some more. She was thankful the cow was still giving plenty. "Jist a empty silo, like always," she grumbled, mostly to fill the silence.

David was too busy wolfing the beans to answer, but he nodded.

"They said you robbed Elliot's Grocery," Lucy said, suddenly bold, sitting up straighter in Papa's lap.

David squirmed in his chair, looked up embarrassed, "So I heard."

"Everybody at school said it, 'specially Richard Elliot."

"Well, Richard Elliot's got hisself in a pickle over it," David said.

When he didn't explain himself, Abby prodded,

"You mean you've seen Richard since you got back?"

David paused from his eating, his eyes downcast, still self-conscious. "I went by there this evenin' so I could clean up some before I came home. His Daddy jumped me out and Richard come clean. See—" He gripped his glass for a moment. "Richard loaned me twenty-five bucks when I left. Got it at the store. I was goin' to pay him back later on when I got a job. And he got hisself twenty-five dollars while he was at it. Then he got scared the next day, he said. He got so scared he told them I broke in."

"Well, I'll jist say," Mama exclaimed indignantly. "If he ain't got the gall! I jist knew you couldn't take no money that wasn't yours."

"It's okay now—all squared away. Richard told them everything." David grinned.

"But what about the twenty-five dollars?" Abby asked, sitting back down at the table, feeling weak from struggling for composure.

"I'll pay them back. Buzz Elliot said I could."

Abby breathed a sigh of relief, wondering at the same time how David would ever get that much money.

"Did you spend that much?" Lucy asked in disbelief.

David grinned one-sidedly, still eating as fast as he could. "Easy," he said.

"Did you git a job?" Abby asked.

"Cleaned up a lady's back yard in Seminole. For two sandwiches. Swept the streets one time in Wewoka after they had some kind of doin's. Hauled a little wood with some guy's truck up by Sallisaw. Nobody's hirin' much right now." He wiped a grimy hand over his mouth. "I guess they all side with that English dude that said everybody but idiots knows the lower class has got to be kept pore, so they'll stay industrious."

Papa spoke, his voice barely rising or falling. "Arthur Young needed his head examined when he wrote that."

David nodded, barely glancing Papa's way. "Yeah. Yeah, it was Arthur Young that said that. I couldn't remember his name." He drew a deep breath, thinking for a minute, then raked up another bite of beans. In silence he finished eating and pushed back his plate.

"Best meal I've had since—" He stopped abruptly, gave a little self-conscious grin. "Since I left here."

"How come you left, David?" Lucy asked, innocent and wide-eyed.

David kept looking at his plate, putting his knife and fork just so across the edge, then picking up his empty milk glass.

"You want some more milk?" Abby asked hastily.

"No, I had enough."

"We couldn't figger out where you was," Lucy continued.

David tried to smile again, shrugging his wide, boney shoulders. "I should of stayed home," he said in a low voice. "At least I should of let somebody know where I was goin'."

"Was you hungry a lot?" Abby asked.

"You know me," he said, smiling. " Always hungry."

"You could of jist bought somethin'," Lucy said.

"There was this problem of runnin' outa money," he said self-consciously. "A few times—" He glanced almost, but not quite, at Papa, then down at his hands. "A few times I thought about stealin' something to eat. Only I couldn't do it." He took a deep breath, a bit shuddery. "But I started to see how—a person might get desperate enough that he could go against all he ever knew that was right—and even go outside the law.

Especially if he had a family to see to. I started to see how that might happen sometime."

That was meant for Papa and Abby looked anxiously at him to see what he would say. But Papa was still just sitting as though he was too beat down to speak.

"We didn't have to fix near as many fried taters when you was gone," Lucy said thoughtfully.

David laughed, relieved to get on another subject. "I guess I shoulda stayed away."

"We don't care," Lucy said, shrugging. "It's Abby that has to peel 'em, anyways."

"We had some cobbler left," Mama remembered suddenly. "The apricots was kinda old tastin' because they have been canned too long. But I put a lotta butter and cinnamon in it and it tasted purty good, if I do say so."

She spooned cobbler out on the side of David's plate that wasn't covered with bean juice. Lucy Belle jumped up unexpectedly. "David we still got your Christmas presents."

"Yeah?" David asked, so busy digging into the crusty cobbler that he didn't even look up.

"I'll git 'em." She paused looking at Mama. "Unless we're gonna save 'em for next year."

Mama laughed softly and said for Lucy to go ahead and get them.

Abby happened to think of the letter from Aunt Myrtle. She was uncertain whether to mention it, but she knew Uncle Lewis' offer still stood because in a recent letter it was mentioned again. Decisively, she slipped out of her chair and went to the back room. There on Mama and Papa's dresser lay the letter, sorely in need of dusting. She blew a little fog of dust off then wiped the rest off with her hand.

In the kitchen Lucy was anxiously standing by, but

David seemed determined not to open the presents yet. Abby knew it was because he was still precariously close to breaking down and he didn't want it to happen again. She laid the letter on top of the three gifts. "Here's something you might want to read sometime. It's about college money from Aunt Myrtle and Uncle Lewis."

He nodded, barely giving it a glance, scraping up the last of the cobbler. "I'll open everything tomorrow. When there's more time."

Disappointed, Lucy went back and sat on Papa's lap. He cleared his throat then, and everybody looked his way, except David, who was rearranging his knife and fork again.

"I want to have my say," Papa said in his oddly flat and dispirited voice, "Then I'll go to bed."

Abby felt a swell of pity for him. She knew exactly how he was feeling. She and Papa and David were all alike in that respect, forever trying to keep a lid clamped on their feelings so they could always appear to be in command of themselves.

He cleared his throat again, scooted his chair back a little and unconsciously patted Lucy's leg. "There comes a time in a man's life—" He breathed heavily and uncertainly, then continued, "When he don't know which way to turn. And sometimes—if he ain't careful—he makes a pore choice."

His hand was smoothing up and down Lucy's back and she snuggled her head down against his shoulder. Papa hadn't held any of them on his lap for a long time, except for that night Abby had found him in the shinnery making whiskey. Now she had a deep, wrenching longing to be near him again, partly for her own comfort, but mostly for his. His voice reflected the loneliness and inner anguish he had been experiencing, the self condemnation, for a body was often quick to condemn his ownself and longer about forgiving his ownself than to condemn or forgive somebody else, Abby had learned. Especially if you were like Papa, and never out to deliberately hurt anyone. Papa needed to know they had all forgiven him—except, possibly, David—a long time ago. But, as was her usual way, she merely stared at her hands and silently ached for him. Besides, it was becoming an increasing concern to her that perhaps Papa would never be able to forgive himself unless David did.

"I don't expect any of you knows how hard it is for a man to say right out in front of his young'uns, that he was wrong. But, that's what I'm a-sayin' now." He took another labored breath and his voice trembled. "I was dead wrong."

The silence was awesome. The bath water on the stove was simmering just enough to make a tiny sighing noise. Mama reached out a hand and squeezed Papa's arm and Abby was glad because it seemed to bolster him just a little. He continued with obvious effort, "Mr. Roosevelt said we don't have nothin' to fear except fear itself. He was partly right, but I'd go him one step. I'd say a body oughta be afraid of pride, too. Not the right kind of pride, the kind that makes you wanta better yourself, or your family and be everything you can be, but the kind of pride that makes you wanta better yourself or your family no matter what lengths you hafta go to, nor how low you hafta stoop. I'm sayin' now that I let my pride git a mite bigger'n it shoulda been. And I let myself start envyin' them that has more'n me." He swallowed, thinking for a minute, and his hand still rubbed back and forth on Lucy's back. "That's how things stands. I wisht it'd never come about, but it did, and I can't take it back. So to say I'm sorry is all I got to stand on, now."

He added, hardly able to hold his voice steady now, "And, Maudie, we'll be a'going to church on Sunday. Anybody that lives in this house'll be goin', too. I got a lotta makin' up to the good Lord."

No one said anything for a minute. Abby didn't dare look at Mama, who would be trying not to cry. Then Mama said softly, almost managing to keep the tears out of her voice, "Lucy's asleep. Look at her, Travis."

Papa looked and nodded and laboriously stood and gathered her up to carry her to her bed. Abby rushed ahead and turned back the cover. And because she knew the others couldn't see her from the kitchen, and because she suddenly understood that there is a time to reveal yourself and a time to remain silent, she did what she had wanted to do at the table. She threw her arms around Papa's middle and hugged him fiercely and whispered, "I don't care. I love you anyways, Papa."

His trembling hand patted her shoulder and smoothed her back, and she knew he couldn't speak.

Then he went back to the kitchen to check the water buckets before he went to bed as he always did. Abby followed, because she had dishes to think about. Even now Mama was getting the food put away and stacking the plates.

Papa's shoulders were stooped, his face lined and weary and old. From over at the washstand he said with difficulty to Mama, "I'll git some water so you'll have some at breakfast."

David stood up, tall—taller even than Papa, and ragged and dirty. "Jist a minute, Papa," he said, and his voice was labored, "I'll git it for you. It's cold out there."

And they looked at each other just for a second, blue eyes piercing blue, eyes that were exactly the same, not only in appearance but in intensity, and Papa said in an odd, shaky voice, "If you want to."

Unsteadily, David said, "I do."

He went over to the washstand and took one of the buckets and then he turned to look at Papa, really looked, and there passed between them some deep, unspoken communication. Suddenly David's shoulders heaved convulsively with an over-powering emotion that could not have been held back any more than a flood could have, and he dropped the bucket because he was crying, a torrent of wrenching sobs that wracked his slender body unmercifully. David, who never cried, was throwing his long, sinewy arms around Papa, who said brokenly, "Davey-*Knabe*," and was suddenly crying, too.

"I love you, Papa," David sobbed.

At the table, Mama steadied herself with a hand on the back of a chair and clutched against her the empty milk jar she had picked up and silently wept. Overwhelmed, Abby buried her face in her hands and tears began squeezing past her closed eyelids and trickling down her cheeks. Tears of gratefulness, an awesome relief, a loosening of the anxiety that had gripped her unmercifully for ever so long. A sudden surge of hope, of love for her family, thankfulness to God, who had returned happiness to their home in spite of them all.

Circumstances had finally made a full turn and they were at last back from where they had descended so many months ago. A complete family, the burst cords and tattered pieces being put back together and mended even at this moment while Papa and David wept and gripped each other as though everything depended on it. In time, perhaps the repaired places would be as strong, or even stronger, than the original fabric had been, the way it was when you stitched and reinforced the underside of a cotton sack with new ducking and diligence, or the knees of a pair of Levi's.

And though the hard times were by no means over—because they never were for a sharecropper—the Easons were all together again, really together, and that's what counted most. They could start from there. They would keep chasing dreams—reachable dreams, and unreachable ones—college-dreams, living-dreams, any kind of worthwhile dreams. They would chase them together. And someday they were bound to catch one.

Epilogue

Though the Easons are a fictional family, they are typical of one variety of the "lower class" who refused to be stymied by circumstances. Like the youth in the poem Excelsior, their watchword was "ever higher." Their goals were varied. Lucy wished for running water or for a can of beet pickles off the grocery shelf. Abby's and Mama's and Papa's dreams were for a close-knit family and a farm of their own. David's for college and an existence that depended not upon physical strength alone, but intellectual as well. I think we may safely assume that each of their goals were realized—if not in that same year, then in the next or even the next.

The particulars of the pursuit of their dreams is not clear just yet. The author has some ideas forming in the back of her mind, though, and an outline for a book tentatively called, *A Meadow Lark Is Singing*. Perhaps if and when that book materializes we will find just how far the Easons were able to go toward realizing their various aspirations. How, with courage and imagination and the help of God, stumbling blocks were turned into stepping stones.

Of course, the catching of one dream usually only fosters the beginning of another, so the cycle is never complete. The story is never really over. Objectives continue to appear and grow as long as ambitions and hope remain. Anything is possible under those circumstances. And probably that is why Robert Browning wrote, "A man's reach should exceed his grasp, or what's a heaven for?"